MEDIA MADNESS

MEDIA MADNESS

DONALD TRUMP, The Press, AND THE WAR OVER THE TRUTH

HOWARD KURTZ

REGNERY
PUBLISHING
A Division of Salem Media Group

Regnery® is a registered trademark of Salem Communications Holding Corporation

Cataloging-in-Publication data on file with the Library of Congress

ISBN 978-1-62157-726-3
e-book ISBN 978-1-62157-756-0

Published in the United States by
Regnery Publishing
A Division of Salem Media Group
300 New Jersey Ave NW
Washington, DC 20001
www.Regnery.com

Manufactured in the United States of America

10 9 8 7 6 5 4 3 2 1

Books are available in quantity for promotional or premium use. For information on discounts and terms, please visit our website: www. Regnery.com.

To Abby, an amazing writer, and Laurie, an amazing talker;
To Judy, an incredible journalist, and Bonnie, an inspiring teacher

CONTENTS

A NOTE ON SOURCES

This is a book based on original reporting. Most of the interviews were conducted on a not-for-attribution basis to achieve the most candid and accurate account possible of Donald Trump's election and presidency. In describing scenes and conversations where I was not present, I have spoken with one or more people with first-hand knowledge of what happened.

I've drawn on a wide array of reporting and commentary from newspapers, magazines, networks, websites, and social media, and have credited them as frequently as possible in these chapters. My thanks to those in the political and media worlds who generously shared their time to help me tell the story of one of the most challenging periods in American history.

CHAPTER 1

A CATASTROPHIC MEDIA FAILURE

Two days after Donald Trump was inaugurated, Kellyanne Conway dived into a media maelstrom with an appearance on *Meet the Press*. It did not go well.

She and *Meet the Press* host Chuck Todd had a history. NBC's goateed political junkie had texted her after four a.m. on Election Night, congratulating her on what he called the greatest upset in the history of American politics. Conway said she was "euphoric."

But their relationship took a bad turn when she taped a *Meet the Press* interview in late November.

When she got home that Sunday morning and told her husband George that it had gone smoothly, he said, "What do you mean? You weren't on for even a minute."

Conway called Todd and asked what happened. The anchor—who had booked Conway under pressure from the Trump team—realized there had been a miscommunication. He explained that he had told a staffer the show was packed and the most they could do was run sound bites.

"I don't give sound bites. I don't speak in sound bites," she said.
Todd asked how he could make amends.

"It's only 8 a.m. on the West Coast," Conway said. "You can run
the whole interview. You've done 8 minutes with Ash Carter," Barack
Obama's secretary of defense, "and I'm falling asleep." Conway was
steamed. NBC News President Deborah Turness called to mend fences,
but Conway did not respond.

Now Kellyanne was doing a live interview with Todd from the North
Lawn of the White House. Todd demanded to know why Trump press
secretary Sean Spicer had made a "ridiculous" statement that was "a
provable falsehood" about Trump's inaugural crowd being bigger than
Obama's. Things turned personal when Todd laughed at Conway's
explanation that Spicer was providing "alternative facts."

"Your job is not to call things ridiculous that are said by our press
secretary and our president," Conway said. "You're supposed to be a
news person. You're not an opinion columnist."

Conway was disgusted and knew her pushback against Todd would
not get replayed on any network. Conway was sympathetic toward journalists, but here she was, trying to talk about Trump's policy agenda,
and getting ripped by a guy she had known for two decades. She thought
it was "symbolic" of "the way we're treated by the press."

Todd regretted letting his emotions show, but not the substance of
his questions. He thought Kellyanne had simply run out of talking points,
and was laughing at the absurdity of the situation. The fact that it was
a satellite interview, lacking the conversational cues provided by a face-
to-face sit-down, made his interruptions look overly confrontational.

The president called Conway to congratulate her on her performance
against Todd. His vice president, Mike Pence, later joked to her: "Does
Chuck Todd have any teeth left?"

But the unfortunate phrase "alternative facts" stuck to her like tar-
paper. She had meant equally accurate explanations, like "two plus two
equals four" and "three plus one equals four," but it quickly became
journalistic shorthand for White House exaggerations and falsehoods.
One viewer, however, liked the phrase.

"In a way, that was genius," Trump told Conway.

"And in another way...?" she asked.

The president was too busy sympathizing. "They do that to me all the time, take one word," he said.

Two days later, Chuck Todd texted her with an offer: "Would love to chat when you have time. I also think we should do a face to face sit down on cam. Maybe something more extended for my cable show sometime next week. Just a thought. All about reminding folks we both prefer cordial back n forths."

Kellyanne happened to be meeting with the president. She asked him how to respond.

"Tell him I thought you were treated with great disrespect," Trump said.

Conway tapped the words into her iPhone: "President Trump said you treated me with great disrespect."

Todd quickly replied: "I respectfully disagree. Of course, I've taken a lot more disrespect than most reporters and never make it public. I'm sorry this was your response."

Kellyanne texted, "That was his response. I typed what he said."

"Well. Let me know what YOU think of my pitch."

Conway put the phone down. She was done with Todd.

She eventually relented, and Turness, the NBC news chief, came to see her and Hope Hicks, the president's loyal young assistant. Conway did not hide her disdain for how NBC and MSNBC were treating the administration.

"This is a side of me you never see," she said. "I'm usually kind and gracious. Your networks are a hot mess."

Turness said that MSNBC was the province of its president, Phil Griffin.

"No, it's your stepchild," Conway said.

"And you've got *SNL*," Hicks added, the comedy show on which Alec Baldwin was brutally mimicking Trump.

Turness delivered an overall apology. NBC wanted to continue a fifty-year tradition of spending a day trailing each new president with a camera crew. Fat chance, Conway thought, if this is how we're going to be covered.

"I let you guys into the White House and this is what happens," she said.

• • •

Donald Trump is staking his presidency, as he did his election, on nothing less than destroying the credibility of the news media; and the media are determined to do the same to him. This is not just a feud or a fight or a battle. It is scorched-earth warfare in which only one side can achieve victory.

To a stunning degree, the press is falling into the president's trap. The country's top news organizations have targeted Trump with an unprecedented barrage of negative stories, with some no longer making much attempt to hide their contempt. Some stories are legitimate, some are not, and others are generated by the president's own falsehoods and exaggerations. But the mainstream media, subconsciously at first, have lurched into the opposition camp, are appealing to an anti-Trump base of viewers and readers, failing to grasp how deeply they are distrusted by a wide swath of the country.

These are not easy words for me to write. I am a lifelong journalist with ink in my veins. And for all my criticism of the media's errors and excesses, I have always believed in the mission of aggressive reporting and holding politicians accountable.

But the past two years have radicalized me. I am increasingly troubled by how many of my colleagues have decided to abandon any semblance of fairness out of a conviction that they must save the country from Trump.

I first got to know Donald Trump three decades ago and never made the blunder of underestimating him during the campaign. I saw all his weaknesses—the bluster, the bullying, the refusal to admit mistakes— but I also saw strengths that most of my colleagues missed, especially an ability to channel the anger of millions of voters who despise the press—including the old-guard conservative press—and other elite institutions.

This was part of an all-out culture war that stretched well beyond journalistic operations to late-night comics, musicians, Hollywood celebrities, and Broadway actors, all of whom ripped and ridiculed Trump at every opportunity. From Alec Baldwin to Meryl Streep, from Stephen Colbert to Seth Meyers, they depicted the president as being beyond the pale, an aspiring dictator, feeding Trump's sense of being under siege and prompting him to lash out at those across the media-and-entertainment complex.

This is, at bottom, a battle over the truth. Who owns it, who controls it, who can sell their version to a polarized public that increasingly cannot agree on basic facts.

Everything you read, hear, and see about Trump's veracity is filtered through a mainstream media prism that reflects a lying president—and virtually never considers the press's own baggage and biases.

Everything you read, hear, and see from the Trump team is premised on the view that media news is fake news, that journalists are too prejudiced, angry, and ideological to fairly report on the president. Trump and his acolytes use these attacks on the Fourth Estate to neutralize their own untruths, evasions, and exaggerations.

Organized journalism is built around rules, traditions, and the careful parsing of words. Traditional politics is built around polling, spinning, and the careful deployment of words, which are often drained of meaning to avoid giving offense. While the two sides are nominally adversaries, they are also joined in a mutually dependent relationship. They speak the same language. They know they will be penalized for reckless rhetoric, for statements that can be proven wrong.

Trump doesn't believe in any of that. He is loose with his language. He makes little attempt to vet his presidential pronouncements. He watches cable news endlessly and sometimes regurgitates half-baked comments. And the media's truth squadders punch themselves silly but rarely seem to land a blow.

What many journalists fail to grasp is that Trump's supporters love his street talk and view the media critiques as nonsense driven by negativity. They don't care if he makes mistakes. As paradoxical as it sounds, negative coverage helps Trump because it bonds him to people who also feel disrespected by the denizens of the mainstream press. The media take everything literally, and Trump pitches his arguments at a gut level. It is asymmetrical warfare.

My greatest fear is that organized journalism has badly lost its way in the Trump era and may never fully recover. Even if the Trump presidency crashes and burns—in which case the press will claim vindication—the scars of distrust might never heal.

My view doesn't reflect some evolution or epiphany on my part. I haven't really changed. My profession keeps moving the goalposts.

When Trump first declared his candidacy, I sat on endless television panels with prognosticators who said he was a joke, a sideshow, a summer fling, and then that he was going to implode the next week, the next month, that he wouldn't make it to Iowa, that he had no shot at winning the nomination. They pronounced last rites each time he caused a media uproar with controversial comments. And then in the fall the cognoscenti knew that of *course* he could never win a general election, right up to the evening of November 8, 2016.

When I would say that Trump wasn't going to self-destruct, that he was media savvy, that he was connecting with alienated voters, that bad press only helped him, I was dismissed in some quarters as being in the tank for a bombastic billionaire. Or being a naïve soul who didn't really understand politics. Or being a closet right-winger who somehow kept his disturbing views hidden all these years. Or a person who had imbibed the Kool-Aid at Fox.

The truth is that I wasn't pro-Trump at all, I was pro-reality.

The point here is not that I was right, but that so many in the news business couldn't see beyond their own biases. Or they would say Trump might win, but the prospect was so frightening that the media had to stop him by convincing voters he was a racist liar, *and dammit, why aren't they getting it?*

It turns out they were the ones who failed to recognize what was unfolding before their eyes. It was the most catastrophic media failure in a generation.

CHAPTER 2

TRUMP WORKS THE REFS

The first time I met Donald Trump, he told me that if he ran for president, he would win.

It was 1987.

We were in his twenty-sixth-floor Trump Tower office, where he was promoting his book *The Art of the Deal*, and he had recently taken an exploratory trip to the first primary state. Which he was more than happy to discuss.

"When I go up to New Hampshire—I'm not running for president, by the way—I got the best crowd, the best of everything in terms of reception," Trump told me. "The politicians go up and get a moderate audience. I go up and they're scalping tickets. You heard that? They're scalping tickets. Why? Because people don't want to be ripped off, and this country is being ripped off. I think if I ran, I'd win."

He sounded exactly the way he does now—brash, self-congratulatory, over the top, and utterly convinced that his wealth and success meant he could accomplish virtually anything.

I didn't exactly envision him in the White House, but he was great copy for a reporter based in New York, feuding with everyone from hotel queen Leona Helmsley ("a disgrace to humanity") to the mayor Ed Koch (a "moron," "jerk," and "disaster"). Trump admitted he had a "thin skin" about negative press, which had to be one of history's great understatements.

The real estate magnate had strong views on world issues, complaining that the U.S. military was subsidizing Japan, Saudi Arabia, and Kuwait, and that Japanese trade policy was taking America to the cleaners.

His staff, even then, had decidedly mixed feelings about the man. Blanche Sprague, a top Trump lieutenant, told me that "to work for Donald you absolutely have to love him, because he will absolutely drive you crazy. There are days when I could cheerfully bludgeon him to death."

I called Trump periodically and he always called right back—even in the first days of the tabloid frenzy over his divorce from Ivana, triggered by his relationship with Marla Maples.

Trump was such a creature of the *New York Post* and *Daily News* that I somehow felt comfortable asking him why he had offered his estranged wife just $20 million of his $2-billion fortune. He called it "a very, very substantial amount of money," backed by a prenup that was "sealed in gold."

And what about her argument that she had contributed to his tycoonery? "You know me pretty well," he said, attributing a greater intimacy to our relationship than I had dared imagine. "Do you think anybody helped me build this fortune?"

Trump always spit out the sound bites and signed off: "I gotta go, baby. You take care. I'll read you tomorrow."

But our relations, such as they were, had the roller-coaster quality that would become so familiar. When he was building the Trump Taj Mahal in Atlantic City, and I had to ask him about reports of cash-flow problems, he snapped: "I don't know why I even talk to you. You've never written anything nice about me." Which was demonstrably untrue, but didn't stop him from taking my call. (His casinos later went into bankruptcy.)

Two decades later, when I had long since decamped to Washington and we hadn't spoken for some time, Trump was at the top of the polls for a possible presidential bid in 2012. I called his lawyer to ask about allegations by customers at several business ventures that they had been ripped off. To my surprise, Trump called back, going on about what a great writer I was and how he was delighted to talk to me.

"What about the 50 deals that turned out great—are you going to cover that too?" he asked. Some of the allegations, Trump said, are "really bullshit stuff."

After flirting with the idea for decades, Trump was ready to take the plunge on June 16, 2015. Unlike most of my colleagues in the media, I knew instinctively when Trump came down that golden escalator to declare his candidacy that he would be a formidable candidate.

Every time Trump said or did something stupid, they would declare him to be toast, only to find him climbing higher. And the same cycle repeated itself during the general election. They were misreading both the man and the mood of the country.

There was no middle ground. I was called a Trump sycophant when I argued that the billionaire shouldn't be counted out, and when I criticized him on some issue, his loyalists would savage me as a Trump hater. Both were way off the mark.

I don't like either party. I believe even the best politicians can be self-serving hypocrites. My brand has always been fairness. I've been a reporter and columnist for the *Washington Post* and *Newsweek*. I've been an anchor at both CNN and Fox. I've got plenty of opinions but I don't take political sides.

And I've always tried not to be trapped in the airless bubble of establishment media types. My father sold shirts for a living. I grew up in a city-subsidized apartment building next to a sewage treatment plant in the non-trendy part of southern Brooklyn. I went to the state university in Buffalo, which is practically Ohio, though I did get a master's at

Columbia. My first job was working the night shift at a newspaper in Hackensack for $10,000 a year.

So I may have been quicker than most of my colleagues to grasp that the country was fed up with the empty promises and utter dysfunction of Washington. I was sensitive to the fact that many Americans we blithely categorize as working class had lousy jobs, were bouncing between jobs, or worried about losing their jobs, and were brimming with resentment. I didn't dismiss them as racist yahoos. This novice candidate, I thought, is connecting on a visceral level.

I had the sense that Trump appreciated my fairness. But he can be quick to feel slighted.

Two weeks after his announcement, when I arrived at Trump Tower for our first interview for my Fox News show *Media Buzz*, he ushered me into his office for a good-natured chat about the race. He wanted to know how I thought he was doing.

When we sat down in front of the cameras, the man who starred in *The Apprentice* for fourteen seasons didn't like the shot.

"Your side is perfect for me, but for some reason they have me sitting in this seat," he said, though he had the skyline backdrop.

He looked at the lights that had been set up. "Can you move it over a little further?" he asked the crew. In the lull he told me, "You're doing a great job."

Trump wanted to examine the shot again: "Can I take a look at it now?"

More instructions: "Could you turn down that heavy light on top? So much better. Okay. Well, a little darker than that."

I admired his persistence in perfecting the image. But as the crew scrambled, he started getting impatient. "Let's go, fellas, are we ready?" Then he said, "It looks very orangey, but I guess that's my face."

When I stumbled on a word out of the gate, Trump graciously suggested we do it again to fix it.

I noted that while he was in second place in the polls, his critics, including Ari Fleischer, who had been George W. Bush's White House spokesman, had called him "irresponsible" and "divisive." I asked, "Does that hurt your feelings?"

He pushed back, as I expected.

The rest of the interview proceeded without a hitch, notable for his forecast that he had a 15 to 20 percent chance of winning the nomination.

But as soon as the cameras were off, Trump let me have it. "It was so negative. It was very negative. I mean, you quoted every person—"

"To give you a chance to hit back," I said.

"You started out by quoting seven people who killed me. Then you quote Ari Fleischer, who's a loser."

He wished me well, and I was puzzled at how pissed he seemed. But when I passed his office on the way out, he waved me in and we shot the breeze for another fifteen minutes.

After the next interview—he greeted me by reciting his great poll numbers—he was more upbeat. Although we had shot at least ten minutes more than I could possibly fit on the show, he said: "You should run the whole thing. You were good, I was good. Use the whole thing."

Suddenly I was on his good side. When I went to a Trump Tower news conference, Trump announced as he called on me that "I love Howie Kurtz"—which proved a tad more embarrassing when I learned that the session had been carried on CNN. But in his eyes you were only as good as your last sound bite.

As our interviews proceeded—in New York, in Las Vegas, at Mar-a-Lago—Trump took hard shots at the pundits who were criticizing him, on the right as well as the left. He told me that Fox News in general—and Megyn Kelly's show repeatedly and in particular—was slanted against him.

One time he told me off camera that I was "not good" on one of Megyn's recent shows, because I had made an unspecified criticism that bothered him. Another time he told me on camera that "you were not fair." We aired it, of course, and whatever my transgressions, he kept sitting down with me.

Trump was less available after he clinched the nomination, and during a phone call in the summer of 2016, he sounded frustrated. "You are marginalizing me," he insisted. I had no idea what he meant, since we covered his campaign intensively, but he had a long memory for even the slightest criticism.

Trump was obviously working the refs, trying to get a better call next time. He did that more vociferously with his biggest critics. I once saw him walk over to Karl Rove, the Bush White House aide turned Fox commentator who frequently ripped his candidacy, throw an arm around him and vow to win him over. They later had a three-hour lunch at which Rove tried to convince him he couldn't win New York, California, or Oregon.

In the final weeks of the campaign, when the entire media establishment was convinced that Hillary Clinton was a lock, I thought the pundits were falling into the same trap they had when they predicted he couldn't win the Republican nomination. Sure, things didn't look good for Trump as he lagged in the battleground state polls, even as Kellyanne Conway kept insisting they had a path to 270 electoral votes. On *Media Buzz* the Sunday before the election, I said it was irresponsible for journalists to count Trump out.

It wasn't until the wee hours of November 9, sitting on the Fox set in New York, the anchors' voices betraying a sense of disbelief, a pro-Trump crowd outside roaring its approval as each state turned red, that I realized how right I had been. What Trump had told me back in 1987 turned out to be true: if he ran, he would win.

• • •

Kellyanne Conway liked to say that she was the most pro-press person in the White House.

She was certainly the one with the deepest relationships with journalists and the greatest savvy about working the media, the most ubiquitous performer on television, and the rock star of the new administration.

But she wound up getting badly burned. Many of her old friends turned on her with a vengeance she had never imagined.

These journalists would act oh so friendly: *Kellyanne, how are the kids? Did you find a house in Washington? Love that dress.* Then they would eviscerate her.

Conway had forged her future from a difficult childhood in which she grew up not knowing her father. He had ditched the family when she was a toddler, with no alimony and no child support, leaving her to be raised in New Jersey by four strong-willed Italian Catholic women—her mom, her grandmother, and two aunts. She didn't see her dad until she was twelve. She spent eight summers working long shifts picking blueberries at a nearby farm. And she developed a fierce streak of independence, getting a law degree, and launching a business when she was twenty-eight.

Despite Conway's growing prominence over the years, her staunch position against abortion and her embrace of "femininity" over "feminism" alienated some women in media and politics who would otherwise be cheering her on.

I first knew her as Kellyanne Fitzpatrick, a pollster by trade who did stand-up at open-mike clubs, melding self-deprecation with pointed barbs at various Beltway players. She embraced the label "pundette," one of a group of conservative blonde women blanketing the cable networks.

Conway had joined the Trump camp after her first candidate, Ted Cruz, dropped out. Trump soon soured on his campaign chairman Paul Manafort, especially after the *New York Times* reported that he had gotten millions in undisclosed cash payments from Ukraine's pro-Russia party. Three days later, on August 17, 2016, Trump made Conway his campaign manager. She immediately pressed him to manage the media, rather than trying to make news around the clock.

Hillary Clinton was lying low, basking in the afterglow of the Democratic convention and sitting on her lead in the polls.

"I get 10 times as much coverage as she does," Trump boasted.

"Is that a good thing?" Conway asked.

She paused before explaining: "You're not making a new golf course, you're not on *The Apprentice*, you're not marketing a hotel. All the press is not good when you're running for president of the United States."

Trump was unpersuaded. Saturating the airwaves and giving constant interviews had worked extremely well for him so far.

But if he kept it up, Conway said, "You'll destroy my strategy. My strategy is this has to be a referendum on her, not a referendum on you."

Under pressure from Conway and other staffers, Trump began cutting way back on television interviews, appearing mainly on Fox News. He was accustomed to picking and choosing shows, but the team quietly conspired to keep most of the invitations away from him. With Conway in charge, Trump would not hold another news conference for the rest of the campaign.

By the time she stepped in, Trump had already made the media a major target, having yanked the credentials of *Politico*, the *Washington Post*, the *Huffington Post*, the *Des Moines Register*, *BuzzFeed*, and others.

In October, when a dozen women accused Trump of sexually assaulting or harassing them, in the wake of his comments on an old *Access Hollywood* video that if he liked a woman he would "grab her by the pussy," Conway stood by her man, even knowing full well that his poll numbers would plummet. And her loyalty was crucial.

"The reason you survived this was Kellyanne Conway," Newt Gingrich told Trump. She and her long blonde tresses were the face of the campaign. The candidate didn't disagree with the former House speaker, one of the few close advisers with the fortitude to tell Trump he was wrong—first privately, and then, if he didn't listen, on the airwaves.

Conway was adroit in her defense, viewing her job as explaining Trump, not justifying his behavior. When she saw a couple of CNN pundits describing Trump as a sexual predator, she called Jeff Zucker, the network's president, and said his talking heads were wrong to imply that Trump was guilty of a criminal act when not one allegation had been proven.

"You can't have people on your panels calling him a sexual predator," she insisted.

Conway pressed the same case with Anderson Cooper, the globe-
trotting CNN anchor and son of Gloria Vanderbilt, when she was on his
show. "I'm trying to do you a favor," she said. Conway later saw Cooper
challenge a panelist who tried to use that description.

As Election Day approached with Clinton leading in most battleground states, Kellyanne tried to keep Trump's morale up, despite his
hearing the constant media refrains of "you're going to lose, you're going
to lose big, and you're going to destroy the Republican Party." When she
insisted in TV interviews that the Trump campaign had a real path to
270 electoral votes, she knew the anchors were thinking, "We love Kellyanne, but she's full of it."

Kellyanne believed what she said, but it was also her duty to say it,
and in the final days of the campaign, she privately feared that Trump
might lose. She asked friends if the Republican Party would ostracize
her. As it turned out, of course, her faith in Trump was rewarded, and
in the early morning hours of November 9, 2016, she became the first
woman to manage a winning presidential campaign.

CHAPTER 3

TRUMP TRAUMA

President-elect Trump remained amazed—and proud—at how his words echoed across the media and American landscape.

When Conway told him that a church leader had spoken of ripping babies out of the womb—using language Trump had used in the third presidential debate to describe abortion—he was pleased.

"This is a trending item," Trump announced. "It became a news story. I did that."

The bigger news story, naturally, was how Trump's White House team was taking shape. Reince Priebus, the chairman of the Republican National Committee, was named chief of staff. Priebus, a plain-spoken Wisconsin native, lacked an easy rapport with Trump, and thought it odd that Steve Bannon was simultaneously named White House chief strategist, as if they were co-equals, especially as Priebus represented the Republican establishment and Bannon represented the populist rebellion against the Republican Party. It was clear that Trump's daughter Ivanka, and her husband Jared Kushner, would wield considerable clout, inside or outside the White House. But Conway's role remained undefined.

She was nevertheless highly visible. When Trump weighed making former Republican presidential candidate Mitt Romney secretary of state, Conway was upset. Romney had attacked Trump during the campaign as a "fraud" and "con man." She was appalled he might be rewarded with such a plum job.

Conway did something remarkable for a staffer. She went on *State of the Union*, the CNN show hosted by aggressive anchor Jake Tapper, to speak for the large "number of people who feel betrayed to think that a Governor Romney would get the most prominent Cabinet post, after he went so far out of his way to hurt Donald Trump." She made the same argument on *Meet the Press*.

The media world was stunned. Was Kellyanne defying her boss?

It seemed that way the next day on MSNBC's *Morning Joe*. Joe Scarborough, the former Republican congressman who was gradually repairing relations with Trump after their friendship blew up during the campaign, declared that Conway was "going rogue," citing as his source, "the top three people in the Trump organization." And, he added, the president-elect was "furious."

Conway, watching the show, couldn't believe it. She had cleared her anti-Romney diatribe with Trump, who put out a statement confirming her account.

Conway texted Scarborough during the show that his report was "false" and "sexist" and that despite his disparagement of her career, she could have any job she wanted in the White House. Scarborough, denying any sexism, read her comments on the air.

Conway suspected Joe's main source was Reince Priebus. She confronted him.

"Go ahead and keep telling Scarborough lies about me," she said.

Priebus looked startled. "I don't know what you're talking about."

Priebus told friends that while he had not discussed the matter with Scarborough, he did believe that Kellyanne had gone rogue; she had no authority to go on TV and say a Romney nomination was a terrible idea.

Several weeks into the transition, Kellyanne still had no official position. Some, including Kellyanne, assumed that Trump's family—Don Jr., Eric, Ivanka, and Jared—did not want her in the White House.

Conway herself agonized over whether it was feasible for a mom raising four kids to work on a backbreaking White House schedule, and felt guilty for hesitating to go into the speaking and punditry world where she could make far more money with more flexible hours. Beneath her warm smile and pleasant demeanor, no one was a rougher infighter than Conway, who was accustomed to being the only woman in a male-dominated profession. Her journalistic connections came into play when Trump wanted to arrange a summit meeting with the *New York Times*, whose negative campaign coverage so rattled him that he had threatened to sue the paper.

At the same time it was his hometown newspaper, delivered every morning to his glittering three-story apartment, and Trump yearned for its approval.

Trump's press secretary Sean Spicer, an intense, combative Republican operative, often chewing cinnamon gum, quickly voiced his opposition: "Mr. President, I think that's a very bad idea. They're never going to treat you fairly. They'll twist what you say."

Trump exploded, yelling at his new spokesman for the first time. "I know how to fucking take care of myself," he shouted.

Priebus hated the idea too, but Trump seemed determined to do it—until the meeting date approached and Trump asked, "Why are we doing this?"

Hope Hicks answered, "Because that's what you asked us to do."

But Trump had changed his mind, saying, "This is ridiculous."

Priebus agreed. The last thing they needed was thirty attackers from the *Times* peppering him with questions.

"I agree with you 100 percent," Trump said. Priebus fell on his sword and came up with a pretext to cancel the gathering. He said the paper was insisting it all be on the record, rather than just a confidential chat with the publisher, Arthur Sulzberger Jr.

Trump took to Twitter, his favorite weapon for firing off insults against the media: "I cancelled today's meeting with the failing @nytimes when the terms and conditions of the meeting were changed at the last moment. Not nice."

Times executives balked, and Kellyanne Conway not only got the meeting back on the calendar, she made sure her boss wasn't blamed.

The paper quoted unnamed sources as saying Priebus "had tried to scuttle the meeting at the Times by telling Mr. Trump, erroneously, that the newspaper was shifting its terms." Priebus wanted the session canceled because Trump "could face questions he might not be prepared to answer." The *New York Times* had just called Reince Priebus a liar.

• • •

Every president gets pounded by the press. But no president had ever been subjected to the kind of relentless ridicule, caustic commentary, and insulting invective that has been heaped on Donald Trump.

I have a name for this half-crazed compulsion to furiously attack one man. It's called Trump Trauma.

It started during the campaign, when the media geniuses were certain that Trump was a joke. New York's *Daily News* depicted him as a red-nosed bozo, with headlines like "Dead Clown Walking." The *Huffington Post*, in an act of awesome arrogance, relegated Trump to its Entertainment section, and stuck with that stupid decision until the day after the election.

As if that wasn't enough, Arianna Huffington's website held its nose by ending every Trump article with this editor's note: "Donald Trump regularly incites political violence and is a serial liar, rampant xenophobe, racist, misogynist and birther who has repeatedly pledged to ban all Muslims—1.6 billion members of an entire religion—from entering the U.S."

Other media outlets openly moved into the anti-Trump camp as well. Subtlety was not required.

In the *New Yorker*, Editor David Remnick wrote: "The election of Donald Trump to the presidency is nothing less than a tragedy for the

American republic, a tragedy for the Constitution, and a triumph for the forces, at home and abroad, of nativism, authoritarianism, misogyny, and racism."

Noah Shachtman, executive editor of the *Daily Beast*, wrote that "if you're renting in a Trump building or playing a round of golf at a Trump resort, you are supporting racism and neo-fascism." And he flat-out called for "a boycott of Trump's businesses," presumably addressing all those racist golfers. This was the man supervising the site's reporters.

At *New York* magazine, writer Emily Yoshida tweeted this appeal: "Men of NYC if you want to be good allies please form a perimeter around Trump Tower at 6PM and start peeing."

At the pop culture site *BuzzFeed*, the editor Ben Smith, a former *Politico* reporter, called Trump a "mendacious racist."

Smith was telling his staff that it was perfectly acceptable to use such terms on social media because the candidate was "out there saying things that are false, and running an overtly anti-Muslim campaign. BuzzFeed News's reporting is rooted in facts, not opinion; these are facts."

That might have been the most troubling declaration: that Trump's racism was simply an undisputed fact, not a journalist's assessment, and that there was no room for dissent on this score.

Graydon Carter, the editor of *Vanity Fair*, had a long-running feud with Trump dating to the 1980s, when he helped run *Spy* magazine, which branded the real estate mogul a "thick-fingered vulgarian." (Trump told me it was "a garbage magazine.") Now, after predicting Trump's defeat in his glossy pages, Carter called him a "preening narcissist" who "may well be the most ridiculed man in history."

When these and other editors and commentators railed against Donald Trump, there was no backlash from their peers. By and large, they received knowing smiles and high fives. Most people in their circles, from Manhattan to Malibu, believed pretty much the same thing. Trump was an affront to their refined sensibilities. And if he remained stubbornly popular, well, no one ever went broke underestimating the intelligence of the American people.

A burgeoning resentment of Donald Trump stretched well beyond people in the opinion business, touching major news organizations as well.

Trump had complained to me, for instance, that the Twitter account of Jonathan Martin, a top political reporter for the *New York Times,* was "just horrible." And that wasn't the end of it.

Weeks before the convention, an RNC staff member called Martin one night to challenge one of his stories. The reporter shot back, "You're a racist and a fascist; Donald Trump is a racist and a fascist, we all know it, and you are complicit. By supporting him you're all culpable."

During the fall campaign, the party staffer called him again, and Martin accused the staffer—and everyone working on Trump's behalf—of supporting a racist campaign and a racist candidate.

This time the staffer was distraught and relayed the conversation to the boss, Sean Spicer. Spicer called a top *Times* editor and unloaded about Martin's behavior. The editor thanked Spicer for the information.

Half an hour later, Martin called Spicer and demanded: "How dare you go behind my back? What are you doing calling one of my editors?"

"Excuse me," Spicer replied, "you call one of my people and say this and I don't have a right to complain?"

The bias even seeped into routine coverage. When protestors snuck onto a Trump golf course in California and carved six-foot letters into the greens, this was the lead sentence in a *Washington Post* news story: "Environmental activists pulled off a daring act of defiance." It was impossible to imagine such a description of vandalism at property owned by any other president. The paper acknowledged the blunder in an editor's note.

Sometimes the smug certainty was cringe-worthy. Stephanie Ruhle, a daytime news anchor at MSNBC, tipped her hand by asking Kellyanne Conway how she could possibly justify working for Trump.

"You've got to look at your kids when you go to bed at night," Ruhle said, noting that she didn't let her own children watch Trump.

Conway was deeply offended at such an unfair comment that clearly insinuated her candidate was beyond the pale; given the struggles of her own childhood, she didn't need any lectures about family.

Perhaps the starkest contrast in the coverage of candidate Trump was at the major newspapers, which devoted untold acres of newsprint to challenging and correcting him, digging into everything from his real estate dealings to his casino bankruptcies to whether he cheated at golf.

Taken one at a time, some of these stories—such as the *Washington Post*'s Pulitzer Prize–winning series on problems with his charitable donations—were perfectly legitimate. But the sheer tonnage was overwhelming, as if part of a coordinated campaign to undermine and expose a single candidate.

In the summer of 2016, it fell to Jim Rutenberg, the savvy media columnist at the *New York Times*, to justify the massive imbalance of press coverage in a remarkable and much-quoted piece that reflected the mindset of his newspaper and so many other media outlets:

> If you're a working journalist and you believe that Donald J. Trump is a demagogue playing to the nation's worst racist and nationalistic tendencies, that he cozies up to anti-American dictators and that he would be dangerous with control of the United States nuclear codes, how the heck are you supposed to cover him?
>
> Because if you believe all of those things, you have to throw out the textbook American journalism has been using for the better part of the past half-century, if not longer, and approach it in a way you've never approached anything in your career. If you view a Trump presidency as something that's potentially dangerous, then your reporting is going to reflect that. You would move closer than you've ever been to being oppositional. That's uncomfortable and uncharted territory for every mainstream, non-opinion journalist I've ever known, and by normal standards, untenable.

"Let's face it," Rutenberg acknowledged, "Balance has been on vacation since Mr. Trump stepped onto his golden Trump Tower escalator last year to announce his candidacy. For the primaries and caucuses, the imbalance played to his advantage, captured by the killer statistic of the season: His nearly $2 billion in free media was more than six times as much as that of his closest Republican rival."

This figure, based on an endlessly repeated estimate, missed the mark. Yes, early on, the cable news networks provided live coverage of many Trump rallies because he was so unpredictable and entertaining. But much of the so-called free media was actually earned by Trump in the process of doing hundreds and hundreds of interviews. From network morning shows to nighttime cable shows to Sunday shows, Trump exposed himself to constant questioning, even when negative stories were in the air and he knew he would get beat up, and that meant he dominated press coverage of the Republican primary campaign.

It was far harder for these shows to book Marco Rubio, Ted Cruz, Jeb Bush, and the rest, and when they did appear they made little news (and were often asked about Trump). Hillary Clinton was rarely available, even on such friendly outlets as MSNBC, and largely hid from her press corps, while Trump regularly answered reporters' questions.

Rutenberg's bottom line was that the media suspended their "normal standards" because Trump was not a normal candidate. But when journalists changed the rules for one White House contender, they abandoned fairness for activism. They became crusaders against the supposed menace of Trumpism. And, of course, they assumed they would be vindicated in the end because Trump couldn't possibly win the election.

After Trump was sworn in, Rutenberg told me: "This is an extraordinary administration, President Trump is an extraordinary public figure, and there is going to be a different way of covering him."

Margaret Sullivan, the *Washington Post* media columnist, and a respected onetime editor of the *Buffalo News* and former *New York Times* ombudsman, argued that Trump could not be treated like any other president.

In a post-election column titled "A Hellscape of Lies and Distorted Reality Awaits Journalists Covering President Trump," Sullivan opined that "we can expect President Trump to lie to the media, manipulate reality and go after those who upset the notion that adulation is his birthright." Another column was headlined, "How Much Normalizing Does an Abnormal President Deserve?"

This newfound mission of policing the Trump presidency came at a time of deep decline in the news business. The newspaper industry had lost nearly half its editorial jobs over a quarter-century. Network news divisions employed far fewer correspondents. Two of the three major newsmagazines essentially disappeared as print products. The result was a decimation of original reporting, and while many jobs shifted to newsy websites, the plain fact is original reporting was far less valued by the new media culture.

The coin of the realm was now the hot take, batted out for quick clicks. Even people in straightforward reporting jobs were expected to provide instant punditry, to make pronouncements and predictions on rapid-fire cable news segments, to build a snarky persona on Twitter. The lines between news and opinion were not just blurred, they were all but obliterated.

In a fiercely polarized political climate, media outlets increasingly took sides on the left or the right. For media moguls anxious, appalled, or horrified by the forty-fifth president, there were undeniable financial incentives to cater to an anti-Trump audience hungry for stories critical of the president.

When the *Washington Post* suddenly emblazoned a slogan under its masthead—"Democracy Dies in Darkness"—you had to wonder why no threat of darkness was perceived during the Obama administration, which conducted secret surveillance of journalists and dragged them into criminal leak prosecutions. *Slate,* which is owned by the *Washington Post,* pitched subscribers with the slogan "Help Us Hold Trump Accountable."

And it was working. At the *New York Times,* print and online subscriptions grew at ten times the usual rate—132,000 people—in the days after the election, and Executive Editor Dean Baquet credited Trump.

But such financial gains came at a steep price for the reputation of the mainstream press, because the more that these outlets emphasized what Rutenberg called oppositional reporting, the more they seemed overtly anti-Trump, the more they eroded their credibility with conservatives and many independents.

And because there is a natural human tendency to push back when the president is calling your network "fake news" or your newspaper "evil," the anti-Trump mindset of the media became a self-perpetuating cycle: Media outlets overdosed on negative stories about Trump, who in turn attacked them with harsh language, which in turn drove them deeper into anti-Trump territory, which they defended by cloaking themselves in the First Amendment.

The damage cuts deeper than day-to-day reports. Many people no longer believe the polls or the fact-checking columns trumpeted by news organizations. Conservatives have complained for decades about media bias, but many liberals now join in the indictment.

The press has always tried to function as a referee in factual disputes. But the whistle has been yanked away and all too often we no longer agree on a common set of facts. Now each side, whether it's Trump or the mainstream media, tries to utterly discredit the opposition.

Donald Trump feels he is awash in phony news, the journalists feel deluged by presidential chicanery, and Americans wrap themselves in media cocoons that validate their opinions and shut out contrary views. If truth is the first casualty of war, it is also increasingly the victim of the Trump wars. And that is especially bad news for the media, which once claimed a monopoly on the truth but have frittered away much of the public's confidence.

I certainly don't think journalists are bad people, although there are a few mean-spirited folks on both sides. Many are misguided in their belief that they are doing the right thing, and myopic in their rationalizations about why it's perfectly fine to treat Trump differently than other presidents.

They are not "enemies of the American people," as Trump puts it, a phrase that goes way too far with its traitorous overtones. They are, however, their own worst enemies.

CHAPTER 4

A QUESTION OF LOYALTY

Sean Spicer thought it was such a journalistic outrage that he didn't even have to pick up the phone.

Here was a national reporter who had smeared both the president-elect and his daughter in the most obscene fashion possible, and *Politico* had already terminated her contract. Julia Ioffe, who ticked off the campaign earlier with a condescending profile of Melania Trump as a trophy wife, had accepted a job offer from the *Atlantic*.

But that was before she posted a nasty tweet about Ivanka Trump's growing influence in the new White House: "Either Trump is fucking his daughter or he's shirking nepotism laws. Which is worse?"

The incoming White House press secretary called Jeffrey Goldberg, the nationally known foreign policy writer who had recently become the *Atlantic*'s editor.

"I'm just doing due diligence here," Spicer said. "I assume you're going to fire her."

"Well, she apologized. Everyone deserves a second chance," Goldberg said.

Spicer was stunned. "She didn't get a fact wrong," he yelled. "She suggested the next president of the United States might be fucking his daughter."

Goldberg pleaded for understanding: "Come on, haven't you said some stupid shit in your life?"

"I say stupid shit every day," Spicer shot back. "I have never suggested anyone, much less a president, is fucking his daughter."

Goldberg thought what Ioffe had done was terrible, but after long management meetings discussing the matter, he had decided not to destroy her career over this misstep.

Goldberg told Spicer they would have to agree to disagree, then softened his tone: "I know our relations haven't been great, I'd like to reset things for the future."

Spicer stood his ground, saying that if Ioffe were to work there, "we'll never talk to you."

"Sean, you never talk to us anyway."

Goldberg later told colleagues that Spicer had guaranteed Ioffe's employment, because he couldn't let an incoming administration tell him whom to hire or fire.

A veteran political operative, a Navy Reserve officer, and a graduate of the Naval War College, the compact, sandy-haired Spicer was willing to take plenty of incoming fire for his new boss. Yet he was an unlikely choice as press secretary.

Laura Ingraham, the radio host and Fox News commentator who spoke at Trump's convention, had declined to join the White House, concluding that as the single mother of three children she would be better off tending to her media empire. Steve Bannon, the president's chief strategist, along with Kellyanne Conway and the Trump kids, had pushed for Kimberly Guilfoyle, a Fox News host and former prosecutor. But Trump told people that he "had to keep a promise"—that Reince Priebus and Sean Spicer, both from the Republican National Committee, had come as a package deal.

Spicer hadn't always been in the Trump camp. As a protégé of Priebus, who made him senior strategist when he ran the RNC, Spicer had grown agitated during the primaries when Trump would complain about a "rigged system," feeling that was demoralizing to the field troops who were working so hard.

Priebus himself had strained relations with Trump during the campaign, especially after lecturing him for announcing his candidacy by saying that rapists were among the illegal immigrants coming into the country from Mexico. And Priebus seemed to endanger any chance he had of joining a potential Trump administration a month before the election.

After the *Washington Post* posted the *Access Hollywood* tape, the nominee gathered his top advisers at Trump Tower: Priebus, Bannon, Jared Kushner, Hope Hicks, Rudy Giuliani, and Chris Christie were there. Most of them were down in the dumps.

"What are you hearing?" Trump asked.

"You're going to lose big and you should withdraw," Priebus said. Republicans were saying that he faced a landslide loss of Barry Goldwater proportions.

Priebus was tired of what he regarded as the sycophancy of other Trump aides who said things weren't so bad. He felt he owed Trump a blunt assessment. But the candidate insisted he would not lose, and warned that if the party abandoned him, "I will take you all down with me." Corey Lewandowski got into a shouting match with Priebus before the second debate, saying, "Go fuck yourself, Reince."

Trump's team had doubts about both Priebus and Spicer as establishment Republicans. Trump aides heard rumors that the day before the election, Spicer had briefed top people at the networks on the RNC's data that explained why Trump would lose.

The rumor was, in fact, a slight exaggeration of what actually happened. Spicer didn't predict Trump would lose but had told media figures like Rupert Murdoch at Fox and Joe Scarborough at MSNBC that Trump was not likely to win, and had been at RNC briefings where a colleague had used stronger language. The tale had reached the president-elect.

At a dinner at Mar-a-Lago, Trump told aides that he was reluctant to pick Spicer because "he wasn't loyal."

Once Trump tapped Priebus, who had the support of Ivanka and Jared Kushner, however, his new chief of staff made it clear he wanted Spicer as press secretary. Trump appreciated Spicer's fighting, Navy side that had been showcased on television during the campaign, and went along. Joining Spicer would be veteran spokesman Jason Miller, who was going to be named White House communications director, and who had been a key campaign and transition team spokesman.

Reporters found Miller easy to deal with, but he was soon at the center of a soap opera.

Miller, whose wife was about to have a baby, had a secret. As the press release announcing his appointment was being prepared, another Trump staffer, a blonde lawyer named A. J. Delgado, fired off an email to top White House aides.

She told them what some colleagues already knew: she was embroiled in an affair with Jason Miller, and said he was not treating her well. It was a blatant attempt to block Miller's appointment.

The next day, the transition team announced the appointments of Miller and Spicer. As if on cue, A. J. went public with a fiery series of tweets, including, "Congratulations to the baby-daddy on being named WH Comms Director!"

The political world was stunned. Delgado didn't stop there, calling Miller "the 2016 version of John Edwards," the onetime presidential candidate who had fathered a child with an aide. And: "When people need to resign graciously and refuse to, it's a bit…spooky."

Trump was furious that this had become gossipy embarrassment for the press. Reince Priebus and the White House counsel's office were alarmed, looked into the matter, and decided to rescind the appointment.

Forty-eight hours after the press release naming him communications director, Miller put out a statement that his family was his top priority and he wouldn't be taking the White House job after all. It was no coincidence that Kellyanne Conway, asked in an interview how she could balance four children and a top White House post, said that "I don't play golf, I don't have a mistress."

CHAPTER 5

A LEAKY SHIP OF STATE

In what would become a hallmark of the new White House, it was clear soon after the election that just about everything leaked to the press.

Every feud. Every spat. Every disagreement. Every power play. Even the delicate process of who was jockeying for which job.

The media had a voracious appetite for White House infighting. These were juicy stories, far easier to do than analyzing policy initiatives. And many in the top echelon of Trump World were all too happy to dish.

It often seemed that these unnamed aides were out for themselves rather than worrying about what was best for the president-elect. This was not a tightly knit squad of loyalists who had worked together for years. It was an oddball collection of disparate personalities who frequently planted stories in the press.

What emerged was a portrait of a dysfunctional operation, which happened to jibe with the media's predominant view that Trump knew next to nothing about running a government.

Corey Lewandowski was expected to be on the team. He was the ultimate Trump loyalist, and that was evident when he phoned Trump after the networks called the race on Election Night.

"Nobody believed in me," Trump told him. "Literally, just you, Hope and one or two others," he said, referring to Hope Hicks, the elegant former fashion model who had become his campaign press secretary and confidante. But Trump joked that Hope "had about as much experience as a coffee cup."

A lean, tough-minded, fast-talking operative who had managed nothing more than a losing Senate campaign in his home state of New Hampshire, Lewandowski was an unknown when he took over Trump's tiny campaign at the start of 2015. He told Trump he had a 5 percent chance of winning; Trump said it was 10 percent.

Lewandowski wound up guiding Trump to the brink of the nomination, but made his share of enemies along the way. He also unleashed a tidal wave of bad publicity when he grabbed the arm of a *Breitbart* reporter, Michelle Fields, while blocking her from asking Trump a question. Various videos showed there was a bit of contact, though Fields was not knocked off balance as she had claimed. Nevertheless, the incident—especially when a criminal charge was filed and then dropped—left him with a rough image.

Trump fired Lewandowski in April 2016, replacing him with veteran lobbyist Paul Manafort. Corey was shocked when Donald Trump Jr. delivered the message. "What am I being fired for? We won," he said.

"You feed into his worst instincts on the plane," Jared Kushner told him. He blamed Corey for allowing Trump to publicly criticize the Mexican-American judge presiding over the Trump University case. "I don't *let* him do anything," Lewandowski replied. "He's 70 years old."

But it turned out to be an amicable parting, and Lewandowski fiercely defended his ex-boss in his new role as a CNN commentator. Jeff Zucker took plenty of heat for giving Lewandowski a half-million-dollar contract, especially since Lewandowski was still drawing severance payments from the campaign.

After Lewandowski praised Trump's acceptance speech at the GOP convention from the CNN set in Cleveland, Trump called him.

"Hey man, you're the greatest. You did the greatest job," Trump said. He paused. "Of course, it helps that you had the best candidate."

Lewandowski quit CNN the day after the election, and when Trump called him again, the talk quickly turned to his next job.

"You get whatever you want," Trump said. "You want to be in the White House, what's the holdup? That's where the action is gonna be."

But Trump had set up a White House with competing power centers, with Reince Priebus on one side and Steve Bannon, the former chairman of *Breitbart*, the conservative website, on the other, and Jared Kushner wielding as much if not more influence. Lewandowski had clashed with Priebus and didn't want a mid-level White House slot where other people were constantly leaking stuff on him.

That fear was well grounded. A week after the election, *Politico* ran a hit piece that Lewandowksi thought had Priebus' fingerprints on it. The story said that some of Trump's "key loyalists" were "quietly lining up in opposition" to Lewandowski getting a top job, given that he was a "loose cannon" with a "penchant for bitter infighting." The piece explicitly claimed that Priebus and Jared Kushner were trying to block him.

During another call Lewandowski told the president-elect, "You know, sir, you've got a bunch of guys sitting up there who don't even fucking like you. Three months ago they weren't even for you."

"I'm so sick of this shit," said Trump, who wanted his people taken care of.

But the blow-by-blow action was still unfolding in leaked media accounts. When *Politico* carried a story on complaints from the loyalists who felt frozen out, Trump was furious. He hated getting bad press for what he viewed as someone else's screw-up.

There was another path for Lewandowski. He had four children, and could make enough on the outside in one year to put them all through college. He could go to big corporations and say, you have no relationship with the new president; well, now you do. Everyone knew he could get Trump on the phone. He could make $5 million in a year. Who knew if he'd be this hot after a couple years in the White House?

Lewandowski told Trump that he would pass. Trump asked him to reconsider.

Steve Bannon tried one more time: "Wait, I'll get you in," he said.

"I'm going to put out my own announcement before you do," Corey said. "I'm done."

Lewandowski immediately leaked word that he was starting a Washington consulting firm. Within a week he had eighteen clients.

• • •

Kellyanne Conway's stay-or-go melodrama also played out in the glare of the media.

She knocked down a reporter's tweet quoting "sources" as saying she was "reluctant" to take an administration job because she wanted to stay at her polling company. "False," Conway said, adding, "Could it be those 'sources' want the WH job I've been offered?"

True, she had talked to Fox and other networks and was trying to forge a double deal, one broadcast and one cable channel. But there were complications.

Conway had become such a ubiquitous television presence for Trump that he could not afford to lose the woman he called "my Kellyanne." Priebus and Bannon insisted she could have a family-friendly schedule in the White House, but she knew that wasn't realistic.

Still, after talking it over with her husband George, a lawyer who wanted an administration job, they decided they were ready to move their family from New York to Washington. Conway accepted the coveted title of White House counselor.

A fascinating mixture of charm and ambition, of barbed humor and steely message discipline, Kellyanne had friendly relations with most reporters and anchors. There is no question she would have been celebrated as a magazine cover girl if she had been a Democratic strategist. But even though she had started the campaign as a Ted Cruz operative, her devotion to Trump made her a lightning rod for the press and a target for shows like *Saturday Night Live*.

With four children to care for—ages twelve, twelve, eight, and seven when she entered the White House—and under a constant media spotlight, Kellyanne would need every bit of toughness she could muster.

• • •

Not a single primary vote had been cast when *National Review* declared war on Donald Trump.

This did not take the form of a stinging editorial or opinion column. The magazine's editor, Rich Lowry, published a special issue—"Against Trump"—with essays from twenty-two leading conservative thinkers, all denouncing the Republican front-runner. Even Bill Kristol, editor of the rival *Weekly Standard*, contributed a piece.

"Donald Trump is a menace to American conservatism who would take the work of generations and trample it underfoot in behalf of a populism as heedless and crude as the Donald himself," the lead editorial said.

Trump responded shortly after the issue was posted online: "The National Review's a dying paper. Its circulation's way down....I guess they want to get a little publicity. But that's a dying paper. I got to tell you, it's pretty much a dead paper." This was the opening salvo in what became a bitter slugfest between Trump and the conservative commentariat, which, for the most part, opposed the GOP's leading presidential prospect.

Trump relished the fight. He was determined to portray his adversaries on the right as out-of-touch elitists, whose influence was confined to their conferences and cruises, and who had more in common with the liberal elite than with rank-and-file conservatives. They were what George Wallace, in a very different context, once described as pointy-headed intellectuals. As a onetime Democrat, Trump didn't quake at being called a fake conservative; he was a Republican populist with a few moderate or liberal ideas, even overlapping with Bernie Sanders on trade issues.

National Review and its allies believed Trump was an opportunist, a onetime New York liberal who rejected the policies of free trade and interventionism abroad that many of them had long supported. But whatever their policy differences, the battle between the incoming president and the #NeverTrump conservatives turned excruciatingly personal.

Charles Krauthammer, the syndicated columnist and Fox News contributor, assailed Trump as a "schoolyard bully" who was "beyond narcissism....His needs are more primitive, an infantile hunger for approval and praise, a craving that can never be satisfied."

David Brooks, the moderately conservative *New York Times* columnist, framed Trump in psychiatric terms: "He displays the classic symptoms of medium-grade mania in more disturbing forms: inflated self-esteem, sleeplessness, impulsivity, aggression and a compulsion to offer advice on subjects he knows nothing about."

Peggy Noonan, the onetime Reagan speechwriter turned *Wall Street Journal* columnist, agreed that "when you act as if you're insane, people are liable to think you're insane...a total flake."

George Will, the syndicated columnist, lashed out at Republican voters and Trump supporters "who persist in pretending that although Trump lies constantly and knows nothing, these blemishes do not disqualify him from being president."

Trump hit back hard. When I asked him about the criticism, he said that "Krauthammer has just absolutely been a disgrace when it comes to me. Don't forget he was a big war hawk, going to Iraq."

He said Stephen Hayes, another Fox commentator and *Weekly Standard* writer, "treats me terribly. It wouldn't matter what I do."

A mention of Brooks prompted Trump to ruminate about how these pundits despised him. "This has nothing to do governing. This has to do with a personal hatred that is unbelievable."

And in Trump's mind, they were taking potshots from afar: "They don't call me. I've never spoken to any of them to the best of my knowledge. So, you would think that if they're going to write something about me, they'd call, they'd talk to me." It wasn't easy to just ring him up, but his mindset was still that of the Manhattan developer who constantly chatted with reporters.

Since several of these conservative critics were associated with Fox—Lowry, Hayes, Krauthammer, Will, Jonah Goldberg—Trump was souring on the network. "I think Fox treats me terribly," he told me. "I will say CNN treats me much better than Fox does." (He would come to dramatically reverse that view.)

Trump's constant counterpunching soon divided the Fox audience. Some viewers who had long admired its conservative commentators turned on them, often adopting the Trump view that they were part of a failed establishment. Trump's electoral victory proved, among other things, that he understood political combat and conservative voters better than many pundits on the right did.

Some assumed that after he won the election, Trump's conservative critics would swallow hard and close ranks behind him. But, for the most part, that never happened. So deep was their distaste for the new president that conservative Never-Trumpers largely stood their ground—and in some cases paid a price.

"There are a lot of pundits on the right who think their job is to be a cheerleader for their team," Jonah Goldberg told me. "That is not my job. My job is to tell the truth as I see it, and that has gotten a lot of people angry."

Goldberg, who occasionally offered praise when he thought Trump was right, took a financial hit. He lost a sizable sum of money, having to pass up speeches where he was expected to be a Republican surrogate. His appearances as a Fox contributor dropped precipitously, he says, because he no longer fit the format of many left-right debate segments. "Every day, on social media, I am attacked, dismissed, or otherwise declared an illegitimate analyst or fake conservative because of my criticisms of President Trump," he says. That became the new world for those on the right who don't accept Trumpism.

Lowry also remained a sharp critic. "Our role is not to get on anyone's bandwagon," he told me. "It's not to read the polls, it's not to get with the program or fall in line, it's to represent conservatism and these ideas and our principles that Bill Buckley created for us, founded us for that role."

I asked Steve Hayes, who became editor of the *Weekly Standard*, about Newt Gingrich's contention that we were getting "anti-Trump propaganda" from "the same idiots" who failed to understand that Trump would win.

"Being one of those idiots," Hayes allowed, "I didn't think Trump was going to win the nomination. I didn't think he was going to win the election. I don't think that that somehow invalidates the things that I say about his Cabinet. Whether I'm praising them, which I have in some cases, or criticizing and raising questions, we've never been sort of a mouthpiece for the Republican Party. We are an independent conservative voice....Look, we're not on the team. We've never thought of ourselves on the team."

When I spoke with Charles Krauthammer, he said, "it's very simple: I call them like I see them....I don't make any secret of the fact that I didn't think he should have been president, but that doesn't matter on the day he's sworn in. He is president. At this point, whatever I thought about his ascendance is irrelevant."

It is hard to fault the conservative critics for standing by their principles, even as they knew they were alienating part of their natural audience. And yet that added to the president's sense of being under siege by a full panoply of media antagonists, rather than just the target of liberal bias.

But Krauthammer made one larger point echoed by the others in various forms. Despite his criticism of Trump, he said, "I want him to succeed. I'm a patriotic American."

CHAPTER 6

THE DOSSIER SURFACES

Donald Trump was freelancing again. And his closest advisers knew the drill.

The president-elect ignited a media firestorm by tweeting, with absolutely no evidence, that millions of people had voted illegally in the 2016 election. The press found this especially odd because, well, Trump had *won* the election.

Whenever Trump went off script, the coverage was almost universally negative. Most politicians would backtrack, admit error, or change the subject. Trump invariably dug in his heels. Reporters were convinced they had him cornered, but like Houdini, Trump would conjure an escape, somehow convincing his supporters that he was the victim, that biased journalists were distorting his meaning or missing the point.

Corey Lewandowski knew all too well that his former boss sometimes misfired on Twitter. Trump talked to plenty of people; they would say things, and he would repeat those things. A couple of folks might have said they saw people voting illegally in their state. But now Trump's microphone was so big that every word was national and international news.

The problem with the media, Lewandowski believed, was that journalists took Trump's words all too literally. Sometimes he would shoot off his mouth like a guy at the bar, not weighing every syllable, but people loved that he didn't sound like a focus-grouped politician. The press still hadn't figured him out.

Trump viewed journalists as nonstop nitpickers. If what he said was "off by one-hundredth of a percent," Trump said, "I end up getting Pinocchios," awarded by the *Washington Post* fact-checking column.

During the campaign, Lewandowski and his successors had endured a remarkably consistent pattern. Trump would hone a successful message, stick to the script, and wind up chafing at the rhetorical shackles.

Lewandowski could always tell when Trump wasn't having fun. And that meant he would rebel. He would create a new narrative: a phrase, a tweet, an extended riff in front of a rapturous crowd. And if in doing so Trump marred his own story line, he blamed the media for twisting his words, and doubled or tripled down (while sometimes tweaking) his remarks.

His staff had a name for when Trump utterly ignored their collective advice: *defiance disorder.*

That's what happened when Trump started criticizing Khizr Khan and his wife. Their son, an Army captain, had been killed in Iraq, making them Gold Star parents. But after the Muslim couple appeared at the Democratic convention and Khan gave a fiery speech against Trump, he lashed out at them. "You're getting killed on this," Lewandowski told Trump after he had dropped 7 points in the polls. As his staff frantically tried to change the subject, Trump would not let go—and was convinced he had done nothing wrong.

"The media was not treating the statements fairly," Trump told me at the time. "I mean, they would chop them up and then shorten the statement, and it didn't sound as proper or didn't sound as good when they did that. It was very unfair."

There were growing calls for Trump's team to boot him off Twitter. But Kellyanne Conway knew Trump would, in the end, say and do what he wanted. When Trump said things she couldn't defend, she simply deflected reporters' questions.

The ultimate example came when Trump's team was prepping him for the third and final debate in Las Vegas, drilling him on one answer dozens of times. With Trump having spent weeks declaring that the election was "rigged," the inner circle urged him to say that while the media were unfair, of course he would accept the outcome on Election Day. He was explicitly warned that any other response would guarantee forty-eight hours of bad press, wiping out the rest of the debate.

But when Fox's Chris Wallace asked that very question, Trump went with his gut. He said he didn't know what he would do and would keep the country in suspense. Conway and Bannon watched in amazement. A modified statement was issued the following day, but the damage was done. Those who knew him best grasped the truth: he would not be managed.

• • •

As Donald Trump stepped up his war on the media, filling the Twittersphere with attacks on CNN and NBC, some of his aides felt that he needed to tone it down, that the campaign was over and a new president should pick his targets more carefully. But one member of his inner circle believed Trump wasn't going far enough.

"I fucking hate the press," Steve Bannon would tell anyone who crossed his path.

In his view, Trump was always trying to mend fences with the media, trying to get them to like him. Bannon viewed journalists like scorpions. If you engaged, you would simply get stung. He liked some journalists personally but they were "killers," he would say, adamantly opposed to his worldview.

Bannon believed that Trump's sit-down interview with the *New York Times* had been a mistake, a misguided attempt at appeasement. Trump had the power of Twitter behind him; he didn't need the mainstream press. During the campaign, Bannon read the Twitter feeds of the network embeds, the young producers who were always on the trail; they did not hide their contempt for Trump; neither did even seasoned journalists who continued to both underestimate Trump and snipe at him.

Bannon understood that Trump's detractors in the press were on both the left and the right, and he was proud of the way the campaign had neutralized the old-line conservative media, whose thunder Bannon tried to steal when he ran *Breitbart*. Bannon loved the way his candidate took on the Never-Trump conservatives; for Bannon, Trump's campaign was not only about defeating Hillary Clinton and the Democrats; it was about shattering the Republican Party and forging a new conservative movement.

Bannon had also learned how to handle the boss. Trump had yelled at him throughout the campaign, demanding that he fire this or that staffer. Bannon let him vent and ignored the orders.

As much as Kellyanne gravitated toward the spotlight, Bannon did his work in the shadows. Despite his pedigree as a Harvard Business School guy, Goldman Sachs executive, and Hollywood entrepreneur, Bannon walked around shaggy-haired and unshaven in well-worn combat jackets and multiple shirts. He had barely known Trump before, but from the moment he became campaign chairman, he was the most reviled man in politics.

Press reports depicted Bannon as a white supremacist and anti-Semite, attributing to him every creepy *Breitbart* headline, such as "Bill Kristol: Republican Spoiler, Renegade Jew" (an article written by David Horowitz, who is Jewish). Bannon was seen as the malevolent force behind the throne.

Whatever his dark view of the world, Bannon barely lifted a finger to defend himself. He was proud of the fact that he went through the entire campaign without granting an interview.

Bannon viewed himself as an economic nationalist, not a white nationalist. He believed that *Breitbart*'s web traffic soared because he channeled a populist fervor that took on Paul Ryan's Republican establishment, and that the same impulse had enabled Trump to connect with frustrated working-class voters. Bannon had a grandiose vision of overthrowing a corroded Republican apparatus whose embrace of global trade and large-scale immigration served the interests of the elites, but left millions of Americans worse off.

Bannon's view was that politics was war by other means and that the press—as much as the Democrats and the establishment Republicans—was the enemy. He believed you couldn't co-opt the media. You had to steamroll them.

Bannon's political strategy for President Trump was to "flood the zone," football lingo for sending more receivers into an area of the field than the defense can cover. That's why he wanted Trump to sign a flurry of executive orders in his first week.

In mid-January, on the eve of Trump's first press conference in six months, aides debated whether to limit the session to its stated purpose, which was addressing possible conflicts of interest involving the president and his global real estate empire. Bannon argued that every topic should be fair game.

Suddenly they had to call an audible. At six a.m., CNN's Jake Tapper texted Spicer that he needed to talk to him about something important. Spicer said he would be available. At two p.m., Tapper got in touch to say that his network was about to air a story that U.S. intelligence officials had briefed Trump about an unverified dossier, assembled by a former British spy, that claimed the Russians had compromising information about him.

"These are classified documents," Spicer said. "It's complicated stuff that I have to go through. I can't just respond off the top of my head." He asked for more time.

Tapper said they would update the story when Spicer came back with a response.

Spicer quickly called Jeff Zucker and pressed for more time to respond. The CNN president's answer was the same: "We'll update the story with your comments."

Soon afterward, *BuzzFeed* posted the entire thirty-five-page document, which made outlandish allegations, such as that Trump had consorted with prostitutes at a Moscow hotel and had watched them engage in golden showers, a porn term involving urination, even as the site said it had no idea whether such allegations were true.

Kellyanne Conway tried to knock down the dossier story on *Good Morning America.* "You're wrong—I'm not spinning," she told investigative reporter Brian Ross off camera.

Trump huddled with his team. Would these sexual falsehoods now dominate the news conference?

Spicer argued that the *BuzzFeed* scoop—which was drawing criticism from major news organizations that had refused to report the unsubstantiated rumors—was already the biggest story in the country. It was the elephant in the room, he said, and they had to tackle it head on.

"How do you want to start?" Trump asked.

"I'd like to write something," Spicer said. He later showed his opening statement to Trump. Spicer suggested he call it "frankly outrageous and highly irresponsible" for a "left-wing blog" to dump "highly salacious and flat-out false information" just days before the inauguration.

"Perfect," said Trump.

The president-elect added his own choice words at the Trump Tower event, calling *BuzzFeed* a "failing pile of garbage," and broadened his attack to include CNN, which hadn't printed the actual dossier.

When CNN correspondent Jim Acosta repeatedly interrupted Trump, loudly demanding a question, Trump finally snapped: "You are fake news." Spicer confronted Acosta afterward, telling him that if he pulled such a stunt again, he'd be kicked out of the press conference. And when Acosta later reported that he'd been threatened with expulsion if he asked a hard question, Spicer called him a liar.

The die was cast. Donald Trump had denounced "fake news" and weaponized Twitter to battle what he viewed as the dishonest media. Steve Bannon disdained the media as a malevolent force. And Sean Spicer was on the front lines against confrontational reporters.

But away from the cameras, Spicer had his reservations. People were posting online that he was evil, and his wife, a former television producer, was freaking out. She stopped putting pictures of their two young children on social media. They had never been through anything like this. And Spicer knew that it was only going to get worse.

• • •

Eleven days before taking office, Donald Trump was at his desk on the twenty-sixth floor of Trump Tower, being briefed on the latest media coverage.

Nothing had changed, and yet everything had changed.

Nothing: With his longtime assistant Rhona Graff sitting next door, Trump still barked out the names of the people he wanted called, still greeted visitors with a smile and a backslap, still roamed the halls filled with framed magazine covers bearing his visage.

Everything: With Secret Service agents filling the suites, with Jared Kushner popping in and out as he prepared to accept a White House post, Trump was holding meetings this day on who to name to the Supreme Court, not where to build his latest golf course. And that's when I walked in.

With the weight of the presidency just days from descending on his shoulders, Trump wore the mantle lightly, pausing to gossip about the news business, taking a shot at Arnold Schwarzenegger's sagging ratings on his old show, *The Apprentice*—then casually remarking that one of the tougher problems on his desk was North Korea.

It was still hard to fathom how he won the election in the face of so much media hostility, Trump said, relishing the moment. "Can you believe it?"

He noted that NBC's Kristen Welker had just reported that he broke his promise that Mexico would pay for the wall. Not at all, said Trump, he had always planned to start it first with American funds and get the Mexicans to reimburse the cost through border fees.

Hope Hicks, who was almost always by his side and had just been named an assistant to the president, pulled out her phone to play footage of Kellyanne Conway on the CNN and Fox morning shows. She was deflecting Meryl Streep's slam against Trump at the Golden Globes, where Streep attacked him for, among other things, having allegedly mocked a disabled *New York Times* reporter during the campaign. Kellyanne said that that charge had been repeatedly refuted and added that if the actress was so concerned about the rights of the disabled, she should have spoken out about a disabled boy who had been badly beaten by young thugs shouting anti-Trump epithets in a video that had been posted on Facebook and generated national outrage. Trump loved Kellyanne's answer, and that got him revved up about his media coverage.

Trump asked why Fox had given airtime to Kurt Eichenwald, a *Newsweek* writer who claimed without a scintilla of evidence that Trump had once been in a mental institution—even if the point was to debunk the claim.

And "CNN is terrible," he told me. "I've never seen anything like it." He was convinced that he had gotten Jeff Zucker, who ran NBC when Trump was doing *The Apprentice*, his job as CNN president by recommending him. It was personal. Trump felt betrayed.

Zucker and Trump used to speak regularly, and Zucker had been a guest at Ivanka's wedding to Jared. But as a candidate, Trump occasionally cursed out the CNN chief over segments that angered him.

During the campaign, Jared Kushner called Zucker after CNN's fact-checkers had declared much of a Trump speech false, from the candidate saying he "started off with a small loan" (it was $1 million from his father) to claiming foreign governments hacked Hillary Clinton's email server ("no conclusive evidence").

"Jeff, this is just unfair," Kushner said. "You're looking for things to pick apart." He told Zucker that Trump "told me to say he doesn't want to do CNN anymore."

"Look, you can't win without CNN," Zucker said, citing an audience study by David Axelrod, the Obama aide he now employed as a commentator.

Jared begged to differ: "You have 1 million viewers, and 70 percent of them aren't in swing states."

The conversation was not going well. Zucker, for his part, felt Trump was trying to delegitimize the press.

"You're so arrogant, you think you know everything," he told Jared.

Trump was more pleased with Rupert Murdoch, whose global media empire included Fox News, the *New York Post* and the *Wall Street Journal*. The two men stayed in touch. Trump told me that the mogul was more supportive after Roger Ailes was ousted from Fox over sexual harassment allegations and Murdoch took day-to-day control. Murdoch thought Trump had great potential but paid too much attention to the media.

Trump had invited French business magnate Bernard Arnault to join him at the press pool that day. Arnault was considering expanding his U.S. factories and Trump thought that was news. "The press didn't care," he lamented. "It was all, 'What about Jared?' 'What about Russia?'"

On a happier note, he was pleased that the *Wall Street Journal* had declared his presidential Twitter feed to be a major media force. As an example of its power he told me that he had tweeted criticism of General Motors' exporting jobs to Mexico and now "General Motors doesn't know what to do about its new Mexican plant." "I move markets," he proclaimed.

Trump had a message for me as well. With everything swirling around him, he was somehow keeping an eye on my coverage. "Your problem," he said in a friendly tone, looking me in the eye, "is that you're too down the middle." I said that was my job. In my world, of course, that was a compliment.

Hicks retreated to a nearby desk, where she spoke to *New York Times* reporter Patrick Healy. He had called Trump's personal cell phone during the Golden Globes, and then quoted him as saying he wasn't surprised by criticisms from "liberal movie people."

Hicks took him to task. "I'm not a confrontational person, but calling the president-elect of the United States at midnight over an entertainment program is crossing the line." If he wanted a comment from the president-elect, he should have called her; the fact that he didn't "makes me look bad. I'm usually very responsive." She ended on a conciliatory note: "It's not the end of the world, we'll move on."

Trump knew he had greater problems than Meryl Streep. He broke with Republican leaders who wanted to replace Obamacare with health savings accounts, telling the *Washington Post* there would be "insurance for everyone." Days later, in another interview he said, "We have to make sure that people are taken care of," which, to the press, again put him at odds with his own party.

What most journalists missed was that Trump was trying to find a compromise plan that would appeal to more moderate voters. It was a collision course in the making, against both parties.

• • •

Carl Bernstein, the onetime Watergate sleuth now working for CNN, was ripping Kellyanne Conway as a "propaganda minister."

Conway dismissed the slap, for while Bernstein was defending his story on the unsubstantiated dossier about Trump and Russia, she knew that his former partner Bob Woodward was now criticizing the ex-spy's dossier as "garbage."

Moments before Bernstein's remarks, Conway had really gotten into it with Anderson Cooper. "CNN and BuzzFeed have a lot in common," she told him. "You both were absolutely convinced and told your viewers Hillary Clinton would win this election."

When Cooper accused her of pivoting away from the question, Conway punched back: "Anderson, you can use words like 'pivot,' 'distract,' 'red herring' all you want. The fact is that the media have a 16 percent approval rating for a reason. It's been earned. And it's crap like this that really undergirds why Donald Trump won."

And then, recalling the gushing coverage of Barack Obama, her sense of resentment emerged: "We get no forbearance. We get nothing! We get no respect. We get no deference!"

The more that Kellyanne fought back, the more she made herself a target. Late-night comic Samantha Bee called her a "spokes-cobra" and "soulless Machiavellian." Bee played an old clip of Conway saying that femininity is replacing feminism for many women. Bee observed: "I know Kellyanne doesn't believe those homophobic, sexist things in her heart, because Kellyanne doesn't believe anything in her heart."

Conway had a seemingly impervious hide. She didn't spend much time thinking about such attacks. People were going to take their shots, that was politics. It wasn't really about her. Conway felt she was being ridiculed for the sin of working for Donald Trump.

What was strange about the growing chorus of attacks was that they didn't accuse her of being an incompetent hack; she was derided for being too good at her job. "Kellyanne Conway Gave a Master Class in Not Answering Questions in Her Fox News Interview," said the *Washington Post*. *Slate* declared her "the Slipperiest Political Flack in History," one who was impossible for anchors to pin down.

In Conway's view, being a woman brought her special grief, especially from other women who made comments like "she's aged 10 years since working for Trump." Conway's standard reply was, "I'm 50 years old, honey, not a beauty queen."

The media environment even penetrated her home. Her daughters had asked why she wasn't voting for the woman in the race. It's about backing the person with the right vision, she told them.

Media fame proved a double-edged sword. It made her a household name, but it also made her subject to terrible death threats that included her family. A package with a suspicious white powder was mailed to her home. She was forced to get round-the-clock Secret Service protection. And Kellyanne blamed it on a press that had seemingly decided to target her.

CHAPTER 7

SPICER GOES TO WAR

Donald Trump had been president for just one day when Sean Spicer got into his first full-blown confrontation with the press.

Running against the media had been Trump's signature move throughout the campaign, a way to discredit, belittle, and intimidate his critics while riling up his base. He had a counterpunching instinct, and attacked reporters by name—sometimes to set the record straight, sometimes because he just couldn't resist.

These denunciations, as well as his tendency to make exaggerated and sometimes untrue statements, served a larger purpose—by fueling coverage about the coverage, hand-wringing over whether he'd gone too far, they helped Trump dominate the media. Trump hated the negative stories but knew that they nevertheless helped him by infuriating his supporters—it always kept the spotlight on him.

Spicer was expected to be his chief enforcer with the media, and on January 20, 2017, he had an opening to fill that role. When the Trump team let journalists into the Oval Office, *Time*'s Zeke Miller reported that a bust of Martin Luther King Jr. had been removed. Actually, it was still there—Miller had just missed it—and he apologized. Spicer scolded him on Twitter for getting his facts wrong.

The morning after the inauguration, Trump grew incensed as cable news reports denigrated the size of his crowd, saying it was far smaller than Barack Obama's in 2009.

Trump was convinced this was more media phoniness and struck back during a visit to the CIA. Standing in front of a memorial wall, he declared a "war" on the so-called dishonest media and blamed them for accusing him of feuding with the intelligence community. The truth was that Trump had, in fact, feuded with outgoing intel officials, accusing them of leaking information.

Trump remained obsessed with affirming the size of his inaugural crowd, especially after some cable networks gave gargantuan coverage to the massive women's protest marches in several major cities. He wanted Spicer to call a special Saturday briefing and denounce the press coverage.

Much of his staff was against it. Picking this fight was no way to kick off the president's first full day in office. Kellyanne Conway tried to talk Trump out of it. She invoked a line that she often employed when Trump was exercised over some slight.

"You're really big," she said. "That's really small."

Spicer knew that his job was to do what the new boss wanted. A veteran spokesman who had enjoyed cordial relations with reporters for years, he was personally fed up with what he viewed as a relentlessly negative media narrative that the incoming administration was perpetually on the brink of failure. His anger rose as he delivered a scolding from behind the lectern.

The Martin Luther King Jr. bust mistake was "irresponsible and reckless." The crowd photos used by some cable networks were "intentionally framed" in a misleading way. "These attempts to lessen the enthusiasm of the inauguration are shameful and wrong," Spicer declared, and for all the media chatter about holding Trump accountable, "we're going to hold the press accountable as well." He took no questions.

Reporters who had long known Spicer were stunned that he had escalated his tone on such meager matters. Several accused him of lying. The *New York Times* accused him of peddling falsehoods. Spicer felt stung. He had never been called dishonest before.

This wasn't really about the crowd size; it was a proxy fight in a larger battle. Reince Priebus, Spicer's mentor, believed the press was actively trying to delegitimize Trump's presidency at the outset.

The president called Spicer later. He was not happy. "You didn't go far enough," Trump said. He didn't like Spicer's look, grumbling to others that he should have worn a better-fitting dark suit. Trump preferred that men wear white shirts. He really cared about television visuals.

Spicer knew he needed help. He called Corey Lewandowski after midnight, seeking advice. Lewandowski said there was a Sean Spicer brand out there that the new spokesman had to protect.

Trump remained boastful about his inaugural crowd. When Conway, who had taken up residence on the third floor, was contacted by a freelance photographer who sent her a panoramic shot of the inauguration, Trump loved it so much he hung it on a wall near his office.

But as the crowd debate raged for days, Trump made a rare admission to Conway, Spicer, and other staffers.

"You were right," he said. "I shouldn't have done that." Trump had paid a penalty for his defiance disorder, for refusing to let the matter go and, as the new leader of the free world, focusing on more important topics.

When Trump went off script in this fashion, it was Sean Spicer who invariably took the heat, given his daily clashes with the press corps.

The president repeated to a group of congressional leaders that as many as five million immigrants had voted illegally in the election, thus explaining his popular-vote loss to Hillary. The president, again, offered no evidence to back this claim; it was just another Trump hunch. A front-page *New York Times* headline called it a "lie." His advisers said privately that once a notion like that got into Trump's head it was going to come out, that he couldn't help himself; when he thought something was true, he just said it.

Spicer was the one who had to face down the press, telling reporters that Trump believed there was massive voting fraud and "continues to maintain that belief based on studies and evidence people have presented to him." He looked uncomfortable as he tried to avoid personally vouching for the unsubstantiated claim. He was caught between the rock of Trump's exaggeration and the hard place of not embracing that falsehood. The *Washington Post* said Spicer was "killing his credibility." *New Yorker* correspondent Ryan Lizza said he should resign. Spicer believed that Lizza wasn't a reporter but a left-wing commentator.

Already, just days into the administration, there were rumors of political infighting in the White House. Someone quickly leaked to the website *Axios* that at least one White House official was talking about replacing Spicer.

The danger for Spicer was that Trump's attitude was: the media hate me, and I get bad press because of you. Some thought Spicer, who was acting as both press secretary and communications director after Jason Miller's withdrawal, had been set up to fail.

· · ·

Donald Trump was in a joking mood as he walked down a corridor near the Oval Office, looking as relaxed as if he had the day off.

He walked over when he spotted me. He pointed at Hope Hicks, whose confident demeanor masked a natural shyness. "You should get Hope to go on TV," the president declared. "That would be it for you, Sean," he said to Spicer. And looking at deputy spokesman Boris Epshteyn, he said, "You'd never get on again. She would be the biggest star."

No conversation with Trump was complete without an assessment of how I was doing. He said he would give me an interview, but first he had a message. "You've gone neutral on me," Trump said in a good-natured tone. He turned to his team and loudly proclaimed, "Howie's gone neutral on me!" I hadn't changed a bit, though his station in life most assuredly had.

He quickly guided me to the framed photo on the wall showing a seemingly massive crowd for his inaugural speech. A week after the event, Trump was still focused on the chatter that his crowd hadn't been the largest ever.

"Can you believe that?" he said, admiring the shot. "Look at that, there are more people over here. And Obama had fences here and here." He grew more animated as he spoke. "But you'll never see this picture on TV."

A casual visitor would never have guessed that less than two hours earlier, Trump had signed an executive order that would create an international firestorm for his fledgling administration. He had banned all refugees from entering the United States for 120 days, and all travel from seven predominantly Muslim countries for ninety days, in an effort to tighten security screening for potential terrorists. This was what Trump had vowed to do during the campaign, but the reality came as a shock.

Downstairs in the briefing room, Kellyanne Conway, who had kicked off her heels, was finishing a remote interview with Fox News. Reporters quickly surrounded her, peppering her with questions about the executive order. The administration had not yet identified the seven targeted countries.

"Kellyanne, can you give us any guidance about this EO?" asked NBC's Hallie Jackson. "They're killing us on the broadcast today."

Conway offered no details but a vivid rationale: "Everyone's going to wait until the next savage murder and say, 'Oh, we should have done something.'"

"Can I have two sentences on the extreme vetting?" asked ABC's Jonathan Karl. "I go live in 10 minutes." Conway complied.

Within twenty-four hours, the world was consumed by what was being dubbed a Muslim ban, which was technically wrong, although Trump had said he would favor Christian refugees seeking asylum. There was chaos at several U.S. airports as hundreds of people who had gotten on planes expecting to be admitted, including legal green-card residents, were detained for questioning, and protests broke out at JFK.

Trump's top aides knew that the rollout was something of a debacle. The order had been rushed out on a Friday evening, key officials hadn't been consulted, there was no messaging strategy. Spicer felt they had needed a couple of briefings and a raft of fact sheets. Policy people, he believed, often didn't grasp the need for strong communications and thought it was a waste of time.

Steve Bannon, who had spent years warning about the radical Islamic threat, was driving the policy and had a larger agenda. He thought the press, focused on the chaotic rollout of the travel ban, was too dumb to figure out that his real intent was to provoke Democratic outrage, freezing the party into a left-wing resistance movement that would drive more voters to Trump and eventually raise support for the mass deportation of illegal immigrants.

But it was Trump, with his bing-bing-bing business approach of getting things done, who had shoved through the sweeping order after just seven days in office; for him it was matter of quickly tackling his campaign promises.

The next morning, Kellyanne was in the makeup chair at Fox, her iPhone earpiece in place, listening intently to her colleague Stephen Miller as her mascara and false eyelashes were applied. Jared Kushner texted her, but she said she would have to call him later. There were many legal nuances to absorb about refugees and regulations, and Miller, the earnest domestic policy chief who had helped Bannon draft the order, was spearheading the damage control.

Jotting notes on a pad, Conway started asking questions:

"And the reason these people were detained is they happened to be traveling?"

"How do you relate this to Nice and Brussels and Paris?"

"But can I say that publicly, Stephen?"

Conway suggested a point to counter the reports that some families had been split up during the detentions: "How many children lost parents on 9/11?" She paused. "You like that?"

Moments later, Conway was telling Chris Wallace on air: "The whole idea that they're being separated and ripped from their families, it's temporary, and it's just circumstantial in terms of whether you are one of those 300 and some who were already on an aircraft or trying to get on an aircraft, as opposed to the over 3,000 children who will be forevermore separated from the parents who perished on 9/11."

Conway seemed drained after the interview. She was coping with her own family separation, the longest she had ever been apart from her children, who were finishing the school year in New York. Melania Trump, who was remaining with ten-year-old Barron at Trump Tower, had convinced her that a new home and new schools would be too disruptive for the kids while their mother worked all the time.

Finally, Conway had a chance to go to church. As she walked toward a waiting car on North Capitol Street, flanked by her Secret Service agents, she was ambushed by a man in a gray sweatshirt from *TMZ*. Without missing a beat, Kellyanne looked into the camera lens and defended the refugee ban for one of television's most gossipy shows.

She called back Kushner. Several newspapers had reported that he wanted to limit Conway's access to Trump. She had walk-in privileges to the Oval Office but was careful not to abuse them.

"I just want you to know that is not true," Jared said of the stories. "You know I love you."

"You know," Kellyanne said, "these leaked stories aren't flattering to you. They're meant to make you look like a misogynist." But they patched things up and Kushner became extremely cordial to Conway.

Meanwhile, *Washington Post* opinion columnist Josh Rogin reported that Steve Bannon had visited retired General John Kelly, the Homeland Security secretary, at his office and pressured him to include green card holders in the travel ban, and that Bannon had joined other officials in a two a.m. conference call about the executive order. Both those stories were untrue.

Spicer called Fred Hiatt, the *Post*'s editorial page editor, and unloaded on him: "What the fuck kind of operation are you running over there? He literally made it up out of whole cloth. There was no staff meeting."

Hiatt said the best way to clear up any discrepancies was for Spicer to talk to Rogin.

"You ratfuck us, and you want me to call him and get it straight? Fred, your paper went after me viciously, you said I was a liar, I have no integrity. He didn't even do the basics." Hiatt, trying to be transparent, updated the story with Spicer's denials and said in an editor's note that Rogin should have contacted the White House, rather than just leaving a message for Homeland Security.

Trump soon assessed the travel ban with Corey Lewandowski.

"You know," Trump told him, "the rollout wasn't really that bad."

"No one's questioning the policy, it was the rollout."

"It really wasn't that bad, it's the goddamn media," Trump said.

On this issue and others, Newt Gingrich had told him that his tweets were hurting him, that his scattershot attacks on the media and his political opponents were too much of a distraction.

"No, I have to be on offense," the president said.

The pundits targeted Stephen Miller for much of their rage about the travel ban. Joe Scarborough, backed by his co-host Mika Brzezinski, called Miller an inexperienced "Little Napoleon" whose policy "was a disgrace" and who should resign.

The thirty-one-year-old Miller, a rail-thin man who had recently quit smoking, was bewildered. He felt that he was simultaneously being described as incredibly powerful and incredibly incompetent. Miller knew that you couldn't achieve real change without making some people angry, but he viewed himself as part of a team; he hadn't gone rogue with this policy; it was a Trump campaign promise.

Conway rose to his defense. She marched into the Oval Office and said, "Mr. President, I feel compelled to tell you that Stephen Miller is being mistreated, by name, by Joe Scarborough. He said the guy screwed up and shouldn't be here." This, she said, was totally inappropriate for a cable news host.

Joe and Mika had just been at the White House for lunch on Sunday. Things had gone smoothly, except when Jared Kushner had praised the "genius" of Steve Bannon in targeting working-class voters and Trump had loudly proclaimed, "That wasn't Steve Bannon's strategy, that was my strategy!"

As Scarborough was leaving the set on Tuesday, his phone rang and an angry president was on the line. Trump shouted, "It's not for you to tell me who shouldn't be here. I could have invited Sean Hannity here, he didn't attack me. I invite you and you attack me. I know what your deal is. You have to attack me to prove you're your own man."

"No, Donald, that's not it at all," Scarborough said, What Miller had done "was deeply offensive" and "undemocratic."

Scarborough knew Trump watched the show, and used his platform to give him advice that he might not accept privately. But Scarborough got the message: the president was pissed. He had played the gracious luncheon host, showing Joe and Mika his Andrew Jackson memorabilia in the Oval Office, and then they had turned around and attacked him on their next two shows. Trump valued loyalty above all.

CHAPTER 8

BANNON AS DARTH VADER

The press was obsessed with Steve Bannon, but while Reince Priebus defended Trump on the Sunday shows and had the loftier title of chief of staff, Bannon, the White House strategist, stayed out of public view. Behind the scenes, he was the driving force behind Trump's populist, establishment-be-damned agenda, and the press, viewing him as a sort of Svengali, made him the focus of some vicious coverage.

Bannon, in a rare public comment, said the press should "keep its mouth shut and just listen for a while." Trump backed him up the next day, embracing his charge that the media were the "opposition party." *Time* put Bannon on its cover as "The Great Manipulator." The *New York Times* ran an outraged editorial titled "President Bannon?" *Washington Post* cartoonist Tom Toles depicted him behind a toilet, calling him the power behind the throne. Bannon had officially been anointed the administration's evil genius.

All this attention bothered Trump. What was Bannon—a staff guy—doing as *Time*'s cover boy? Bannon needed to understand there was only one star in this White House. Conway thought it would be better if Steve did an occasional interview. The hit newsmagazine *60 Minutes* wanted him, but she didn't want Bannon getting sliced up on the show. George Stephanopoulos of ABC's *This Week* wanted him too. But Bannon texted Conway, "LOL."

When Trump reorganized the National Security Council, he made Bannon a permanent member, but excluded the head of the CIA and the chairman of the Joint Chiefs of Staff. Inevitably, the Washington establishment freaked out. While Bannon had been a naval officer and had a graduate degree from Georgetown in national security studies, his presence was deemed an affront. He was a practitioner of the black arts of politics; he jokingly called himself Darth Vader. Now he had a media bulls-eye on his back.

● ● ●

After hundreds of interviews in which her words came pouring out in great rivulets, Kellyanne Conway made a mistake—a big one.

And the media, relishing the chance for a little payback, beat her up so badly that she plunged into some serious soul-searching.

The blunder took place on MSNBC, a network that most Trump officials avoided. Conway was defending the president's travel ban in an interview with Chris Matthews, the former Jimmy Carter and Tip O'Neill aide who had become the nonstop talker defending Beltway liberalism.

During the Obama years, Conway said, "two Iraqis came here to this country, were radicalized, and they were the masterminds behind the Bowling Green massacre"—which, she said, "didn't get covered."

But there had been no massacre in Kentucky. She had screwed up. Her larger point was right: two Iraqis living in Bowling Green had been convicted of helping al-Qaeda in Iraq kill American soldiers. But invoking the non-existent "massacre," which she had done a couple of times before, caused an explosion.

MSNBC didn't catch her error; a Kentucky reporter tweeted it hours later.

The mockery online was brutal as Kellyanne was accused of inventing "alternative facts." She said she had "misspoken one word" while newspapers regularly ran three-paragraph corrections, but that didn't matter. Some people in Bowling Green created a phony memorial. The *Washington Post* gave Conway its "Worst Week in Washington" award. CNN, Trump's least favorite network, said it declined to book her on Jake Tapper's show because of her "credibility" issues. (Actually, Conway was spending the weekend with her family in New York—her oldest daughter was in a school production of *Annie*—and had made plans to go to church with her family.)

The backstory was that CNN was miffed that Mike Pence was appearing on every Sunday show except Tapper's *State of the Union*. Still, the liberal *Huffington Post* ran a screaming headline: "KELLYANNE CRISIS: TOO DISHONEST FOR TV!" Conway had actually argued against what was becoming a White House boycott of CNN, but she now believed that the network's president, Jeff Zucker, was attacking her as a way of embarrassing President Trump.

On *Saturday Night Live* Kate McKinnon portrayed Conway as a slut who is so desperate to get on television that she tries to seduce Jake Tapper and then threatens him with a knife.

The media battering pushed Kellyanne into a deep period of reflection. She felt she had to stop being so naïve. She was no longer a single woman living with her dog. The media hits she took affected not just her but her family. In the past, she had regarded herself as a pollster who happened to go on TV. She could walk through an airport or into a Cinnabon unmolested. Now she was mobbed everywhere she went, and she and her family needed Secret Service protection.

During the campaign, Kellyanne felt like a happy warrior, delivering a fresh dose of honesty and fighting the good fight against Hillary.

But now the media were turning themselves into her enemy, and her head spun at how media people could be so nice to her off camera, and so mean to her in their reports.

Kellyanne knew she didn't come off as very feminine, but she didn't like how the press portrayed her as harsh and shrill. She resented being treated as a talking head and nothing more, and she desperately wanted to get off television. She turned down more and more invitations. The vice president sympathized with her, saying that she should save her media appearances for really big issues. "I think we're using Peyton Manning in the preseason," Mike Pence told her. "I think you should spread it out."

But Trump wanted her out there defending him, and for now, that was her fate.

Conway ended a tumultuous week with another unforced error. After Nordstrom abruptly dropped Ivanka's clothing line, Trump retaliated on Twitter, saying his daughter "has been treated so unfairly by @ Nordstrom. She is a great person—always pushing me to do the right thing! Terrible!"

As criticism mounted that the president was using his office to help his daughter's business, Conway put in a plug on *Fox & Friends*. "Go buy Ivanka's stuff," she said from the pressroom. "I hate shopping and I'm gonna go get some myself today.…I'm gonna give a free commercial here, go buy it today everybody, you can find it online."

The condemnation was fierce. Conway had violated a federal regulation against promoting one's own business or that of a colleague.

The *Washington Post* and *New York Times* splashed the story on the front page. A Republican congressman demanded an investigation. Spicer summoned Kellyanne to a meeting and told her that he would inform the press that she had been "counseled" on the matter and it wouldn't happen again.

Conway had detractors both inside and outside the White House, and gave them ammunition when she appeared on Jake Tapper's weekday show and acknowledged that CNN was not "fake news." Her administration critics said she was out for herself, not the president, and circulated a *Washington Post Magazine* cover story in which Conway said she had passed up millions of dollars by not selling her polling company. Kellyanne went to the president and apologized for her mistake involving his daughter. Trump was sympathetic. He knew she was trying to defend Ivanka, and that taking flak was part of the job.

"It's fine. I'll take the hit," Conway said.

"Why should you take the hit?" Trump asked. He hated the official line that she had been "counseled." "It makes it seem like you're a child," he said.

. . .

On the morning of February 16, Trump abruptly told Reince Priebus in the Oval Office, "We're having a press conference in two hours." There had been no warning. He was ready.

Trump was feeling boxed in, convinced that he wasn't being adequately defended by Conway and Spicer, and decided to do it himself. He savaged the media at a rambling, stream-of-consciousness, seventy-seven-minute news conference, denouncing the *New York Times*, the *Wall Street Journal*, and CNN for "fake news" and "disgraceful" reporting. He accurately predicted that the headlines would say he was "ranting and raving." Minutes later, Jake Tapper called the president "unhinged" and said he should "stop whining" and do his job. The *Morning Joe* team said he had lost touch with reality.

The president had stirred things up as he intended, but the next day he crossed the line. He tweeted that "fake news" outlets—CBS, ABC, NBC, CNN, and the *New York Times*—were "the enemy of the American people."

Even sympathetic commentators were taken aback by the president calling the press unpatriotic and intimating that its practitioners were guilty of treason.

The language was too rabid even for "Mad Dog" Mattis, the retired Marine Corps general and secretary of defense. He told reporters that while he'd had "some rather contentious times with the press," he had no serious issues with the media.

The president's words were thrown back at Kellyanne Conway, who would never have used such language. She argued—again trying to explain Trump rather than defend him—that what the president meant was that the media weren't his personal enemy, but were hurting the public by misleading them.

Corey Lewandowski understood what had happened: Trump's staff had over-managed him and tried to keep him under wraps. That, he knew from long experience, never worked. The approach only made Trump feel like a caged animal, and it was only a matter of time before he broke free and started roaring.

What people failed to understand, in Lewandowski's view, was that Trump always needed an enemy. That was true when New York's high-society crowd treated him like an outsider. It was true when Augusta National wouldn't accept him as a golf member. It was true with Trump's Republican primary opponents and then with Hillary Clinton. Now Trump was casting the media in the role of the enemy. That showed his supporters he was fighting for them, and it fired him up as well.

Lewandowski visited the White House only days after he had criticized Bannon, Kushner, Conway, and Priebus as inexperienced. He got an earful. "Some people here were unhappy with your comments," a top official told him.

"Well, I'm not happy with the way things are going," Lewandowski shot back.

He was there at Trump's request—Lewandowski knew Reince didn't want him in the building—and he was stunned to learn that his friends in the administration were dejected and miserable.

Lewandowski told Trump in the Oval Office that he should do more press conferences. The president countered that Corey should go on television more often, that Lewandowski's unsmiling demeanor was very effective.

"I'm 100 percent loyal, sir."

"I know that," Trump said. "I just wish everyone in this building was."

• • •

Reince Priebus was chairing a 7:30 a.m. intelligence meeting when one of the participants, Andrew McCabe, asked to speak to him privately.

McCabe, the deputy FBI director, closed the door and told Priebus: "We want you to know that everything in this *New York Times* story is bullshit."

The *Times* had quoted unnamed sources in reporting that Trump campaign aides and associates had repeated contacts with senior Russian intelligence officials. CNN had carried a similar report.

Priebus pointed to the three televisions on his office wall: "Here's my problem, they're going 24/7. Can the FBI say what you just told me?" McCabe said he would have to check. Priebus thought he might come out of this a freaking hero.

A few hours later, McCabe told him the bureau couldn't start the practice of commenting on newspaper stories or it would never end.

"Give me a break," Priebus said. "I'm getting crushed all over the place, and you won't say publicly what you told me privately?"

James Comey called later. "We really can't do anything about it," the FBI director told him. But Comey said he'd be willing to tell the Senate Intelligence Committee that the charges were bogus; he was sure its members would repeat that for the cameras.

Now, a week later, CNN was airing a breaking news story naming Priebus. According to "multiple U.S. officials," the network said, "the FBI rejected a White House request to publicly knock down media reports about communications between Donald Trump's associates and Russians known to U.S. intelligence."

Priebus was stunned by the implication that he was pressuring law enforcement. Had he been set up? Why was the FBI leaking this information when one of its top officials had initiated the conversation?

Comey assured Priebus that afternoon that he hadn't done anything wrong, but the story reverberated for days. "Is Reince Priebus Lying About the FBI?" *Slate* asked. "Reince Priebus Should Resign," a *Boston Globe* columnist demanded. The damage was done.

CHAPTER 9

KELLYANNE UNDER SIEGE

From the moment he was named national security adviser, Michael Flynn was a target for the media. The retired general, who had been fired by the Obama administration, was a Trump loyalist with a taste for conspiracy theories. Trump had yet to be inaugurated when the press began reporting that Flynn had questionable communications with the Russian government.

The story took off when the *Washington Post* reported that according to nine unnamed officials, Flynn had potentially broken the law by discussing U.S. sanctions with the Russian ambassador before Trump took office—and had lied about it to Vice President Mike Pence. Trump said it was fake news, but he was wrong; the story was right on target.

Each day brought new revelations, and the White House went into damage control mode. The *New York Times* reported that Flynn had gotten on Trump's nerves "because of his sometimes overbearing demeanor." Kellyanne Conway went on MSNBC and assured viewers that the general "does enjoy the full confidence of the president." But late

that night, Trump fired Mike Flynn, which made Conway look disconnected from the decision-makers.

At six the next morning, Kellyanne was groggy when her phone rang.

It was the president. He wanted his chief cable combatant to go on
the morning shows.

"Sir, we decided not to send anyone because we were all at the office
until midnight," she said.

"No, I want you out there," Trump said.

Conway didn't want to be accused of seizing the spotlight. "If I go,"
she said, "I have to say you want me to do this."

The boss gave her some guidance. She would say that Flynn had a
fine thirty-year career but that the situation had become unsustainable.
She would try not to say that he lied to Mike Pence and the White House
about his Russian contacts; she would say he provided inaccurate or
incomplete information.

Conway made the case on *Today*, *Good Morning America*, and *Fox
& Friends*. She particularly got into it with Matt Lauer when she said
that Trump was a loyal person and that "Mike Flynn had decided it was
best to resign." When Lauer countered on *Today* that the Justice Department had told the White House weeks earlier that Flynn was vulnerable
to Russian blackmail, all she could say was "well, that's one characteriza-
tion."

Kellyanne felt she was being protective of Trump. She had known
for weeks that Flynn was in trouble. But with Democrats calling for his
scalp, she didn't want press accounts to say they had capitulated right
away. Of course the president had fired Flynn, but she insisted on saying
he resigned because that's what you do when you're about to be fired.
She believed the media were nitpicking over semantics.

Trump singled her out in a private meeting with education advocates.
"Did everybody see Kellyanne on the *Today* show?" he asked. "They
tried to beat her up. She's tough."

Kellyanne had to be tough, because she had become a target of many
news shows, especially *Morning Joe*, which paired Joe Scarborough, the
ex-Florida congressman, with Mika Brzezinski, a former CBS reporter

and daughter of Jimmy Carter's national security adviser Zbigniew Brzezinski.

When Conway joined the campaign, Scarborough was in a Twitter war with Trump. But after the election Jared Kushner helped arrange a kiss-and-make-up session at Trump Tower. "Of all the people I thought would walk through that door," Spicer told Conway, "Joe and Mika were not on the list."

They had courted Kellyanne for months. Their executive producer often sent text messages trying to book her for *Morning Joe*. Was she in New York? Was she free this week? And after one appearance on set, "You nailed it."

Brzezinski had invited her to a Florida bar where Joe's band was playing, and said she'd even like to invite Trump; she stayed in touch with Conway by text. "It's Mika, call me when you have 30 seconds." There was an appeal to the sisterhood: "Let's talk as girls this week."

Mika sent Kellyanne a handwritten note: "You're the best person ever in this job." But Brzezinski also warned Conway that not everyone in the White House was on her side. She encouraged Kellyanne to stay out of the administration and pursue a private career for the sake of her kids—and offered help her find a media perch.

But now, Scarborough and Brzezinski turned on Conway, banning her from their program.

"Every time I've ever seen her on television, something's askew, off, or incorrect," Brzezinski announced on air one morning. "Kellyanne Conway does not need to text our show, just as long as I'm on it, because it's not happening here....She's not credible anymore."

Scarborough chimed in: "She's out of the loop, she's in none of the key meetings, she goes out and books herself often....She's just saying things just to get in front of the TV set and prove her relevance."

Kellyanne shrugged it off. Trump had stopped watching the show two weeks earlier, and so had Ivanka. She knew Scarborough and Brzezinski were catching flak for not being tough enough on the president, and now that they no longer had any access to him, they turned hostile toward Trump and her. She thought Scarborough might even be planning a future presidential run himself and felt he need to establish himself as an anti-Trump force.

Despite Scarborough's claim, Conway was deluged with media requests. Chuck Todd had recently invited her on three days in a row. She had received seven media invitations, including one from *The View*, the day before Scarborough and Brzezinski's assault.

She felt the business about her being on the periphery was also hogwash. She was in a daily meeting every morning with the president, Reince Priebus, Sean Spicer, Jared Kushner, and Hope Hicks. She was the point person on veterans' issues and heroin addiction.

Although Conway was under siege, she had an uncanny ability to maintain diplomatic relations with her critics. She called Jake Tapper, after *Saturday Night Live* ran the skit of her stalking him, and apologized that he'd been dragged into a debate about her credibility. Tapper said he didn't know who at CNN had said his show wouldn't have her on.

"Normally we'd be honored to have you on *State of the Union*," Tapper said. The issue wasn't her credibility, it was that the White House had stiffed CNN by putting Pence on every other Sunday show.

Conway thought much of the media's grilling of her was merely a way for anchors to get high marks from their colleagues: *You didn't let the president's counselor lie!*

Kellyanne knew her detractors said she looked haggard and drained; she knew that her nails were uneven, there was no time for such niceties as a manicure. But, she asked me on the air, what was she supposed to do—get a face lift like so many female anchors did?

Conway was convinced that the media were trying to marginalize her because she was effective at her job. She was a proxy for Donald Trump.

She wasn't the one saying that major media organizations were "fake news." She wasn't out there talking about the "dishonest media." She wasn't the person who had called the press the "opposition party." That was all Trump and Bannon. But she took the heat.

Her colleagues egged her on, saying, "You do things nobody else can do, Kellyanne; you have nerves of steel." She knew that in Washington people built you up only to tear you down later. She also knew that she was in the record books as the first woman to run a winning presidential campaign. What were they going to do, add an asterisk that said "Bowling Green massacre"?

Conway believed the usual media double standard against conservatives was greatly magnified in the case of Trump, and that a routine misstatement for someone else would be made into a huge controversy for her because he was her boss. She had dismissed advice to wait on joining the administration, to cash in on lucrative offers and then ride to the rescue after the inevitable screwups. Kellyanne felt she had a duty to be there on day one. And now she was paying the price.

CHAPTER 10

TRUMP TARGETS MEDIA "ENEMIES"

onald Trump was supposed to be preparing a speech for the Conservative Political Action Conference (CPAC) in Maryland, but he spent the
morning telling Steve Bannon how mad he was at the press. The president grew more agitated as he spoke with Bannon and others on that
morning. The press, he said, was fundamentally dishonest, and the *New
York Times* was "evil."

Bannon reinforced Trump's darkest feelings toward the news business. The media have complete contempt for you, he would say; they
want to destroy you, delegitimize you, and overturn the election.

Bannon knew that Trump was more ambivalent about the press than
he let on. Trump was an optimist and a dealmaker. He liked many
reporters; he wanted to work with them; he thought he could win them
over.

Bannon was unburdened by such thoughts. He had wanted to kick
the reporters out of the White House and exile them to the Old Executive
Office Building. He thought it was patently absurd that they could walk

in and out of a building loaded with classified material. He joked that he'd rather see them on the other side of a wire fence.

The day before Trump's speech, Bannon, in a rare public appearance, told the CPAC audience that the "corporatist" media, the "globalist" media, were opposed to Trump's nationalist revolution. CNN, MSNBC, the broadcast networks, the *Economist*, the *Wall Street Journal*, the *New York Times*, the *Washington Post*, in his view, all represented the Party of Davos, the internationalist, pro-immigration consensus that included the Republican establishment. The Democrats were a shattered, broken, regional party with enclaves in New York and San Francisco, the Hamptons and Hollywood. The real enemy were the media.

Bannon fumed about the coverage of immigration issues. Trump was committed to enforcing existing law and reinforcing America's borders, but the media treated his plans as draconian, even barbaric. There were always stories on families being disrupted and small children suffering.

Steve Bannon felt that his influence on the president was vastly overstated. He wasn't privately pulling Trump's strings. The president was a newcomer on some social conservative issues, but he had been an economic nationalist, a believer in national sovereignty, and a foreign policy skeptic for more than two decades.

Bannon told the president that the press would never give him credit for these ideas. Media people were history and English majors, they weren't wealthy, and they could not accept that Trump, a Wharton School graduate, was smarter than they were.

Bannon believed Clausewitz was right: War is politics by other means. Bannon made his office a war room. He used a standup desk and had Trump's agenda scribbled on a large whiteboard nearby.

Bannon didn't care how the media blackened his reputation. They were trying to make him into Svengali or Rasputin. He wore their hate as a badge of honor. He dismissed media reports about his feuds with Reince Priebus and others as ill-informed gossip. And he believed the more Trump's agenda succeeded, the worse his media coverage would be.

As Bannon and Trump groused about the press that morning, the president got fired up. They talked about adding a couple of lines to the

CPAC speech. But when the moment came, Trump did more than that. He delivered the most lacerating attack on the media by any president in history. There was no script. No one on his staff knew what was coming. Trump just riffed for twelve long minutes.

He said much of the news was "fake, phony, fake." He said those outlets were "the enemy of the American people." He said journalists "shouldn't be allowed to use anonymous sources." He cited one story that said "'nine people have confirmed.' There's no nine people. I don't believe there were one or two people." That was the *Washington Post* piece on Mike Flynn—which was so on the money that Trump fired Flynn.

Bannon was pumped up about the speech. His only regret was that the self-referential media focused on Trump's criticism of them rather than on the president's conservative agenda. Trump of course knew exactly what he was doing and that journalists would devour his anti-media diatribe, enabling him to dominate the headlines.

Later that day, Spicer, not wanting to compete with the president for air time, dropped his usual televised briefing in favor of an off-camera session in his office. But he made a major misstep.

In making up the invite list, he invited the press pool, which would distribute the comments to their colleagues. But he added reporters from *Breitbart* and the conservative-leaning *Washington Times* and One America News, while leaving off reporters from CNN, *Politico*, *BuzzFeed*, the *New York Times*, and other outlets.

Spicer belatedly realized that coming just hours after Trump's "enemy of the people" attack, it looked like retaliation against the administration's least favorite media outlets. The press was in high dudgeon. The AP and *Time* boycotted the briefing in solidarity with the excluded reporters. Jake Tapper, on CNN, called the move "un-American." *Washington Post* Executive Editor Marty Baron said it was "appalling."

Lost in the uproar was that Spicer had also added CBS and NBC to the session. The exclusion of CNN and the others was essentially a coincidence once the list had filled up. He wasn't trying to send a message, hadn't checked with the president, and didn't explain himself very well, but his miscue got wall-to-wall coverage and wound up bumping Trump's speech from the cable news cycle.

Spicer was disgusted with the accusatory coverage and thought the *New York Times* and the rest of the liberal media were whiners with a sense of entitlement that he found mind-blowing.

The pressure was getting to him at times. Spicer seemed constantly agitated. He sometimes yelled at his staff. He picked fights with journalists on Twitter. After two *Times* reporters described him in a piece as "New England-born," Spicer, who grew up in Rhode Island but was born elsewhere, tweeted that they "can't even get where I was born right and failed to ask." One of them, Glenn Thrush, shot back that he had sent the press secretary two emails with no response: "Did u get them, Sean?" Spicer wouldn't let up, saying the birthplace question was not in the email: "More excuses for why you get it wrong."

More troubling was Spicer's decision to launch a one-man leak investigation. He called together ten staffers who had been in a meeting where information had leaked and asked for their government-issued phones. One by one, they handed them over. White House lawyers were there to supervise the process. Spicer said that message-encryption apps like Confide were not allowed. He also asked for their personal phones and said he would check on whether certain numbers had been called. And, of course, insiders quickly leaked that story.

Spicer's surprise confrontation displayed a striking lack of trust in in his staff, but also a way to show his boss he was serious about stopping leaks.

Trump, however, did not back him up. While praising Sean as a "fine human being," he told Fox: "I would have done it differently. I would have gone one-on-one with different people." It was hardly a vote of confidence.

CHAPTER 11

THE WAR OVER WIRETAPPING

Kellyanne Conway woke up on Saturday morning, March 4, and found out, like the rest of the world, that Donald Trump was making an explosive charge with absolutely no evidence.

The president of the United States had gone on Twitter to accuse the former president of the United States of wiretapping him during the campaign. He had charged that Barack Obama was engaged in "McCarthyism," was using "Nixon/Watergate" tactics, and that he was a "bad (or sick) guy."

It was the most self-destructive act of his young presidency. None of his aides knew it was coming. This was the height of defiance disorder.

Sean Spicer, getting the kids out of bed in his Alexandria, Virginia, home, was also blindsided and hopped on the phone. Nobody in the White House knew quite what to do.

The president called Reince Priebus at his Alexandria home.

"Did you like my tweet?" he asked.

"What tweet?" Priebus replied.

"About the wiretap. I've been wiretapped." Priebus was frantically searching his phone for Trump's Twitter feed. While they were talking, the phone exploded with emails and texts. Priebus knew the staff would have to fall into line to prove the tweet correct, the opposite of the usual process of vetting proposed pronouncements. Once the president had committed to 140 characters, he was not going to back off.

Conway decided that this time she would just say no. She canceled a planned television appearance. She was not going to put herself out there and defend the president without any facts. She would not be the lightning rod on this story. She was done with that.

Kellyanne called Trump at Mar-a-Lago that morning, but he had already left for the golf course.

Trump was reacting to right-wing media reports without any attempt to determine the facts. A staffer had given him a *Breitbart* article, recounting a monologue by conservative radio host Mark Levin on how the Obama administration might have conducted surveillance at Trump Tower. There were references to past newspaper reports that the FBI, as part of its Russia probe, had asked a special national security court for permission to investigate a Trump company server, but it was all very murky. Yet Trump simply stated it as fact.

The problem was there was not a shred of evidence to support his stunning charge that his predecessor had committed a felony. This wasn't an exaggeration or a vague declaration. But Trump, who once told his staff that "I hate backing down," wouldn't budge.

As president, he could have called the FBI or CIA and demanded the information. But instead he indulged his itchy Twitter finger. Trump had always been drawn to conspiracy theories, most notably the one that launched his political career, the bogus birtherism charge against Barack Obama. But now these musings had international repercussions.

In some ways he had yet to grasp his own power. After four hours on the links, still filled with anger, Trump asked a friend if the tweets were having an impact: "Are they talking about it? Is it out there? I'm hoping it's the lead." He had no idea of the media furor he had caused. And he had no doubt that his gut was correct.

"This will be investigated," Trump said. "It will all come out. I will be proven right."

. . .

For days, the president had been furious with his attorney general. Jeff Sessions had been an early supporter of the Trump campaign and played a crucial role in the transition, so he recused himself from any investigation of Trump associates and their contacts with Russia—a recusal that Trump thought entirely unnecessary. He was angry at the staff as well. Reince Priebus and Steve Bannon met with the president in the Oval Office, along with Sean Spicer, Jared Kushner, and Ivanka.

"Why would he capitulate like that?" Trump demanded.

When he unloaded on his White House counsel, Don McGahn, Bannon grew animated and started pointing his finger at Trump.

Bannon told the president that no one—not Sessions or Rudy Giuliani or Chris Christie—could have been confirmed as attorney general *unless* they promised to bow out of the Russia probe. Chuck Grassley's Senate Judiciary Committee had made that clear, especially given Sessions's own contacts with Russians during the campaign.

But Trump berated Sessions, calling him an idiot and saying he should resign. The president insisted Sessions had panicked and screwed up.

"That's not what happened," Bannon said. "We talked about it with them. He wouldn't have been your attorney general otherwise."

"Well, you should have told me that," Trump said.

"We did tell you that," Bannon shot back.

The president, who nonetheless rejected Sessions's resignation letter, was especially livid that the media's endless chatter about Sessions's recusal had overshadowed the favorable coverage of his first address to a joint session of Congress. He had been praised for delivering a substantive and unifying speech. A day later, that story had vanished.

This place is a mess, Trump declared.

Among the messes were an endless stream of hostile or gossipy press reports based on White House leaks.

Priebus, for instance, had to dismiss what he considered a silly rumor that Trump ordered him not to attend an RNC donor retreat at Mar-a-Lago. Priebus and Bannon told reporters, off the record, that Trump wasn't mad at them and hadn't kicked them off *Air Force One*, they had just stayed behind to work.

• • •

Conway had missed the meeting in the Oval Office—instead attending a health care strategy session with Hope Hicks—but accounts of Trump's tantrum quickly leaked to the press.

Conway told Priebus sardonically, "Well, we know Hope and I aren't the leakers." She was distressed by reports that Trump had sworn at his staff: "You'd better clean this up," she told Reince. "They said he used profanity and he did not."

Meanwhile, the president spoke by phone with Newt Gingrich and said how glad he was to have unloaded on Obama through Twitter. He said he fully grasped that he was in a war with the *Washington Post* and *New York Times*. Gingrich told Trump that at least 95 percent of donations from federal employees had gone to Hillary Clinton; the bureaucracy was full of leakers, he said, and they are not for you.

• • •

Kellyanne needed answers on how to respond to questions about Trump's tweeted Obama wiretapping allegations. She was thinking of possible on-air defenses as she worked out on a treadmill. She finally reached the president late Saturday afternoon, but there was no consensus on how to respond, so she abruptly canceled a scheduled interview with Fox's Jeanine Pirro. Conway didn't want her information to be false or wrong or incomplete or to be a replay of the Mike Flynn fiasco, where she declared on air the president's "full confidence" in the general hours before he was fired.

The next morning, minutes before the Sunday shows aired, the president had Spicer put out a statement urging Congress to investigate the "very troubling" allegations and saying the White House would have no further comment until then. They were trying to tamp down the wildfire that the boss had started.

Now that she had some marching orders, Conway agreed to tape a segment with Jeanine Pirro. She played her weak hand as best she could.

Did Trump know for sure he had been tapped? "He may." The president sees "different intelligence than everyone else," Conway said, and "there were politically motivated stories and investigations all through the campaign season, and those come from credible news sources, and the president wants to get to the bottom of it. What is everyone afraid of?"

What she didn't say was that the allegation was true or that she believed it to be true.

That was fortunate for her, because that afternoon sources leaked word to the *New York Times* that FBI Director James Comey wanted the Justice Department to issue a statement saying there was no truth to the wiretapping allegation—essentially calling the president a liar.

Spicer answered reporters' questions with great caution, as Conway had. "I think the president's tweets speak for themselves," he said. When asked if the administration had intelligence reports to confirm these allegations, Spicer replied that the answer to that question was "above my pay grade." He got hammered nonetheless, with Chris Matthews branding him "Baghdad Bob," after Saddam Hussein's famous lying information minister.

This controversy was different from Trump's other Twitter eruptions, because the media were stunned that a sitting president would hurl such an unsubstantiated charge at a former president. And the story was even bigger than that: the nation's intelligence services appeared to be leaking against the president, and congressional intelligence panels were gearing up to investigate.

Trump's closest aides knew he had done himself long-term damage. Pundits on the right as well as the left were questioning his mental stability. It was the Lewandowski theory on steroids: Trump had been confined, sticking to the script of his speech to Congress, and hadn't been allowed to break free. When he did, all hell broke loose.

Despite the storm, Conway didn't believe this was the apocalypse depicted by the media. People didn't focus on every jot and tittle of these convoluted stories, they saw the big picture. They were more likely to have watched a clip of Trump's speech to Congress than to be closely following the Sessions controversy.

The press was treating Kellyanne like a piñata. A harmless picture of a shoeless Conway in the Oval Office, with her legs tucked under her on the couch, went viral and brought her all kinds of abuse, accusing her of everything from flouting protocol to being disrespectful of minorities (because she was taking pictures of visiting officials from historically black colleges). Trump hated the image, but the media could not get enough of it. A Democratic congressman, Cedric Richmond, even joked that she "looked kind of familiar" on her knees and referred to what happened in "the '90s" with Monica Lewinsky. He eventually apologized.

The media portrayed a tempestuous administration that could do very little right, which was a major source of embarrassment to Trump and his family. Virtually everything seemed to leak. Even Reince Priebus's walking into a senior staff meeting and giving a little pep talk prompted a wave of bad press.

Priebus believed that some of his colleagues had come in with a fantasy of what West Wing life was like. He realized that he had the title of chief of staff but not the authority that went with it.

Politico ran a story titled "Knives Are Out for Reince," with unnamed sources saying he was incompetent, that he couldn't manage, that he was stacking the White House with RNC types, and that he was blocking the true-believers' access to Trump.

The reality was that Trump ran the White House with ten direct reports and Priebus was one of them, with slightly more authority than the others. Priebus felt that he could not be a traditional chief of staff, because this was not a traditional president; he had less power because all of Trump's deputies represented power centers of their own. Reince believed that he—by pumping millions of dollars into television ads and data collection for the Trump campaign when he ran the RNC—was responsible for Trump's election, and he needed to be there, despite the frustrations and limitations of his job. But he knew it would be a short-term gig.

· · ·

Kellyanne Conway was also getting bad-mouthed inside the White House, but she tried to stay focused on media strategy. She wanted to end the administration's boycott of CNN. She told the president that whenever she went on *Fox & Friends*, Fox would run the best clips throughout the day. They needed to get similar facetime on CNN. "You've got to get people back on CNN," she said. "They're going to be on 24/7 with or without our people."

When Trump learned that Mika Brzezinski had called him a "fake president," he decided to watch *Morning Joe* for the first time in a month. Wow, he told Kellyanne, they are vicious. Conway herself avoided consuming most of what was said and written about her; why keep reading that she was stupid and ugly?

Trump, like Conway, had once been pals with Joe and Mika, and they had touted his chances of winning when almost no one else did. But late in the campaign, Trump tweeted that they were "two clowns" and, at a time when their romance was secret, Trump hit Scarborough "and his very insecure long-time girlfriend." Jared Kushner tried to repair the relationship, with Trump even offering to officiate at a White House wedding, and Scarborough was encouraged enough to offer Trump advice on Cabinet picks during the transition. But their relationship was now in a deep freeze.

Kellyanne thought Trump wanted, and deserved, more respect from his media antagonists. She was struck by what Trump had said in a private session with the network anchors. They asked him what had most surprised him about becoming president. "The fact that you never changed your coverage," he said. "The fact that it never got better."

. . .

Madonna was live on cable news, dropping F-bombs as she spoke.

She was a featured speaker at a women's protest rally the day after Donald Trump was inaugurated, and she was letting loose.

"Yes, I'm angry," she railed. "Yes, I am outraged. Yes, I have thought an awful lot about blowing up the White House."

No, she didn't mean it literally. But what was eye-popping was how little attention the media gave Madonna's outrageous comment; if it had been reversed, if a conservative entertainer had threatened to blow up Barack Obama's White House, the media would have been in a full-blown frenzy.

Instead, the constant stream of inflammatory invective from celebrities against Trump was simply woven into the larger news culture. Their diatribes generated segments on cable news and endless online gossip items. Some of them appeared on political talk shows and Sunday shows, the better to goose the ratings. Their swipes and slams were covered so matter-of-factly, or with raised-eyebrow acquiescence, that it sent a signal that this was perfectly ordinary discourse.

Robert De Niro called Trump "totally nuts." Susan Sarandon said he "made hatred and racism normal." A petition from "Artists United Against Hate," including Bryan Cranston and Mark Ruffalo, said "Trump wants to take our country back to a time when fear excused violence, when greed fueled discrimination, and when the state wrote prejudice against marginalized communities into law."

Lena Dunham described sobbing in the shower on Election Night, and suffering such "soul-crushing pain and devastation and hopelessness" that her weight dropped.

They had every right to speak out, but they often seemed like actors reading variations of the same script.

Sarah Silverman went on Conan O'Brien's show dressed as Hitler and compared the Nazi leader to Trump, down to the size of their manhoods. Chelsea Handler tweeted a near-naked, rear-view picture of herself, with "Trump is a butt hole" scrawled on her body.

Rob Reiner, the liberal director and actor, said that "This is not normal. We've had the greatest attack on this democracy since 1941.... Our democracy is being compromised." Yes, he was comparing the president's election to Pearl Harbor, and went on to call for "all-out war" against Trump's "treason."

The cast of *Hamilton* felt compelled to lecture Mike Pence when he took his family to the hit Broadway show. "We are the diverse America who are alarmed and anxious that your new administration will not protect us," a cast member announced.

At the Oscars, it was de rigueur to take shots at Trump. *La La Land* producer Marc Platt said that "repression," meaning by Trump, of course, "is the enemy of civilization." Barry Jenkins of *Moonlight* told viewers that "the ACLU has your back. For the next four years we will not leave you alone, we will not forget you." And Jimmy Kimmel, who hosted the awards, said they were all hoping to give a speech "that the president of the United States will tweet about in all caps during his 5 a.m. bowel movement tomorrow."

Kimmel and other late-night comics formed an almost united front against Trump. The lone exception was Jimmy Fallon, the apolitical *Tonight Show* host who took enormous abuse for tousling Trump's hair during a playful interview. Fallon was "devastated" by criticism that he had been "humanizing a well-documented, xenophobic, racist and misogynistic serial liar," as the *Huffington Post* put it. And he soon lost his top spot in the ratings.

The openly liberal Stephen Colbert, who made Trump-bashing a staple of his program, drew glowing reviews and a bigger audience. Comedians ranging from Samantha Bee to Seth Meyers to John Oliver to Trevor Noah followed suit. Hey, they could be funny; all presidents get bashed. But after eight years of gentle humor aimed at Obama, comedians brandished a much harder-edged, more intensely personal brand of satire against Trump, one that was increasingly mixed with serious politics.

And then there was *Saturday Night Live.*

The iconic program surged to its highest-rated season in decades, powered by Alec Baldwin's over-the-top impersonation of the president as a doofus. Trump, of course, hit back, tweeting that it was "time to retire the boring and unfunny show" and that Baldwin's "hit job" on him "stinks." And Baldwin, an unabashed New York liberal who once hosted a talk show on MSNBC, attacked Trump at every opportunity.

"When we woke up the day after the election it was like 9/11," Baldwin told Howard Stern, likening a free election to the worst terrorist attack in American history. He confessed that he no longer speaks to his brother Steve Baldwin: "If you support Trump, there is no common ground."

That about summed up the celebrity culture's attitude toward Donald Trump: no common ground. And that sense of ridicule constantly reverberated through the news echo chamber.

CHAPTER 12

"THE KNIVES ARE OUT"

Kellyanne Conway seemed off her game.

She could be flawless in a long interview—sharp, funny, and charming, with an encyclopedic command of statistics. And then, without warning, she could step in it.

On March 12, in a video interview with her hometown Jersey paper, the *Bergen Record*, she was asked: "Do you know whether Trump Tower was wiretapped?"

"What I can say is there are many ways to surveil each other," Conway said, referring to a new WikiLeaks disclosure about CIA spying techniques. "You can surveil someone through their phones, certainly through their television sets—any number of different ways, microwaves that turn into cameras."

Conway was simply deflecting the question by changing the subject, but it seemed like she was insinuating something.

The next day, Conway made the rounds on the morning news shows. On CNN, she got hammered over the *Bergen Record*'s piece: "Kellyanne

Conway Alludes to Even Wider Surveillance of Trump Campaign." The hosts of course demanded to know what evidence she had of wider surveillance.

"I'm not in the job of having evidence. That's what investigations are for," she told *New Day* anchor Chris Cuomo. She insisted she was offering a more general point about surveillance capabilities, not making new allegations, and criticized the *Record* headline, saying: "I know I'm great clickbait."

And then there was this: "I'm not Inspector Gadget. I don't believe people are using the microwave to spy on the Trump campaign."

It was the same drill on *Today* and *Good Morning America*. All day, her defensive answers replayed in an endless loop. She was the microwave lady. The Inspector Gadget line went viral. Mika Brzezinski attacked her again. Even on Fox, anchor Shepard Smith introduced the story by saying, "Kellyanne Conway, whom we really don't quote much anymore because, well, history..."

Had a lower-profile official used the same dodge, it wouldn't have been news. But this was Kellyanne, and the media were waiting to pounce on the merest misstep.

The most stinging part wasn't the criticism, it was the mockery. Stephen Colbert did a bit peering out from inside a microwave oven. CNN's Jim Acosta made Inspector Gadget jokes. Kellyanne was adept at producing colorful phrases, but as with "alternative facts," these could also be thrown back in her face.

After her morning blitz, Trump tweeted: "It is amazing how rude much of the media is to my very hard working representatives. Be nice, you will do much better!"

The president was now having to defend the woman whose job was to defend him on television, and that left him feeling perturbed. He sent word that Kellyanne should take some time off from the airwaves. "She's worn out, making mistakes," Trump told a top aide.

Jared Kushner, widely viewed as one of Conway's antagonists in the Trump White House, actually became one of her defenders. He felt she didn't get credit for the 999 times out of a thousand that she did a good job, and got too much blame when there was a misstep. He knew that campaigning and governing required different skills and standards, that they all had to make the adjustment, and Kellyanne, he thought, was making the transition as well as anyone.

Still, the media firestorm over Trump's accusation of wiretaps ordered by Obama raged on. Trump tried to muddy the waters by having Spicer say that his boss's use of "wiretap," in quotes, included any kind of surveillance. Journalists were openly skeptical, and felt vindicated when, on the morning of March 16, the Senate Intelligence Committee issued a statement saying there was no evidence that Obama had ordered Trump wiretapped.

The president gave Spicer his marching orders: "Let's make sure we're pushing back on this."

What followed was Spicer's most contentious press briefing. He angrily accused journalists of pushing a "false narrative." He charged the press with a blatant double standard for focusing on the lack of evidence for Trump's wiretap claim, while simultaneously ignoring the lack of evidence for any Trump campaign collusion with the Russians, which was now the subject of an FBI investigation. The press of course regarded the collusion allegations as newsworthy precisely because they were under investigation; and no major news organization had flatly accused Trump or his associates of conspiring with the Russians. The president, by contrast, had flatly insisted that Barack Obama had ordered surveillance for him and his campaign associates, and by offering no evidence, he had made the press criticism fair game.

Spicer had come prepared to make his case. He devoted seven minutes to citing news reports, from the *New York Times* and *National Review* to Fox News, about surveillance during the campaign. But the articles didn't say what he said, having focused mainly on intercepts of Russians that apparently picked up contacts with certain Trump people.

In the president's defense, Spicer approvingly cited Andrew Napolitano, Fox's top legal analyst, who said that three unnamed sources had told him that the Obama administration had asked British intelligence to put Trump under surveillance. Fox anchors made a point of saying their news division found no evidence to support that claim.

Spicer's move caused an international incident, especially after Trump, at a news conference, defended Spicer, saying that "all we did was quote a certain very talented legal mind." The British government called the charge "utterly ridiculous," and U.S. officials apologized.

The pundits hit back hard. Jake Tapper said after the briefing that Spicer can't "defend the indefensible" and was arguing that "the earth is flat."

Four days later, when James Comey testified that there was no evidence to support Trump's wiretapping tweets, the president's media detractors took a victory lap. They had tried for two years to prove that Trump did not tell the truth, had struggled to make the public care—and now they felt vindicated.

"The president has no facts," Anderson Cooper said on CNN. Lawrence O'Donnell, a former Senate Democratic aide, said on MSNBC that Trump should be considered incapacitated and removed under the Twenty-Fifth Amendment—a ludicrous suggestion even by the most partisan standards.

But some outlets continued to push stories saturated with speculation. CNN reported the FBI had learned that Trump associates had "communicated with suspected Russian operatives to *possibly* coordinate the release of information" damaging to Clinton, "*raising the suspicions* of FBI counterintelligence investigators that the coordination *may have* taken place, though officials cautioned that the information was *not conclusive* and that the investigation is ongoing." (Italics added.) The sheer number of qualifiers rendered the story meaningless.

Still, Spicer had to keep deflecting questions about whether Trump should admit he was wrong and apologize to Obama.

Things sank to the point that Spicer was again feuding with Glenn Thrush on Twitter. Thrush was a dogged *New York Times* reporter who previously worked for *Politico* and was now being portrayed as a character on *Saturday Night Live*. He had also, however, been caught on leaked emails admitting to Clinton campaign chief John Podesta that he was a "hack" and asking him not to tell anyone he was sharing an unpublished story in advance for Podesta's vetting. And he had posted plenty of snarky tweets about Trump.

"Name a time in American history—even during Watergate—when the executive branch was this dysfunctional, feral and fragile. I can't," Thrush tweeted. *Feral*? He sounded disdainful of the White House.

Thrush felt he was simply engaging in the same truth-telling as the president. He viewed his tweets as factually accurate and didn't understand why anyone would object to them. No one, in his view, had degraded the national discourse more than Donald Trump.

Spicer did not like how Thrush occasionally would call him after a briefing, tell him he had done a great job, and then bash him in print. The last straw came when Thrush co-authored a story saying that Spicer and other officials had "told allies that Mr. Trump's Twitter habits are making their jobs harder."

That was obviously true, but Spicer angrily tweeted in response, "Just when you thought @nytimes couldn't go any lower, they make this up."

That prompted Thrush to taunt him on Twitter: "Tell the folks out there why u didn't reply to my email running it by you? Gave you hours and hours...." This was, in fact, true as well. Spicer sometimes ignored requests for comment and then complained about the resulting story.

Thrush felt he was making the process transparent, using his Twitter following as leverage to get answers. This was his way of telling the press secretary that he had a responsibility to respond to the Fourth Estate.

Spicer sometimes engaged in such obvious fudging that no one could figure out why he bothered. When news leaked that Paul Manafort was under investigation for his dealings with Russia, Spicer told reporters that Manafort "played a very limited role for a very limited amount of time." On another day Spicer said he had been "hired to count delegates."

Did he think they had forgotten that Manafort had been the campaign chairman for five months, through the Republican convention, and was Trump's top spokesman on television? Why deny what everyone already knew?

It was those little evasions that kept providing fodder for Spicer's detractors.

Some of Spicer's friends were worried that he would have trouble getting a job in corporate America when he was done at the White House. Those fears were underscored when CNN ran a piece titled "How Sean Spicer Lost His Credibility."

. . .

At 3:31 p.m. on Friday, March 24, Trump called *Washington Post* reporter Robert Costa.

"So, we just pulled it," he told Costa, who immediately tweeted the news. The president was using a newspaper he often denounced to tell the world that he couldn't get the votes he needed and was yanking his Obamacare replacement bill. He called Maggie Haberman of the "failing" *New York Times* moments later with the same news.

Revamping health care was Trump's signature promise, along with building a border wall. The House Republicans had voted sixty times for repeal under Obama, when it was purely symbolic. Now the media had cast it as a test of whether the party could govern.

Trump had promised to repeal Obamacare right away, then, when Congress balked, said that it might take until 2018. "Nobody knew that health care could be so complicated," he said, an observation that had Washington cynics chuckling. The president could muster only a weak spin about the Democrats. "The beauty," he told Costa, "is that they own Obamacare" and would eventually be forced to "make one beautiful deal for the people."

Conway was glad that her boss was making the calls. She had been pushing this approach on the president for a long time. The *Times* and the *Post* were tone-setters for the news media. No matter how much Trump resented their coverage, he needed to engage them so that they had his version of events.

Both reporters were TV regulars: Costa was an MSNBC contributor and Haberman a CNN contributor, which meant they would be on the air talking about the calls, amplifying Trump's message. Haberman had covered Trump as a New York tabloid reporter for years. In 2015, Trump had even offered to let her break the story that he was running for president, but she refused, viewing it as another head fake. Their relationship was often contentious. Trump had called Haberman "third-rate" and "totally in the Hillary circle of bias," but respected her and sometimes called to thank her for her reporting.

Reaching out to the press, however, did not stop the flood of negative stories about the administration, many of them related to Trump's tweets, especially his wiretapping charge. The *Wall Street Journal* editorial page decried "the damage that Mr. Trump is doing to his presidency with his seemingly endless stream of exaggerations, evidence-free accusations, implausible denials and other falsehoods....Yet the president clings to his assertion like a drunk to an empty gin bottle, rolling out his press spokesman to make more dubious claims."

A deluge of leaks followed, with White House officials anonymously savaging each other and assigning blame for the administration's missteps.

Politico reporter Tara Palmeri tweeted that a "source close to @POTUS" said he is open to the possibility of replacing Reince Priebus, and "healthcare was the last straw." The *Times* said that Mike Pence's team "has at times questioned whether Mr. Priebus was up to the demands of his job."

Priebus thought these stories were ludicrous. The White House had done everything it could to pass an Obamacare repeal bill, but no one could force members of Congress to vote a certain way. If the knives really were out for him, his life would be a lot easier if he wasn't chief of staff.

But the most negative leaks were aimed at Jared Kushner. He and Ivanka had chosen the week of the big health care vote to go skiing in Aspen. That annoyed Trump, but it also annoyed officials who resented that Kushner was getting credit for so many policy initiatives at home and around the world. Here was the biggest legislative showdown of the administration and Jared was AWOL. It underlined his critics' suspicions that he wasn't a team player, but merely took credit where he could, and deflected blame from himself when the administration failed. Jared was "a shrewd self-promoter," Trump aides told *Politico*, shrewd at grabbing credit and sidestepping blame without being quoted by reporters.

Trump had repeatedly questioned with his staff whether Jared and Ivanka should be in the West Wing. When he was frustrated with them, he told them to their face. Back during the transition, Trump had warned them that life in the White House would not be good for them and perhaps they shouldn't come. More recently he suggested in front of others, in a sympathetic tone, that maybe this wasn't a good fit. Now the feeling was they should have known they were going to get skewered.

He wasn't about to dismiss his family members, but he made other staff changes, accepting the resignations of spokesman Boris Epshteyn and Priebus's deputy chief of staff Katie Walsh.

This shakeup, minor as it might have seemed, only deepened the sense of an administration in turmoil—and the journalistic sharks smelled blood in the water. CNN ran the headline, "Trump's Problem with the Truth." The first in a series of *Los Angeles Times* editorials was titled "Our Dishonest President," which the paper turned into a book.

Spicer complained that reporters were nitpicking and obsessed with "process" rather than substance, though they viewed themselves as the administration's fact-checkers.

Then, however, came a story that much of the press barely seemed interested in fact-checking.

When Fox News and Bloomberg News reported that Susan Rice, Obama's national security adviser, had "unmasked" Trump and his aides when they were incidentally picked up on foreign intercepts, much of the press was dismissive. Rice, while insisting she had no political motive, admitted the practice to MSNBC's Andrea Mitchell, despite having falsely told PBS two weeks earlier that she knew nothing about the allegations.

It wasn't clear whether Rice had done anything improper, but some journalists had no interest in finding out. On CNN, Don Lemon said he would not "aid and abet the people who were trying to misinform you, the American people, by creating a diversion." He had less interest in aiding and abetting journalism.

When Jim Sciutto, CNN's national security correspondent, denigrated the story as "largely ginned up, partly as a distraction from this larger investigation," he failed to mention that he had worked for the Obama State Department just four years earlier.

The president pushed journalists to cover the Rice story. Despite Glenn Thrush's negative tweets, Trump was happy to chat with him and Maggie Haberman in the Oval Office. He insisted that Rice might have committed a crime—an extraordinary statement about a former official under investigation—and he chided their newspaper.

"I think it's a massive, massive story," he said. "All over the world, I mean other than the New York Times."

"We've written about it twice," Haberman said. In fact, her paper, like many others, had greatly played down the Rice allegations.

Trump wouldn't let go: "I mean, I frankly think the *Times* is missing a big thing by not writing it because you're missing out on the biggest story there is."

Later, Trump made a joke about NBC's Andrea Mitchell being "Hillary Clinton's PR person," adding, "Course, you've been accused of that also."

"Mostly by you," said Haberman.

Trump never let up. He was the nation's most relentless media critic.

CHAPTER 13

ANSWERING WITH AIRSTRIKES

The press was increasingly portraying the president as a bumbling reactionary on domestic policy and as dangerously ignorant on foreign policy.

But on the night of April 7, 2017, the mainstream media suddenly went into a collective swoon over Donald Trump. He had ordered the firing of fifty-nine Tomahawk missiles against a Syrian air base, in retaliation for Syria's using chemical weapons in an attack against civilians. Many of Trump's fiercest critics gave him the equivalent of a standing ovation.

They praised Trump for doing what Barack Obama had failed to do in 2013, when he famously drew a red line against any Syrian chemical weapons attack, and then backed away from military action after Syria's dictator Bashar al-Assad used sarin gas against civilians in Damascus.

"Donald Trump has restored the credibility of American power," *Washington Post* columnist David Ignatius declared on *Morning Joe*.

Even CNN host Fareed Zakaria—who detested Trump and twice called him a "bullshitter" on the air—was impressed. With that attack, he said, "Donald Trump became president."

The press loves denouncing politicians as flip-floppers, suggesting that they bend with the wind, but the dirty little secret is that journalists care far less about flip-flopping if you flip in their direction, and on some foreign policy issues Trump had done just that. During the campaign, for instance, Trump said he would authorize the use of torture against terrorists. But after hiring General Mattis as Defense secretary, he ceded the decision to his Pentagon chief, who opposed torture as ineffective.

The president had also mused about reviewing the One-China policy that denied recognition to Taiwan, which the Communist mainland viewed as a breakaway province. He had shattered protocol by accepting a post-election call from the leader of Taiwan. But by the time he arranged a call with Chinese President Xi Jinping, Trump had to put out a statement reaffirming the One-China approach. And when he wanted Xi's help to rein in North Korea, he quietly dropped his insistence that China be punished for manipulating its currency, which China had quietly stopped doing anyway.

The media could have said that Trump was "growing" or "evolving" in office—as happened when Obama came out for gay marriage—but aside from cheering the attack on Syria, they continued to lay into him.

And at certain times Trump was not "evolving," but just working the angles. In a background briefing with network anchors before he addressed Congress, the president suddenly opined that he would be open to a bill that provided a path to legalization, and perhaps even citizenship, for many illegal immigrants. "There's got to be a coming together," Trump said, a compromise that would satisfy both the "far left" and "far right." Sean Spicer quickly interrupted, saying they didn't want to put that on background and allow the networks to report it. But Trump agreed before the anchors left that they could use the information on background. In his hip-shooting way, he had just contradicted a year and a half of campaign rhetoric without a firm idea of what the legislation would look like. But whether it was a moment of candor or a plan to buy a few hours of favorable coverage, Trump didn't include the idea in his Hill speech and it quickly faded.

The media accused Trump of being erratic, and Trump did have a tendency to revise his answers. But he sometimes did so with a politically savvy element of guile. For example, Trump had long argued that the North American Free Trade Agreement was a bad deal for America. In an orchestrated leak in late April, two unnamed White House officials told CNN and *Politico* that Trump was considering an immediate executive order to withdraw from NAFTA.

Within hours, Canada's Justin Trudeau and Mexico's Enrique Peña Nieto had placed pleading calls to the White House.

The next morning, Trump told reporters he had decided against terminating NAFTA and would renegotiate the deal instead—though he reserved the right to pull the plug.

Trump was acting like a New York real estate guy—making unrealistic demands, pulling back, issuing threats, making the other side think you might do something crazy—all in the service of gaining negotiating leverage.

The same pattern emerged on North Korea. When rogue dictator Kim Jong Un stepped up his testing of nuclear weapons, Trump ridiculed and threatened him, prompting a *New York Times* news story to admonish: "The biggest risk, critics say, is that Mr. Trump will talk himself into a war." When Trump later said he'd be honored to meet Kim under the right circumstances, his deputies thought he was masterfully keeping the young leader off balance.

The media were accustomed to covering presidents whose language was carefully calibrated, whose every utterance was vetted by the bureaucracy. Trump's endless talkathon, his habit of making policy on the fly, made for good copy but it also left Washington reporters appalled, as they held him to a standard he had no intention of observing.

. . .

More than most presidents, Trump faced a hostile bureaucracy and previous administration holdovers who wanted to undermine their new boss. Nowhere was that more evident than in Trump's early round of calls with foreign leaders.

Sources told the *Washington Post*, for instance, that Trump had scolded Australia's Prime Minister Malcolm Turnbull over a refugee agreement he had negotiated with President Obama. Of Trump's four conversations with world leaders that day, "this was the worst call by far."

When Trump spoke to Mexican President Peña Nieto, an obviously well-placed official gave a transcript to the Associated Press. The wire service reported that Trump had warned he was ready to send U.S. troops to stop "bad hombres down there" unless the Mexican president did more to control them.

The pattern continued when the president had a call with Vladimir Putin. In another leak, Reuters reported that when the talk turned to the New START nuclear treaty between the two countries, Trump paused to ask his aides what the agreement was.

These leaks were nothing short of extraordinary. The president was unable to conduct confidential conversations with other heads of state without anonymous dissidents spilling the beans to the press. And news organizations were happy to publish the stories that, invariably, depicted Trump as a hothead who was smashing china on the world stage.

. . .

Sean Spicer had an uncanny knack for getting bad press.

But he took that to a new level behind the podium on April 11, when Spicer was explaining Trump's airstrikes against Syria.

"We didn't use chemical weapons in World War II," he began. "You know, you had a—someone who is as despicable as Hitler who didn't even sink to the—to the—to using chemical weapons."

To historians it is common knowledge that Hitler did not use battle-field chemical weapons, which were banned after World War I. But as a spokesman, not a historian, Spicer should have known he was treading down a dangerous path.

An ABC correspondent, Cecilia Vega, saw that Spicer's comment was blowing up on Twitter, so she repeated Spicer's answer and gave him a chance to clarify.

"I think when you come to sarin gas, there was no—he was not using the gas on his own people the same way that Assad is doing," Spicer said. "I mean, there was clearly, I understand your point....I appreciate that.... [H]e brought them into the Holocaust centers, I understand that. But I'm saying, in the way that Assad used them where he went into towns, dropped them down to innocent, into the middle of town....So, the use of it...I appreciate the clarification. That was not the intent."

Spicer's comments were a media disaster. After the briefing, the press secretary plunged into damage control mode. He told Trump how he planned to fix things, and the president was understanding. "I knew exactly what you were trying to say. I know you didn't mean it," Trump said.

Spicer put out two clarifications. When that didn't work, he apolo-gized in successive interviews on the lawn with CNN, Fox, and MSNBC. And at a forum the next day, he was completely contrite.

Spicer said he had "screwed up." His mistake was "inexcusable and reprehensible." What made the controversy worse was that it had hap-pened during Passover. And, he admitted, he had let the president down. Trump was asked about it, of course, and said that Spicer had made a mistake.

But as terribly as Spicer had blundered, the media reaction in some quarters was just as bad. It might be predictable that Nancy Pelosi called on him to resign. But some critics online called him a Holocaust denier. Everyone knew what Spicer had clumsily tried to say, that even Hitler hadn't used chemical weapons on the battlefield. Chris Matthews had made the same point four years earlier. The attempt to paint the president's spokesman as anti-Semitic, with no evidence, was even more pathetic than Spicer's stumbling performance at the podium.

. . .

When the Tea Party movement arose during the Obama administration, some in the media depicted its members as right-wing zealots infused by borderline racism.

Taunting Trump, however, was cool, and the media, as cultural arbiters, adored those who were placed on the hip side of history—especially if they came out as part of the anti-Trump "resistance."

One of them was Dan Rather.

The former CBS anchor was now eighty-five, decades beyond his heyday. He had enjoyed a storied career as a newsman, but had also been widely criticized for his liberal leanings, especially after he made unsubstantiated charges in 2004 that George W. Bush had gone AWOL during his days in the National Guard, a story that collapsed when a key source admitted to lying and experts concluded that the documents in question were forgeries. Rather apologized for the story, but later insisted it was true and unsuccessfully sued CBS for firing him. He wound up with a little-noticed show on the AXS cable station.

But now, as *Politico* put it, Rather was enjoying "an unexpected, career-redefining resurrection aided by Trump's shocking ascent." He was "one of the leading voices of the Trump resistance," with a weekly Sirius XM show and a popular Facebook page, which he used to describe Trump as "unsettling and unstable and incompetent and erratic and gloating and swaggering and petulant and ill-informed."

Rather was "alarmed" at the "potential peril" of a Trump presidency, and weeks after the inauguration declared that "this is an emergency." Rather told *Politico* that he had been thinking a lot about Adolf Hitler: "And I'm not comparing Trump to Hitler, but..."

This was the nature of his comeback.

Ironically, Rather's eventual successor as CBS anchor, Scott Pelley, began using his newscast to score anti-Trump points. And that earned him praise from Margaret Sullivan in her *Washington Post* media column.

Pelley was doing what evening news anchors generally avoid, and that was "abandoning careful neutrality in favor of pointed truth-telling," she wrote. Think about that: neutrality was out. Opinion, dressed up as "truth-telling," was now in on the program once anchored by Walter Cronkite.

Pelley was more "dogged" and "blunter" than NBC's Lester Holt or ABC's David Muir, talking about Trump's "boasting and tendency to believe conspiracy theories."

Pelley would begin the *CBS Evening News* this way: "It has been a busy day for presidential statements divorced from reality." He would speak of Trump having "another Twitter tantrum" or say that "the president's real troubles today were not with the media, but with the facts." He would denigrate "the president's fictitious claims, whether imaginary or fabricated."

Sometimes Pelley would call out presidential statements offered without evidence, but everyone in the business could see that he was using loaded language. Pelley dismissed Kellyanne Conway as a "fearless fabulist." All this earned him praise from Washington's top newspaper.

The *Washington Post* also lionized Keith Olbermann, once a powerful liberal voice on MSNBC, who had left six years earlier in a bitter dispute with his bosses. He was later fired by Current TV, leading to litigation, and subsequently laid off by ESPN. So Olbermann took his fiery diatribes to a low-production web series, sponsored by *GQ* magazine, to fulminate against Trump. He called his online show *The Resistance.*

And he would rail away: "Donald Trump has branded himself a traitor to everything this country has stood for. We will remove him."

And: "I speak for those unlike Trump, unlike the sycophants who surround him, unlike the hate-filled souls and the conscious optional bigots who applaud him, unlike the Russian puppeteers who may be manipulating him."

But such overheated rhetoric, calling the president a traitor, drew no disapproval from the *Washington Post*. Instead, the paper ran this laudatory headline: "Have Liberals Found Their Combative New Leader in... Keith Olbermann?"

Or perhaps their new leader was Stephen Colbert, who was mired in last place at CBS's *Late Show* until he started a nightly barrage against the new president, catapulting himself into first place. This brought a rave review from the *New York Times*: "Mr. Colbert has benefited from his decidedly anti-Trump point of view." And while there were other factors, "Mr. Trump's victory appears to have single-handedly turned the late-night comedy race upside down" based on Colbert's anti-Trump mockery.

But when it came to slamming Trump, fame was not a prerequisite. In what seemed like a spate of disconnected feature stories, newspapers found a subtle way of denigrating Trump by elevating those who found him odious. The stories almost never questioned whether they were going too far; they were cast as men and women of conscience, rallying behind a righteous cause.

The *Washington Post* did a whole spread on an obscure Democratic congressman from California, just for trolling the president online: "Ted Lieu is Out-Tweeting Trump, And It's Making Him a Political Star."

The *Post* even profiled a high school teacher who took on, yes, the White House Easter Egg Roll by investing $5,000 to make protest eggs, telling the paper: "Donald Trump has broken that trust with families and children."

Walter Shaub was an Obama appointee running the little-known Office of Government Ethics, and because he challenged the White House on a few conflict-of-interest matters, some *Washington Post* puffery was inevitable: "How the U.S. Ethics Chief Took On Trump and Became a Reluctant Washington Hero." To make sure we knew he was a hero, Shaub was quoted as saying, "I feel like I'm working for the good guys." (He soon resigned, saying the White House was close to an ethical laughingstock.)

The *New York Times* lavished ink on poets who, according to the headline, "Rage Against the Right." These included Jane Hirshfield, who wrote verse on "climate change denial" and Trump's "dismantling of environmental regulations," and Danez Smith, whose poem mocked Trump and said "you're dead, America."

A *Washington Post* piece on how teen magazines were becoming more serious led off, naturally, with a *Teen Vogue* essay titled "Donald Trump Is Gaslighting America."

Sometimes a gratuitous slap would be inserted into a completely unrelated story. A *New York Times* book review that began with Bob Dylan winning the Nobel Prize for literature suggested that "this is a spiritual disaster on par with Donald J. Trump's election." The animus was blowing in the wind.

The *Times* published a column by Annie Pfeifer titled "Help! My 3-Year-Old Is Obsessed with Trump." This was a crisis because her daughter attended the kind of liberal New York school "that made counseling available" after the election. "Parents stood together comforting one another on Nov. 9 in an act of collective mourning that I hadn't seen since Sept. 11." Of course.

But perhaps the most forehead-smacking piece in the *Washington Post* began with a Passover Seder held by a woman whose guests jettisoned the usual reading of the ten plagues—blood, frogs, lice, and so on—for "Neo-Nazis," "Fake news," "Freedom Caucus," "The American Health Care Act," and other purported plagues from the Trump administration.

This was said to be a trend among Jews. "For some," the paper intoned, "the big question has become: Is it right to cast the president of the United States as the villainous pharaoh?"

There was no hint that this might be an inappropriate question, to liken an American president to the Egyptian ruler who enslaved the Jews. Not even Passover was safe from the anti-Trump virus.

Imagine for a moment that any of these stories and columns had been written during the last administration. Imagine anchors, comedians, has-beens, and ordinary folks drawing a gusher of positive press for calling Barack Obama a traitor, a liar, a fabricator, and someone reminiscent of Hitler and Pharaoh, and chastising him for presiding over an Easter egg hunt. Those critics would have been diagnosed with Obama Derangement Syndrome. But in the Trump era, it was a sure-fire ticket to good press.

CHAPTER 14

WHITE HOUSE GAME OF THRONES

Most journalists thought Steve Bannon was a dangerous guy, and when he suffered a setback, they practically broke into cheers.

It began with a bureaucratic move. Trump had been annoyed when Bannon maneuvered himself onto the National Security Council, and the president allowed Mike Flynn's successor, H. R. McMaster, to remove him, triggering a flood of headlines about how Bannon had been demoted or diminished.

The new narrative, propelled by a gusher of leaks, had Bannon losing power to Jared Kushner, who seemed to be exerting his influence over just about everyone in the White House and several Cabinet departments as well. Behind the scenes, the seemingly invincible Bannon had grown increasingly frustrated, even openly musing about quitting. Bannon's spin, that he went to the NSC temporarily to keep an eye on Flynn, was hardly convincing.

By publicly declaring that he hated the press, by branding journalists as the "opposition party," Bannon had started a battle that they were now happy to fight. And his rivals in the White House moved quickly to supply the ammunition.

Suddenly there were stories about how the president was angry at Bannon for the rushing of the botched travel ban, and displeased with him for threatening Freedom Caucus members during the failed health care negotiations.

The *Daily Beast* said Bannon had referred to Kushner as a "globalist" and a "cuck"—short for "cuckservative," or a right-winger who sells out. The *Washington Post* said the "Bannonites" were losing ground to the centrist faction of New York financiers led by Kushner. *Politico* said Kushner had complained about Bannon's performance in hours of conversations with people inside and outside the White House. The *New York Times* said Bannon told Jared that they couldn't find "common ground" because "you're a Democrat."

That last comment was untrue, and other anecdotes were exaggerated, but Bannon didn't care. Journalists *should* take shots at him, he felt, because he was opposed to everything they stood for. The press was the propaganda arm of the status quo, which he was determined to overturn. You wouldn't hear him whining about the coverage. Bannon thought these *Game of Thrones* stories were the sort of unadulterated gossip that White House correspondents liked, because they weren't terribly bright, had no grasp of history, and were functioning more like bloggers, aiming for quick hits on MSNBC.

There were, what, a hundred stories about him in the *Washington Post*, including one on which books he read? Now the paper was saying he was a "marked man." It was all so juvenile. Some news outlets routinely referred to him as anti-Semitic. How many people knew he had gone to Auschwitz and Buchenwald and confronted the horror of the Holocaust as part of a film he had produced?

Of course he was clashing with Jared, who worked in the adjoining suite of offices, but it was about policy, not personality. In Bannon's view, they actually got along well. He was a firebrand who fought for nationalism, Kushner a soft-spoken guy with a globalist outlook.

Jared had a very different view of their ongoing battle. He thought it was rooted in personality and that though they agreed on many things, they had different values and different ways of pursuing their goals.

Kushner had no doubt that Bannon and his allies were planting unfavorable stories about him. These were usually passed to the same half-dozen reporters. Finally, Kushner confronted him.

There were three options, Jared said.

Bannon could keep leaking against him and he would do nothing in response. That wasn't happening.

Bannon could keep leaking against him and he would retaliate with his own leaks. That wasn't happening, because it wouldn't help the president.

Or Bannon could stop this garbage.

If not, Kushner indicated, Bannon would be gone.

Bannon told friends this incident never happened, but there was no question that he was locked in constant political warfare with Jared and his wife Ivanka. Bannon had told Ivanka early in the administration: "My daughter loves me as a dad. You love your dad, I get that. But you're just another staffer who doesn't know what you're doing." The president's daughter fought back hard.

During one Oval Office meeting between the president and his senior staff, Bannon bluntly blamed Ivanka for a leak, and Trump backed him.

"Baby, I think Steve's right here," Trump told her.

Bannon had, of course engaged in a few strategic leaks of his own. But, in his view, that was nothing compared to the gusher of leaks emanating from the entity he called Javanka.

The infighting drew so much media attention that Trump told Bannon and Kushner to work things out, or he would do it for them. The situation was simply not sustainable.

Bannon understood Trump's frustration, and he didn't blame the president for getting angry when *Time* magazine put him on its cover. Bannon had refused to cooperate with the magazine, but *Time* had taken a black-and-white photo of him that had been shot for Trump's Person of the Year issue and colorized it in an ominous way for the cover. He felt it made him look like Dr. Evil.

Some journalists were practically high-fiving when Trump apparently whacked Bannon in a pair of interviews. The president told the *New York Post* that Steve had joined the campaign late and "I'm my own strategist," and described Bannon to the *Wall Street Journal* as "a guy who works for me." To Bannon, both statements were self-evidently true. He *was* just a staff guy. He wasn't offended.

Bannon hadn't had a boss since he left Goldman Sachs in his early thirties, and he didn't care about his status as a presidential aide. He was the ultimate cause guy. He would fight the establishment from inside the White House or outside the gates. He had said from the beginning, he might be at the White House for eight minutes or eight years. If Trump concluded, or he decided on his own, that he couldn't do the job, he would be gone.

• • •

There was something about Trump in the White House that brought out the worst in left-wing journalists. They were affronted by his very presence. They thought it reflected badly on America. And their angst came to a head when Trump struggled to pass a health care bill. The fact that Trump insisted on covering patients with preexisting conditions and favored more moderate policies than House Republicans mattered not at all to liberal writers. What mattered was that Trump was open to compromises to win conservative votes. The left was aflame that some of the proposed compromises meant an estimated twenty-four million people could lose health care coverage over the next ten years.

Liberal commentators argued that Trump was betraying the very voters who put him in the White House, that his health care plan would especially hurt working-class Americans. Journalists dutifully tracked down families who were worried about losing their insurance. And this struck a deep chord among the pundits who believed that Trump had essentially deceived these blue-collar folks, that he had exploited their cultural resentments but would hurt them financially by catering to the rich.

In their anger against Trump, and their gloating over Trump's alleged betrayal of blue-collar Americans, they showed an ugly side of themselves.

Frank Rich had been a talented op-ed columnist and theater critic for the *New York Times*. Now, in *New York* magazine, he assailed "the hardcore, often self-sabotaging Trump voters who helped drive the country into a ditch on Election Day....If we are free to loathe Trump, we are free to loathe his most loyal voters, who have put the rest of us at risk."

The *Huffington Post* ran a piece headlined, "A Vote for Trump Was a Hate Crime."

Conor Lynch, in *Salon*, said of Trump's "culturally backward" voters: "Let them lose their health care; maybe they'll learn something this time around."

Kurt Eichenwald of *Newsweek* took the next logical step, admitting a deadly wish: "As one w/ preexisting condition: I hope every GOPr who voted 4 Trumpcare sees a family member get long term condition, lose insurance, & die," he tweeted.

Rather than back off after being confronted on Twitter for that hateful statement, Eichenwald upped the ante. He said that the family members of Republican lawmakers should be "tortured."

Tortured was a good way to describe the media anguish. How did people who marched under the liberal banner, who professed to care about the little guy, wind up hoping for lower-income Americans to lose their health insurance, even drop dead? How did they feel comfortable beating up on "hillbillies," the term adopted by Frank Rich? It was another case of Trump Trauma that caused liberals to lose their minds and their sense of decency.

It was one thing to assail the president they despised. But somehow they felt entitled to sneer at the sixty-three million voters who put him in office.

· · ·

Everyone knew it was an ossified media ritual, tied to an utterly arbitrary date, but even a president determined to write his own rules was going to be judged by his first hundred days.

To preempt an inevitable avalanche of bad press, Trump touted his Supreme Court confirmation of Neil Gorsuch as a major achievement and tweeted: "No matter how much I accomplish during the ridiculous standard of the first 100 days, & it has been a lot (including S.C.), media will kill!"

Corey Lewandowski told him to ignore the media hype: "Who cares about this artificial 100-day marker? It's inside-the-Beltway news. If you believed them, you never would have run, never would have filed your papers, would have quit after finishing second in Iowa, and never would have won the general election."

Trump, of course, had campaigned on a hundred-day action plan. And his team had held meetings to "brand" the time period—meetings that, like almost everything inside the White House, quickly leaked to the press. Sean Spicer was deluged with so many requests for interviews and comments that he knew a media hurricane was coming. Kellyanne Conway saw it as an opportunity to defend Trump's agenda.

The press had marked Barack Obama's first one hundred days dramatically differently. In *Time*, Joe Klein called Obama's debut "the most impressive of any presidency since FDR." Mark Halperin called him "instantly comfortable and highly skilled at the hardest job in the world...even temper, cool demeanor, boldness under pressure."

Now the press was ready to give Obama's successor grief for not having pushed a major bill through Congress. That was a critical measurement, but journalists tended to minimize his other accomplishments, from regulatory rollbacks to executive orders, from killing the Pacific trade deal to jump-starting the Keystone pipeline.

Trump broke tradition again by skipping the White House Correspondents' Dinner, since he had no desire to be skewered by hostile journalists and a comedian. Instead, the television veteran decided to engage in some counterprogramming.

On the night of April 29, when 2,500 journalists gathered in a Washington Hilton ballroom, Trump was giving a stemwinder in Harrisburg, Pennsylvania. He mocked the White House Correspondents' Dinner, ripped the media as a "disgrace" and sounded a populist note:

"The Washington media is part of the problem. Their priorities are not my priorities and they're not your priorities."

And he singled out two outlets in particular. "CNN and MSNBC are fake news," the president declared, amid chants of "CNN sucks!"

On the way back to the plane, Trump asked Kellyanne whether CNN had aired that part of his speech. The answer was yes. All three cable news networks had carried the rally live.

The White House Correspondents' Dinner, deprived of its star, was low energy. There were self-congratulatory speeches about protecting the First Amendment and holding a president accountable. Only Bob Woodward, who appeared with Carl Bernstein, found fault with the profession. He said the media made mistakes and had to face up to a loss of public trust. But he still delivered a suitable sound bite: "Mr. President, the media is not fake news."

Before he knew Trump would be absent, Graydon Carter canceled the huge *Vanity Fair* bash that he had thrown during the Obama years. The *New Yorker* abandoned its lavish soiree as well. Once Trump bailed, other parties vanished. Hollywood celebrities, who invaded the capital every spring for Obama, were nowhere to be found; and journalists, in a fitting metaphor, were left talking to themselves. The media's prom weekend was a flop.

Trump, however, knew how to combat the negative press reviews. He returned for a campaign-style media blitz, sitting down with journalists he spent so much time deriding. Trump did interviews with the Associated Press, Reuters, the *Washington Post*, the *Washington Examiner*, CBS, Fox, and Bloomberg, among others. He even wrote an op-ed for the *Post*.

His critics pounced on any wayward phrase. Trump told Reuters that "I loved my previous life. I had so many things going. This is more work than in my previous life. I thought it would be easier."

Aha! He had no clue what the presidency would be like; the president was obviously a dope who had lucked into the world's toughest job—at least that was the media narrative. But really it was simply Trump sharing a candid thought—and unlike most politicians, he shared many such thoughts; he didn't carefully weigh his words as other politicians did.

There was a deeply uncomfortable moment on CBS's *Face the Nation*. Trump liked his interviewer, John Dickerson, but was wary of him, feeling that Dickerson's easy demeanor and pleasant smile masked the ability to suddenly stick the knife in.

The president took a swipe at Dickerson early on: "I love your show. I call it *Deface the Nation*. But, you know, your show is sometimes not exactly correct."

It was toward the end of the interview, when Trump was discussing Obama and what had happened with "surveillance," that Dickerson asked why he had called the former president a "bad" and "sick" man in the initial tweet about wiretapping. Did he stand by that charge?

"I don't stand by anything. You can take it the way you want," Trump said.

Dickerson kept pressing, again and again, and Trump kept deflecting: "I have my own opinions. You can have your own opinions."

With that, the president abruptly ended the interview: "Okay, that's enough, thank you." He walked back to his desk.

But his flash of anger faded once the cameras were off. Trump spent part of the day with Dickerson and they had dinner. The president was personally fond of some journalists, but not of their work. He felt so badly mistreated by the press that, in public at least, he always had his fists up.

The Dickerson incident triggered a much nastier blow. Stephen Colbert, in the guise of defending his CBS colleague, fired off a series of rapid-fire insults on the *Late Show*, including this one: "The only thing your mouth is good for is as Putin's cock holster." That CBS allowed the airing of the bleeped joke, which was scripted for the taped show, was stunning, as was the fact that a talk show host as talented as Colbert would stoop to that level. But when he was criticized for the line, Colbert offered only a lame non-apology.

"I don't regret that," Colbert told viewers. While he would "change a few words that were cruder than they needed to be," he would do it again. The core of Colbert's audience disliked Trump—he had obviously written off conservative viewers—and he did not want to appear to be backing down. What's more, these were not just jokes. Colbert, like his mentor Jon Stewart, had long ago fused satire and serious political commentary.

If Colbert had gone low, comedian Kathy Griffin was willing to go lower with grotesque photos of her holding a severed head resembling that of Donald Trump. The D-list comedian apparently thought this would be amusing—in an age of ISIS beheadings—because Hollywood haters of Trump seemed to reap nothing but praise for any attack on the president, no matter how vile. But this time, CNN, after initially hesitating, fired Griffin from the New Year's Eve show she co-hosted with Anderson Cooper. The president tweeted that she was "sick" and that the image had upset his eleven-year-old son Barron.

Griffin made a video apology, saying "the image is too disturbing. I understand how it offends people....I beg your forgiveness."

But within days she held a tearful news conference in which she attacked Trump. "A sitting president of the United States and his grown children and the first lady are personally, I feel, personally trying to ruin my life forever," she said.

Griffin also accused Trump of retaliating against her because she was a woman. "I don't think I will have a career after this," she said. "I have to be honest, he broke me."

Griffin, who owned a $10-million California home, was casting herself as the victim after behavior that she herself had described as offensive. The brief statements by the first family were not the reason she was losing her gig at CNN and was deemed too gross for her sponsor Squatty Potty. A national wave of revulsion, on the left as well as the right, had finally determined there was a line of human decency that no one should cross, even when it came to Trump.

And yet that line kept getting lowered. Actor Johnny Depp thought it was amusing to tell a crowd at a film screening, "Can you bring Trump here....When was the last time an actor assassinated a president?" He later apologized for his "bad joke."

In a perversion of Shakespeare, New York's Public Theater produced *Julius Caesar* with a Trump figure, complete with orangey hair and a red tie, stabbed to death on stage by a gang of senators next to an American flag. Delta and Bank of America were so offended by this bastardization of the bard and celebration of anti-Trump violence that they yanked their funding.

But not the *New York Times*, which continued to support the production as an affirmation of free speech in the arts. The *Times* ran a front-page story on the controversy that did not mention its financial role, which was relegated to the twenty-seventh paragraph of a twenty-eight-paragraph sidebar. Its corporate association with this ugliness was barely news fit to print.

CHAPTER 15

JARED AND IVANKA FIGHT BACK

It read like a political obituary for Reince Priebus.

Filled with embarrassing details leaked by his colleagues and rivals, the *New York Times* story painted a devastating portrait: The chief of staff's job "often seemed to overwhelm him." He was "a would-be gatekeeper desperately in search of a gate." He had finally "cut back on his stalking-butler tendency to hover over the president," realizing that Trump "had grown resentful of his constant companionship."

And the killer quote, attributed to Trump at a recent meeting around his desk: "What are you doing in here? Don't you have health care to take care of?"

What rendered the long piece by Glenn Thrush and Maggie Haberman remarkable was that it was published on May 5, the morning after Trump pushed the House into approving a bill to revamp Obamacare.

And it was Priebus who played the vital role in reviving the effort after the devastating failure six weeks earlier that appeared to bury health care reform.

His reward? The *Times* verdict that this was "less a victory" than "a reprieve" for him, that a loss would "probably have been an unrecoverable blow to an already weakened Mr. Priebus."

The story dug into the endless infighting, saying Priebus was often "elbowed out" by Jared Kushner and other West Wing aides, that he was trying to curb Steve Bannon's agenda and felt that Bannon was using *Breitbart* and other outlets to wage a "hidden war" against him.

Priebus thought the piece was phony. Its sources were what he liked to call straphangers, people from outside the inner circle. He had talked to Thrush and Haberman, and so had Bannon and Kushner, in front of the PR people, and yet the paper still trashed him.

"You're just getting cut up. They're winning," Bannon told him. The two men had actually become allies after the tension of the early months.

Priebus had complained to Trump about the endless leaks. He felt that he had laid down strict rules against leaking, but that he was being a Boy Scout while all his detractors dumped on him in the press. He had seen too many details published after meetings involving just him, Trump, and a couple of other people.

The president himself leaked to reporters as well, his aides believed, sometimes in late-night calls. And sometimes it was inadvertent: Trump would talk to so many friends and acquaintances that key information would quickly reach journalists.

Priebus also sometimes spoke to reporters on background to push back against anonymous accusations. And there were times when he placed authorized leaks, such as previewing coming announcements. Still, the porous atmosphere fostered mistrust within the administration, and Trump's deputies were increasingly willing to use the press to undermine their colleagues rather than help the president. But Reince was wedded to the belief that that Trump's opinion of him was the only one that mattered.

• • •

The media swiftly shifted from dutifully treating the House's passage of a health care bill as a modest victory for the president (on a narrow, party-line vote), to highlighting how bad the bill was.

Many liberal outlets were apoplectic. The *Huffington Post* ran this screamer: "HOUSE VOTES TO LET 'EM DIE." That scare-tactic banner was followed hours later by "PATIENTS FEAR: 'THEY WANT TO KILL ME.'" The site had used a policy disagreement to brand Trump a killer, echoing some of the most extreme Democratic rhetoric.

Kellyanne Conway was disgusted. Shame on the anchors who didn't correct their liberal guests on outlandish charges of people dying in the streets. Wasn't it part of the media's job, she asked, to challenge such hyperbolic claims?

When the original bill failed in March, MSNBC host Lawrence O'Donnell had announced: "It is impossible—*impossible*—to exaggerate the enormity of what happened to Donald Trump. His presidency effectively ended. He is a powerless president." That prediction had not aged well.

The press did point out some legitimate problems. For one thing, the measure faced a far rougher ride in the Senate. Despite the president's insistence that he had protected people with preexisting conditions, the bill was a convoluted compromise that allowed states to opt out of those rules, and the billions allotted to the states might not be enough to make insurance affordable for them. Journalists noted that Republicans initially tried to ram through the bill without an official "score" of how much it would cost.

But the spate of stories about people who might lose their health insurance was not accompanied by much examination of how Obamacare had faltered, how millions of patients lost their plans and their doctors and faced big premium hikes, or how most insurers had bailed out in some states.

The media, in effect, were tilting in favor of the status quo—Obamacare—against Trump's reforms. He had finally put a win on the board, but they were, for the moment, discounting that victory.

• • •

Ivanka Trump had a golden media image—until her father won the presidency.

Then the press began tarnishing her, not because of what she said or did, but because of who she was.

With her striking looks, cool demeanor, and soft-spoken style, the businesswoman who had branded her own clothing line was part of Manhattan's smart set. She had socially liberal views on such issues as child care, equal pay, and climate change.

And that is precisely what made her a target: Some left-leaning journalists were convinced that she should talk some sense into her crazy father.

Ivanka was stunned that so many people put their hopes and dreams at her feet, that she was supposed to ease her liberal friends' remorse over Hillary's loss. They somehow expected her to contradict his public positions on issue after issue, to change her dad in radical ways. But they had apparently missed the fact that not only had the country had elected him president, but that she had supported him; she did not believe it was her role to "moderate" or change him.

"I'm one of the few people in Washington who doesn't have a hidden agenda," Ivanka told her father. He knew where she stood. She was a senior official now. Her goal was to pursue the issues she cared most about, and on which she and her father had common ground—from supporting female entrepreneurs to larger tax credits for families with children. Ivanka was not there to fight his agenda. She realized, though, that every time her father annoyed liberals, especially on "social" issues, many in the media would blame her for failing to rein him in.

Ivanka Trump was different than her father in that she was low-key, tightly controlled, and a consensus builder. She had never experienced negative press before, and was shocked at how vicious liberal media outlets could be. They had helped her build her brand as a business-woman. But once her father became a candidate for president, she felt that everything was viewed through this cynical prism: *Oh, she's being used as a weapon to sanitize him with women.*

It's not that criticism of the thirty-five-year-old Ivanka was somehow out of bounds. She had worked for her father's company. And she knew she would face charges of nepotism when she took a job in the adminis-tration, relinquishing her role in her company, and working in the White House at no salary.

The media assault really intensified when she flew to Germany for a conference on female empowerment, sharing the stage with Angela Merkel and Christine Lagarde. When Ivanka called her father a "tre-mendous champion" of women's rights, media reports said that the audience booed (though it turned out it was just murmurs).

CNN commentator Amanda Carpenter, a former Ted Cruz aide and an anti-Trump conservative, slammed her: "When I see Ivanka taking on this role, I really see her becoming like Hillary Clinton in the worst ways. She's sort of becoming increasingly unlikable. She's trying to get these jobs she's not qualified for based on family connections."

The *Huffington Post* ran a banner headline: "Trump's White House Family Affair Looks a Lot Like the Most Corrupt Nations in the World."

The *Guardian* carried a snarky column saying that Ivanka "invoked her own impressive achievements as an example of her father's commit-ment to equality....Trump is, indeed, a wonderful example of what women can achieve with just perseverance, tenacity and millions of inherited dollars."

Joe Scarborough defended Ivanka by noting that Bobby Kennedy had done a good job as Jack Kennedy's attorney general. When Mika Brzezinski asked if he was really comparing Ivanka Trump to Bobby Kennedy, Scarborough said she was being "snotty" and taking a "cheap shot."

One of Ivanka's problems was that, like her husband Jared, she rarely spoke to the press, ceding the field to her critics. She did an interview with NBC's Hallie Jackson, defending her father and saying she didn't like being described as his "accomplice." But mostly her voice was muffled.

Finally, at the beginning of May, Ivanka gave two interviews for a carefully orchestrated piece in the *New York Times*. She criticized the media's about-face in reporting on her. As for the president, "maybe along the way I've modified a position just slightly."

The lengthy article included some criticism, but it was a largely sympathetic profile obviously done with her side's cooperation. The lead anecdote said that when her father refused the full-throated apology she had urged after the leaking of the *Access Hollywood* tape, a teary, red-faced Ivanka ran out of the room in frustration.

But whatever residue of good will the article generated was quickly wiped away. When Ivanka's book *Women Who Work*, written before the election, was published, many reviewers trashed it as a collection of insipid advice by an entitled child of privilege. And columnists used it as a reason to tee off on Ivanka's character.

Ruth Marcus asked in the *Washington Post* whether Ivanka could try to "imagine the needs of those who inhabit a world outside your cosseted confines, and use your Trump-whispering skills on their behalf. Say, the kinds of people who have to worry more about finding enough money to get food on the table." Otherwise, said Marcus, there was little reason to swallow "the inherent distastefulness, if not outright brand-building griftiness, of having Jared Kushner and Ivanka Trump in the White House."

The headline on Gail Collins's *New York Times* column captured the media sentiment: "Where's Ivanka When We Need Her?"

Her dad was "going to war against women....Ivanka's a major power in the administration, and she ought to be mobilizing support for things like easy access to contraceptives."

This was now the narrative, that Ivanka was a fraud unless she could change the president's policies. Actress Debra Messing addressed her rhetorically at an awards ceremony for the gay and lesbian group

GLAAD: "Ivanka...girlfriend...what are you doing?...Ivanka, you can change the lives of millions of women and children just by telling your dad stories about real people who are suffering."

Things soon took a toxic turn. Bill Maher, the uber-liberal comedian on HBO, opened with this line: "A lot of us thought, 'Ivanka is gonna be our saving grace.'" And then he dove into the gutter: "When he's about to nuke Finland or something, she's gonna walk into the bedroom and—'Daddy, Daddy. Don't do it, Daddy.'"

And he made what most news outlets had to describe as a crude hand gesture, which amounted to an incest joke—that Ivanka could influence her dad by having sex with him. It was the same sick "humor" that former *Politico* writer Julia Ioffe had used when she tweeted, "Either Trump is fucking his daughter or he's shirking nepotism laws. Which is worse?" Only Maher had a much larger audience.

The media reaction was mostly muted, because the entertainment culture had already condoned saying virtually anything negative about Donald Trump, no matter how personally vicious. Now it was somehow acceptable to slime Ivanka Trump by suggesting she was an incestuous slut, simply because she was the president's daughter.

Ivanka found the Maher joke beyond inappropriate, but she really didn't care. After her first couple of months in Washington, she had become totally desensitized.

• • •

Ivanka's husband didn't have her glamorous image. In fact, he didn't want much of an image at all—hardly a realistic option given his closeness to the leader of the free world.

While he worked in a small suite outside the Oval Office, Jared Kushner felt he wasn't good at politics; he was good at solving problems, and it was that ability at got him slowly sucked into the campaign, as Trump called with one request after another: My schedule sucks, fix it. The pollsters are robbing me. The vendors are ripping me off. By the end, Jared was running everything.

His father-in-law would phone every morning. "Did you see the fucking New York Times?" he would say.

"Donald," Kushner would reply, "if they mattered, you'd be at 1 percent."

The election taught him to avoid the hysterical media voices yelling from inside their bubble. And of all the journalists and producers and commentators whose predictions were so wrong, had a single one been fired? If they were stock pickers, Kushner thought, they would have been wiped out.

Trump relied on Jared's advice, but he had reservations. He warned his daughter and son-in-law that life in the White House might be extremely unpleasant.

"Look, it's going to be nasty and they're going to come after you guys," Trump told him.

And he told Ivanka, "I know you're doing this for the right reasons. But they'll never let you win, because you're with me."

Even with Trump's warning, Kushner was unprepared for Washington's hostile media. But when colleagues told him that the climate was unfair, Jared objected. No, no, he said, this is the White House. This is the game. The other side is trying to kill us.

Kushner was blunt with people, and he realized that probably hurt him. He told Priebus flat out that Sean Spicer was doing a bad job. He didn't say it publicly; he didn't leak it; he realized that feelings might get hurt; but he knew others were more adept at political maneuvering.

Some colleagues thought he should build relationships with the media and go on TV. Even Trump told him, "You should do it." But his default setting was to avoid the limelight. He didn't have a following. He wasn't there to build his brand. He wanted to have a real impact on policy, not a fake impact as measured by pretty stories. What Kushner didn't understand was that in Washington positive news stories can increase your clout.

At the hardest moments Jared would think, what am I doing this for, why don't I go back to New York? But he felt he was doing important work. Still, since he almost never spoke to journalists on the record, there were no gauzy features about him; he was viewed as important but elusive figure.

Kushner was amazed by the constant attacks on his father-in-law, and felt it had become the hip thing to do to trash Trump on television. He wasn't blind to the president's excesses; he knew their lives would be easier if Trump stopped tweeting; but on balance he felt that Twitter was a positive tool for communicating his agenda.

When people told him his father-in-law was unhinged, Kushner had a ready answer: No, he makes other people unhinged.

CHAPTER 16

THE COMEY FIRESTORM

Late on the afternoon of May 9, 2017, Sean Spicer was summoned to a meeting with the president.

Trump had decided to fire James Comey, the FBI director. Brushing aside the few objections from his advisers, he committed the ultimate act of defiance disorder. By canning the head of the agency that was investigating his associates and their ties to Russia, the president handed his media antagonists a devastating narrative. There were many legitimate stories questioning the decision, but many in the press simply went bonkers, casting Trump as criminal or crazy or a malevolent mastermind, especially as his explanation for the firing seemed to change.

The cover of New York's *Daily News*, which detested Trump, called it a "coup," and that word popped up in cable news segments as well. The headline on a McClatchy Newspapers story was "Trump Takes a Dictator's Stand Against Inquiry."

On CNN, Jeff Toobin called Trump's decision "a grotesque abuse of power" and "the kind of thing that goes on in non-democracies." Morning anchor Dave Briggs kicked off CNN's coverage by saying "breaking news, the bedrock of our democracy is under siege." On MSNBC, Chris Matthews said the move carried a "whiff of fascism." John Heilemann said Trump "blew the lid off his own coverup." On Fox, Bob Beckel called Trump "a liar and a buffoon."

John Harwood, CNBC's editor at large, who had been condemned for asking Trump during a debate whether he was running a "comic book version" of a campaign, tweeted that it's "not hard to imagine resulting chain of events that would make Pence president."

So for dismissing the head of the FBI, who serves at the pleasure of the president, Trump was called a fascist dictator who threatened the foundation of democracy and who could be impeached. If he was not a fascist, Trump was at least Richard Nixon, with the press likening Comey's ouster to Nixon's firing of Watergate special prosecutor Archibald Cox. Never mind that Cox was investigating real crimes while the Russia allegations remained murky.

Trump had not informed Spicer that he was firing Comey until the last minute, which left the press office stranded without a plan.

When there was a glitch in emailing the press release announcing the firing, Spicer read it—shouted it, actually—to a handful of reporters outside his office.

That night, Spicer huddled with his staff near a clump of bushes on the North Lawn. He had just done a brief interview with Lou Dobbs of Fox Business, and a pack of reporters was nearby, clamoring for more answers. An aide said Spicer would take a few questions, but only if the networks turned off their lights.

Spicer laid out the White House line: Trump was merely acting on the recommendation of Rod Rosenstein, the deputy attorney general, who had been on the job for two weeks and was overseeing the Russia investigation because Jeff Sessions had recused himself.

"It was all him," Spicer said, meaning Rosenstein. "No one from the White House. That was a DOJ decision."

Spicer promised to get answers to the many questions he couldn't answer, and when he retreated toward the mansion, a pack of reporters trailed his steps.

The surreal scene was described in a *Washington Post* sidebar that cast Spicer as using the bushes for cover. Spicer angrily called a top editor at the paper to complain that he wasn't "hiding" behind the bushes, as the *Post* suggested, that he had taken questions near there for ten minutes. And Sean was upset that the paper, which complained about access, failed to note that he had directed cameras to the Roosevelt Room, where he did one-on-one interviews with every network.

The *Post*'s handling of the episode, Spicer believed, had been disgraceful. And he was perturbed that not one reporter who witnessed the scene stood up for him.

The paper ran an editor's note to clarify what happened. But the "hiding in the bushes" meme took on a life of its own, with sketches of a cowering Spicer even appearing on magazine covers.

Kellyanne Conway was on a road trip when she heard the news and rushed back to the White House. "What do you think of this?" Trump asked.

"I think it's very you," Conway said. "You've been itching for a while about this guy," meaning Comey. Trump had made his decision over the weekend, when he was at his Bedminster, New Jersey, golf club. Jared and Ivanka had been there, but not Conway or Bannon or Priebus, who might have tried to dissuade him.

Trump was upset that he was being trashed by CNN's panels, which he viewed as stacked six to one against him. "Where are my people?" he asked.

With Rosenstein refusing to appear on television, Trump's team tried to reach Chris Christie or Rudy Giuliani. Trump asked Conway to go on CNN, which she viewed as the lion's den.

Speaking from the White House lawn, Kellyanne made the case to Anderson Cooper. "He took the recommendation of his deputy attorney general," she said; and "today's actions had zero to do" with the FBI's Russia probe.

When she offered an aside about how she had tried to tell them that Trump would win the election, Cooper rolled his eyes, which Conway regarded as sexist.

The president told Kellyanne that he loved the interview. At the very least, he said, it cut into the channel's otherwise non-stop negative coverage.

Every official had the same talking points, including Sarah Huckabee Sanders, Spicer's deputy, and Mike Pence, who spoke of "the president's decision to accept the recommendation of the deputy attorney general and the attorney general."

The two-page Rosenstein memo that Trump and his allies kept citing focused on Comey's mishandling of the Hillary Clinton email investigation. It criticized Comey's public trashing of Hillary when he chose not to recommend that the Justice Department bring an indictment against her. And it criticized him for his eleventh-hour announcement of a renewed probe into her emails (which had prompted Trump to praise Comey for his "guts").

But while Rosenstein's memo recommended removing the FBI chief for botching the Clinton email investigation, the president invoked the Russia inquiry in his official letter dismissing Comey: "I greatly appreciate you informing me, on three separate occasions, that I am not under investigation." A gusher of administration leaks followed, which quickly debunked the notion that the firing was all about Hillary and not about Russia.

A *New York Times* account detailed how the president had been fuming about Comey's Senate testimony that he had been nauseated by the notion that he had interfered with the election.

Mike Pence, Jared Kushner, and White House counsel Don McGahn supported the idea of firing Comey. Reince Priebus did not favor the move, but the decision was largely made before he learned about it— underscoring his lack of influence at crunch time.

Steve Bannon, however, had weighed in and was adamantly opposed. He believed that the geniuses who wanted Comey ousted didn't understand the Beltway culture. In real estate and entertainment, Bannon felt, personalities could carry the day. But charm didn't work in Washington. It was all about institutions. And you couldn't fire the FBI, he argued, which is how the dismissal would be perceived. Trump was already unpopular at the FBI, and with much of Congress. The president, Bannon believed, could have gotten away with firing Jim Comey right after the inauguration, or if he waited a few months until things died down. But right now, with Comey overseeing the Russia probe, Bannon was certain it would be the worst political decision of modern times. And beyond that, the probe had been running out of gas. It was a third-tier story going nowhere. It had no oomph.

The others, the New Yorkers, actually thought the Democrats would praise the move, since they detested Comey for undermining Hillary in the campaign's final stretch. And the president, who employed the Socratic method—asking everyone he could find for their opinion—was swayed by the staffers who opposed Bannon. And now they were shocked by the blowback.

The press was obsessed with the issue of Trump's motivation. The *Washington Post* said that Trump, who was tweeting that Comey's Russia probe was a "total hoax," had already "made up his mind" before ordering Rosenstein and Sessions to lay out the case against Comey.

In an interview with NBC's Lester Holt two days after the firing, the president flatly contradicted all the top aides who had been peddling the spin that the decision rested on Rosenstein's memo. Trump admitted he had made the decision beforehand, telling the anchor that "I was going to fire Comey regardless of recommendation." With that one sentence, the president enabled the media to trumpet that they had been right all along.

Kellyanne didn't care if she had been undercut. He was the president, he was her boss, and she had made her argument with the information that was given to her. Even though she had been left out of the loop on Comey, she didn't agree that Trump had blindsided his communications team. She and Hope Hicks were with the president, off-camera, during the Lester Holt interview. Conway saw no contradiction between Trump acting on both his longstanding desire to fire Comey *and* on Rosenstein's recommendation (though Rosenstein later admitted that, before he wrote his memo, he knew Trump intended to fire Comey).

Kellyanne thought the whole story was overblown. Ordinary people outside the Beltway didn't care about Comey. They worried about their jobs, not his. As a New Jersey girl raised by a single mother, she felt she understood ordinary Americans in a way the elite media did not.

Conway was amazed that lawyers like Jeff Toobin could trash the president with loaded language and be back on CNN day after day. She thought it was terrible that the *Washington Post* could anonymously quote "one GOP figure close to the White House"—how close, she wondered, at the Cosi down the street?—as musing about whether Trump was "in the grip of some kind of paranoid delusion." And where, she wondered, were the corrections? The *Washington Post* reported that Rosenstein threatened to resign if he was blamed for Comey's ouster; he denied it. The *New York Times* reported that Comey had asked for more resources for the Russia probe; his deputy denied it.

Conway was once again a prime media target. Mika Brzezinski, her former friend, went into overdrive, denouncing CNN for putting her on the air. "It's politics porn. You're just getting your little ratings crack," she said, because Kellyanne was "a repeated liar."

Brzezinski went further, saying that after Conway's *Morning Joe* appearances during the campaign, "the microphone would be taken off and she would say 'Blecch, I need to take a shower' because she disliked her candidate so much."

Word of Brzezinski's slam on Conway reached the president. "Did you see what Mika said about you?" Trump asked Kellyanne. "I don't believe that for a second."

Many outsiders didn't understand that Trump has a strong sense of loyalty, and that when his people come under fire, he pulls them closer. Trump appreciated Conway's defending him after the *Access Hollywood* debacle; he knew she had given up a gold mine to work for him, telling Mike Pence, "She could have made eight figures and came with us instead."

It may have been a breach for the *Morning Joe* duo to reveal private, off-air conversations. Scarborough didn't know whether Kellyanne viewed it as a betrayal. But he recalled Conway subtly dissing Trump; now she was lecturing the press about its mistreatment of the president.

Conway issued a statement calling Brzezinski and Scarborough "virulent critics of the president and those close to him." She noted that she had walked away from "millions of dollars" that she could have made in the private sector, and said it was "absurd" to suggest that she served the president merely because she needed a paycheck and not because she believed in him.

Joe Scarborough stuck by Mika's story and jumped on Sean Spicer as well, saying "he went into the White House and shattered his reputation." He also called Donald Trump, the president of the United States and his former friend, a "thug" and implied that he was mentally ill: "Donald Trump is not well. He is detached from the reality that most of us live day in and day out."

The president matched his critics with inflammatory language. In over-the-top comments during a three-hour interview with *Time*, he called Chris Cuomo a "chained lunatic," "like a boiler ready to explode, the level of hatred" (which the network called "beneath the dignity of the office"). Trump dismissed CNN's Don Lemon as "perhaps the dumbest person in broadcasting." As for Scarborough, "I don't watch the show anymore, it drives him crazy." Trump also hit back at Stephen Colbert, calling him a "no-talent" purveyor of "filthy" jokes.

Trump continued his press war online. He tweeted that since he was a very active president, "it is not possible for my surrogates to stand at podium with perfect accuracy! Maybe the best thing to do would be to cancel all future 'press briefings' and hand out written responses for the sake of accuracy???" Trump insisted on Fox that the "level of hostility" toward Sean Spicer and Sarah Sanders was "incredible," and maybe he'd just hold a biweekly press conference instead.

Things really spiraled out of control with a *New York Times* report that at a dinner one week after the inauguration, Trump had asked Comey whether he would "pledge his loyalty to him," with the director offering only his honesty. Trump denied the account, and posted this ominous tweet: "James Comey better hope that there are no 'tapes' of our conversations before he starts leaking to the press!"

The media went nuts. Tapes? As in Watergate? After a firing they were all likening to Nixon's Saturday Night Massacre?

Trump refused further comment. Spicer's orders were to duck the question: "I've talked to the president. The president has nothing further to add on that."

Trump might have been trolling the press, but he fueled a whole new wave of negative stories.

Trump never admitted that the Comey firing had been a mistake. But he told Bannon that "it's gotten really hot," that the media reaction to dumping Comey had been "terrible." It was his way of acknowledging that he and others at the White House had greatly underestimated the fallout.

· · ·

After missing two days of briefings while fulfilling his Naval Reserve duty, Sean Spicer returned to find the media filled with stories saying he was practically toast. *Politico* reported that Trump was pleased with Sarah Huckabee Sanders filling in at the podium and "has talked about grooming her" for Spicer's job. The *Washington Post* said Trump had "lashed out at the communications office" for its lousy performance. In the mother of all palace intrigue stories, *Axios* said the president was considering a "huge reboot" that, according to unnamed "White House sources," could knock out not just Spicer but Reince Priebus and Steve Bannon.

Spicer's White House colleagues felt sorry for him. A Melissa McCarthy skit on *SNL* had him begging Trump for his job. Sean Spicer had become a human punchline.

· · ·

During Donald Trump's long-shot campaign, the glib shorthand was that he would be a reality show president.

That, as it turned out, was more prescient than anyone had realized. Trump's insistence on responding to the media in real time, his extraordinary appetite for consuming media, and his use of social media and television outlets to slam detractors and drive his message has been unprecedented.

Every president is a product of his time, whether it was FDR and his fireside radio chats, Jack Kennedy's televised news conferences, or Bill Clinton going on Larry King and MTV. And every president has had his battles with the Fourth Estate.

JFK canceled his subscription to the New York *Herald Tribune*. LBJ called CBS chief Frank Stanton after a report on a Marine using a Zippo lighter to set a Vietnamese hut on fire to say he had "shit on the American flag." And Johnson challenged the loyalties of the Canadian-born correspondent, Morley Safer, saying, "How could CBS employ a communist like Safer?"

Richard Nixon put reporters on an enemies list, had some of them wiretapped, and threatened to "screw around" with the *Washington Post*'s TV licenses during Watergate. Ronald Reagan said he'd had it "up to my keister" with leaks to the press. George H. W. Bush, whose unofficial campaign motto was "Annoy the Media—Reelect Bush," once called CBS to complain about an *Evening News* story while Dan Rather was on the air.

Bill Clinton complained that he had "not gotten one damn bit of credit from the knee-jerk liberal press, and I am sick and tired of it." George W. Bush called a *New York Times* reporter a "major-league asshole." Barack Obama—who said that "if I watched Fox News, I wouldn't vote for me either"—ran an administration that secretly obtained phone and email records from Fox's James Rosen, as well as the Associated Press.

Trump had grown accustomed to favorable media treatment during his long career in New York: brand-building stories from the business press, celebrity stories of feuds and dalliances from the tabloids. He would regularly call the editor of the *New York Post* to plant stories and was rewarded with "BEST SEX I EVER HAD" headlines; he let a *Daily*

News reporter come to the hospital when his second wife Marla Maples was having a baby. So, he was initially stunned when he became a politician and the press pummeled him.

As president, Trump begins his day with four newspapers—*New York Times, New York Post, Wall Street Journal*, and *Washington Post*. He watches the White House press briefings in the afternoon, and spends his evenings surfing cable news. He uses a TiVo ("one of the great inventions of all time") to replay cable shows he's missed while working or traveling. And Hope Hicks, who had Google alerts set up for key surrogates and allies, sometimes showed him clips on her phone.

Sometimes, when Trump saw guests ably defending him, he told Sean Spicer to call them and say the president thought they did a good job. When Trump saw what he deemed unfair reporting or punditry, he used Twitter to trash the offending show or network. And occasionally he tweeted something favorable about *Fox & Friends* or *Hannity*.

Trump told three *New York Times* journalists that he had given up sports and was "consumed by news." Using a remote control and a sixty-inch flat screen, he showed them excerpts of congressional testimony by Sally Yates, the former acting attorney general he had fired, and James Clapper, Obama's national intelligence director and an outspoken critic. And he provided color commentary as he fast-forwarded to key parts. "Watch them choke like dogs," the president said. He was in his element.

Ironically, given his forty million Twitter followers, Trump rarely looked at the web. But if staffers handed him printouts of articles they thought important, he read them.

Trump knows how to hold an audience, and the constant churn of his presidency—the plot twists, the palace intrigue, the threats and retreats and deadline drama—reflects that.

The Trump Show is never dull, which is why he has lifted the ratings and clicks for networks and websites, transformed Facebook into a political battleground, and put national politics at the center of our culture. The media's largely negative approach to the show has produced a paradox: while their credibility has eroded, their bottom line has grown fatter.

CHAPTER 17

THE MEDIA GO
TO DEFCON 1

T he *Washington Post* newsroom broke into applause when the numbers
flashed on the video monitor.

The *Post*'s explosive story on Donald Trump and Russia had just
broken the clicks-per-minute record on its website, previously held by
the paper's posting of the *Access Hollywood* tape.

On May 15, the *Post* reported that during an Oval Office meeting
with Russia's foreign minister and ambassador, Trump had disclosed
highly classified data—dubbed "code word" information—about an ISIS
terror threat involving laptops on airplanes.

The information was so sensitive that the *Post* withheld most details
of the plot at the urging of federal officials, and senior White House aides
contacted the CIA and NSA to discuss the possible fallout.

The White House press team moved quickly. Raised voices were heard
as Steve Bannon met with Sean Spicer and his staff in the Cabinet room.
H. R. McMaster, the new national security adviser (and someone that the
White House told the *Weekly Standard* that Trump held in high esteem,

precisely because there were leaks that he didn't—that he lectured Trump and lacked rapport with him), was tapped to read a statement.

The blunt general did his duty. McMaster said the *Washington Post* story was "false," that he had been in the room, and that "at no time were any intelligence sources or methods discussed." The article, however, hadn't said that sources or methods were compromised, although the leak could have led to that. It was, in journalistic parlance, a non-denial denial.

The paper acknowledged that no law had been broken because the president has the power to declassify information. But the story's obvious news value was enormously amplified because it played into a larger media narrative: that Trump would do anything to help the Russians. That Trump was too unsophisticated to grasp the nuances of intelligence matters. That Trump was a danger to national security.

Glenn Thrush of the *New York Times* snarked on Twitter about "Reported fact-chain: 1) Comey requests more $ for Russia probe 2) Trump cans Comey 3) Trump invites Russians to Oval, divulges state secrets." Even if he hadn't included the debunked story about Comey having asked for more resources, the tweet conveyed a reporter's view that Trump was an unwitting tool for Moscow.

Less than twenty-four hours later, the *Times* quoted from a James Comey memo, read by an unnamed associate, saying the president had suggested to him that he drop the Michael Flynn investigation: "He is a good guy. I hope you can let this go."

The media went to DEFCON 1.

The instant consensus was that this was an obstruction of justice, a scandal of Watergate proportions: the president was trying to pressure his FBI director to stop an investigation of his former national security adviser's ties to Russia. It was a slam-dunk case! Donald Trump had finally been exposed.

Joe Scarborough spoke of "a president that is increasingly isolated, increasingly enraged, and increasingly out of touch with the realities of what is required to run this office."

Lawrence O'Donnell announced that "Donald Trump now sits at the threshold of impeachment." The *Atlantic* declared that "Donald Trump's presidency appears to be on the verge of collapse." The *New Yorker* said that "discussion of Trump's presidency ending before his four-year term is up is no longer an oppositional fantasy." The degree of wishful thinking was astonishing.

The *Weekly Standard* described a "car-wreck presidency." *Slate* announced that "it's the beginning of the end for Donald Trump." The *Huffington Post* asked, "CAN HE SURVIVE?" David Brooks called Trump "a 7-year-old boy" who is "perpetually desperate for approval." Stephen Colbert crowed, "You're a bad president, please resign." And one CNN and MSNBC anchor after another asked Democratic lawmakers whether Trump had committed impeachable offenses.

Comey's account was unquestionably troubling, and while Trump may have had a strong case for firing the FBI chief, his shifting explanations had made the matter a mess. The day after the *New York Times* story hit, Rod Rosenstein named former FBI director Robert Mueller as a special counsel to investigate possible Russian meddling in the presidential election.

The media sharks smelled blood, especially after Sean Spicer canceled his regular, televised briefing with reporters. Then, on May 19, minutes after the president left on his first foreign trip, the *New York Times* reported that Trump had told the Russian diplomats that Comey was "crazy, a real nut job," and that the firing relieved "great pressure" on him because of Russia. (Spicer later said he meant pressure on his ability to negotiate with Russia.) The *Washington Post* reported that investigators were looking at a "senior White House official" as a "person of interest," which raised the stakes. Boom. Boom. Boom. It was hard for anyone, even journalists, to keep up.

Some anchors became short-tempered. Anderson Cooper snapped at Trump loyalist Jeffrey Lord that even if the president "took a dump on his desk, you'd defend him." He apologized for his "crude" and "unprofessional" crack.

There were also backslapping rounds of self-congratulation. A *New York Times* columnist praised the *Washington Post*'s Trump scoops and its adding of hundreds of thousands of digital subscribers as "little short of astonishing." A *Washington Post* columnist said Trump had prodded both papers into producing "one breathtaking scoop after another," listing the names of fourteen journalists.

But here's what the media, in their rush to judgment, failed to consider: that James Comey, fired in humiliating fashion, might have motives of his own in leaking against Trump. The tall, imposing Comey put out through intermediaries that he was so wary of Trump that he once hid from him, ducking behind curtains at a reception and trying, unsuccessfully, to deflect a Trump hug with an arm's-length handshake. Instead of treating this as unusual behavior, even for Washington, the press touted Comey as a man of unimpeachable integrity, with every orchestrated leak from his friends or other unnamed officials regarded as absolute truth. Trump, as usual, got no benefit of the doubt. The press showed no curiosity as to why top government officials were handing journalists story after story designed to damage the president.

Perhaps most important, journalists glossed over the fact that despite all the revelations and headlines, there was still no firm evidence that the Trump campaign had "colluded" with the Russians.

Even Bob Woodward, the preeminent champion of investigative reporting, felt compelled to say that some journalists were biased and "binge-drinking the anti-Trump Kool-Aid."

Trump's media defenders aimed their fire at the mainstream press. On Fox News, commentator Jesse Watters decreed it a "boring" scandal. Tucker Carlson accused the media of "hyperventilating," which he blamed on newsrooms "where every single person has exactly the same political views....They're destroying themselves."

Fox News was increasingly seen as in the pro-Trump camp, but the reality was more complicated. It was undeniably true that the president and his top aides made the majority of their appearances on Fox, in part because they had all but written off CNN and MSNBC. Trump's preferred interviewers were Sean Hannity, Jeanine Pirro, and the hosts at *Fox & Friends*, who were openly sympathetic. And Fox's prime-time opinion shows, while covering damaging controversies, tended not to dwell on them or insisted they were overblown.

But the news division, led by programs such as Bret Baier's *Special Report*, covered Trump fairly, if without the reflexive animosity that marked much of the programming on MSNBC and CNN. The Fox conservative commentators who opposed Trump during the campaign—Charles Krauthammer, Karl Rove, Rich Lowry, Jonah Goldberg, and Steve Hayes among them—remained largely critical, though they sometimes offered limited praise. The Fox audience was split, with some complaining that the network was too soft on Trump and others rebelling at the mildest criticism.

Aside from Fox, most of the media were in fact aligned against Trump. Harvard researchers found that major media coverage of his first hundred days was 80 percent negative, a figure that jumped to 93 percent negative for CNN and NBC, and 91 percent for CBS. (On Fox, it was 52 percent negative, 48 percent positive.)

Even some in the media's liberal precincts were tapping on the brakes, recognizing that the press's normal fixation on scandal might be reaching insane levels. The *New York Times* editorial page said that "really bad stuff could turn up. But Watergate? We're not there yet. That's a word that summons obstruction on a monumental scale, with evidence to prove overt criminal acts." And its ombudsman Liz Spayd, while praising the paper's reporting, worried about "a slide toward coverage that can be misperceived as rooting for Trump's demise." That is sometimes how it looked. (The paper soon abolished her job.)

Yet Trump had also given his antagonists plenty of ammunition: firing the FBI director, shifting his story, telling Russian diplomats that Comey was crazy, and denouncing the probe rather than blandly pledging cooperation. And, as usual, he kept on talking about it.

The day after the Mueller appointment, Trump held an off-the-record luncheon for network anchors, ostensibly to brief them on his first foreign trip. At a time when he was under absolute siege by the media, the president nonetheless devoted two hours, over salad and short ribs, to several of the news organizations he had branded "fake news."

Jared Kushner, an elusive figure to the press, chatted with reporters, saying, "This is probably the weirdest job I've ever had." In his previous life, "I've failed at more deals than I've done but I've closed 250 building deals. I know how to make a deal....This country didn't get fucked up in 100 days and it's not going to get fixed in 100 days."

With off-the-record protection, Trump let loose. He said he was Vladimir Putin's "worst nightmare." He called Comey "a mental mess. Look in his eyes—that guy's got problems."

When ABC's David Muir asked about the naming of the special counsel, Trump said: "I believe it hurts our country terribly, because it shows we're a divided, mixed-up, not-unified country....It also happens to be a pure excuse for the Democrats having lost an election that they should have easily won because of the Electoral College being slanted so much in their way."

As the session ended, the anchors clamored for those quotes to be put on the record. "Wait a minute," Kushner shouted, "you all have to go through Hope!" They knew Trump had given in to such requests before.

As the president started shaking hands, Sean Spicer came running up with a tape recorder to catch any remarks. In the crosstalk, Trump told the anchors "that last part we talked about, yeah," it could be put on the record.

Hicks suddenly took charge: "I will send the quote out at 3 so no one gets a jump. You have to run it in its entirety," she said.

At a news conference an hour later, Trump essentially repeated his remarks, calling the probe a "witch hunt" and denying that he had asked Comey to drop the Flynn investigation. He often tried out his responses in off-the-record settings and then went public.

The battle lines were now drawn: James Comey, whom the press believed to be an honorable man, versus Donald Trump, whom the press did not believe at all. The press backlash was far greater than the White House had expected.

The media also took aim at the president's staff. Trump was ready for "a major shakeup," the *New York Times* said, "probably starting with the dismissal or reassignment of Sean Spicer," who might be pulled from the daily briefings. Fox commentator Kimberly Guilfoyle was quoted as saying she was in talks with the White House for the job—she had been Trump's early favorite for press secretary—but Fox News let it be known that she was under a long-term contract.

This was why the infighting stories mattered, because the anonymous knifing fed a narrative of presidential dysfunction. "They seem to palpate with contempt for him," conservative *Times* columnist Ross Douthat said.

Campaign veterans shook their heads at what one called the administration's "managed chaos" and how leakers, in order to protect their own reputations, sacrificed the president, portraying him as petulant, impulsive, and uninformed. And they knew how frustrated Trump was; he couldn't understand why the press harped on collusion with Russia when he insisted there wasn't any.

Corey Lewandowski, Trump's former campaign manager, spoke out in his defense, saying any staffer who couldn't support Trump's agenda "should not be there" and that those leaking derogatory information "should be fired." The president invited him to the Oval Office; he was back in demand. But it was a sad commentary that Trump loyalists had to defend the president by attacking his staff.

• • •

Mike Pence, the soft-spoken, white-haired former Indiana governor, was a media favorite in the early months of the administration. The main reason was that he wasn't Donald Trump.

The vice president was "a clean-cut 1950s Republican" who seemed "jarringly out of place" in the chaotic White House, a *New York Times* profile said. Some viewed him "as a president-in-waiting," if Trump was "brought down by scandal."

Perhaps the most controversial thing about Pence, at least in the eyes of liberals, turned out to be a fifteen-year-old quote. A sympathetic *Washington Post* profile of his wife Karen, a devout Christian, noted in the twentieth paragraph that Mike had once said "that he never eats alone with a woman other than his wife and that he won't attend events featuring alcohol without her by his side, either."

This prompted a spate of smug essays about whether Pence was sexist, or silly, to observe such old-fashioned morality. Yet it was hardly an uncommon practice among religious Christians. With so many politicians embroiled in sex scandals, Pence was pilloried for trying to avoid temptation.

He had made no mistakes for months, but that wasn't good enough for some in the press. Pence was, according to *Politico*, "the White House's Invisible Man," someone who had earned Trump's trust but had "racked up few tangible accomplishments." Of course, the job of a vice president is to loyally serve the president, not leak stories about how much clout he's wielding.

By the spring, however, the media had turned on Pence. "What Did Mike Pence Know?" CNN asked.

Slate ripped him as "Mr. Complicit." As scandalous doings swirled around the White House, the vice president was a "stooge," following a path of "willful blindness and misrepresentations....He continues to vouch for President Trump and others who conspire, lie, and hide corruption. Pence isn't a victim. He's an accomplice." Merely for standing by the president who picked him, he was a bad guy.

Pence occasionally punched back, scolding "left-wing activists and their willing allies in the media" for spreading "fake news."

It was fair for the press to observe that Pence sometimes seemed in the dark, whether it was defending Mike Flynn on television after the national security adviser had lied to him about Russia, or defending the Jim Comey firing as having been based solely on the deputy attorney general's recommendation. The press treated these episodes as embarrassments.

For the most part, Pence remained unflappable. He was, though, annoyed by media reports that played up protests at his commencement speech at Notre Dame. Only about one hundred of the thirty-two hundred graduates had walked out from his remarks in protest—and they were booed as they did so.

On *The View*, Whoopi Goldberg supported the protestors by offering a KKK analogy: "I shouldn't have to listen to a guy who's wearing a hood, who I know wants to string me up," as if the mild-mannered Pence was anything remotely like a klansman.

I chatted with Pence at the White House an hour before the Comey firing was announced. He seemed relaxed, even serene, as he posed for pictures with schoolchildren. He told me he had grown close to Trump, and he was obviously comfortable as the president's behind-the-scenes confidant.

Ironically, given his loyalty to the president, many in the media wanted this staunch conservative to take over at the White House. It was a measure of their antipathy toward Trump that the pundits now pined for Pence.

CHAPTER 18

COLLUSION CONFUSION

The television commentators were doing something extremely rare—praising President Trump for a signature speech—when breaking news banners began flashing across their screens.

Mike Flynn was taking the Fifth, refusing to comply with a Senate subpoena in the seemingly endless Russia investigation.

It was the morning of May 22 and Trump was on his first foreign trip, having just delivered a sober address in Saudi Arabia that struck a more moderate tone on Islam as he tried to rally the Arab world against terrorism. The press hailed the speech, but Flynn's legal maneuver overshadowed coverage of the president's next stop in Israel.

That was the pattern all week. Trump's strong performance on the world stage, credited even by his critics, competed for ink and air time with each new report on the scandal front. A *Washington Post* story, for instance, said Trump had conversations with national intelligence director Dan Coats and National Security Agency chief Mike Rogers, asking them to push back against Jim Comey's FBI investigation, and that both refused.

And when the media weren't distracted by scandal they plunged into silly debates, such as whether Melania had slapped her husband's hand when he tried to hold hers.

Even a high point of the trip, a cordial meeting with Pope Francis, fed the gossip machine. Sean Spicer, a devout Catholic who had openly yearned to meet Francis if Trump went to the Vatican, was not included in the small group of handpicked aides who joined the papal meeting.

This was cast as a presidential swipe against his long-suffering spokesman, especially when CNN quoted a source close to the White House as saying "wow, that's all he wanted." Reporters felt sorry for Sean. Even Glenn Thrush, his constant antagonist, said Spicer's exclusion "speaks to a small-mindedness that I find incredibly depressing."

But in the media's short-attention-span environment, that was quickly forgotten.

While Trump was in Brussels, scolding NATO leaders about paying their fair share of defense costs, a big story erupted on CNN and MSNBC.

The subject was Jared.

The press increasingly resented Kushner, who was dubbed a "princeling." He had no previous government experience, yet he seemed to be running everything, including foreign policy. Reporters investigated his real estate empire and searched for conflicts of interest with his White House work. The *New York Times Magazine* cast him as a slumlord of low-income apartments in Baltimore. Many stories recycled the fact that Kushner's father, who owned billions in real estate, had served time in prison for his role in a sordid case of illegal campaign contributions (to Democrats), tax evasion, and witness tampering, which included entrapping his brother-in-law with a prostitute and sending a tape of the incident to his sister.

Despite his "cool and unflappable" image and being "soft-spoken, slim and handsome," a *Politico* profile said Jared Kushner played rough and quoted ex-employees as disparaging him. The *Washington Post* highlighted allegations that Kushner had tried to use the newspaper he owned, the *New York Observer*, to retaliate against business adversaries.

Now the *Post* reported that investigators in the Russia probe were "focusing on a series of meetings held by Jared Kushner," with the Russian ambassador and a Moscow banker, the month before the inauguration. And *NBC Nightly News* reported that Kushner was under FBI "scrutiny."

The pieces were strikingly thin, acknowledging that Kushner was not a "target," a "subject," or even a "central focus" of the probe. So the news was essentially that Kushner, who had voluntarily offered to discuss these meetings with Congress, would be a witness in the probe. But the volume was cranked up so high that it *seemed* like he was under investigation and probably guilty of something. Actually, the unnamed "sources close to the investigation" were breaking the law by leaking the information, but just about everything in this criminal investigation was leaked, almost in real time. And the press had what it wanted: the president's son-in-law was under suspicion.

The following night brought another *Washington Post* exclusive and frenzied coverage on CNN and MSNBC (but not Fox, which downplayed the story and similar developments in prime time). The paper said that Kushner had discussed with Ambassador Sergey Kislyak setting up a secure communications channel between the Trump transition team and the Kremlin. Kushner suggested using Russian equipment at its embassy or consulate, according to U.S. intercepts of Russian communications.

The immediate media assumption was that this was nefarious, an attempt by the president's close relative to hide his underhanded dealings with Moscow. It certainly might have been naïve. The Trump team, seven weeks before taking office, clearly didn't trust the Obama administration, and was exploring its own diplomatic channel to the Russians.

This was news, but the media plunged into hyperventilation mode. CNN's David Gergen suggested that Kushner consider a leave of absence. MSNBC analyst Malcolm Nance said if the story was true, "this is now espionage." Another MSNBC analyst, Naveed Jamali, flatly said that Kushner was "either aspiring to be a Russian agent or was in fact a Russian agent." *Foreign Policy* magazine warned of "Jared Kushner's

Growing Stench of Treason." Keith Olbermann, still doing his online rants, proclaimed: "I call for the immediate arrest of Jared Kushner."

The idea that a novice had made an innocent misstep was widely dismissed by the press. It was all seen as part of the Trump/Kushner cover-up. The *New York Times* editorialists said Kushner's behavior might be explained by "stupidity," "paranoia," or "malevolence," but clearly he was "in over his head" and should vacate the White House.

Kushner believed that the media totally oversold the story. To them, this was treason! But where was the substance? He had met with an ambassador. There was nothing wrong with setting up back channels, Kushner felt. He hadn't put the meetings on his security forms because he thought "foreign contacts" meant relationships, not individual meetings. He had done nothing to hide a meeting he had with Russian banker Sergei Gorkov shortly after the election.

Jared believed he knew why this was happening. There had been a blog post suggesting that he had argued the White House should take a scorched-earth approach to dealing with the Justice Department. That had put a target on his back. Now the FBI was leaking stuff against him.

When this was all over, when you asked all these media people what they had found on Russia, what would they say? Would the media, he wondered, ever admit that they were wrong?

When Trump returned home from overseas, where he had avoided reporters, the press had escalated matters to what a *New York Times* headline called the "Growing Crisis Over Kushner." That melded seamlessly into leaks about infighting, with *Politico* announcing: "Russia Scandal Casts Uncertainty Over Kushner's Role."

The media drumbeat grew louder. A couple of stories said the FBI wanted to talk to Kushner, which was legitimate news but hardly surprising since he was a key aide and had dealings with the Russian ambassador. The same stories dutifully noted he was not a subject of the investigation. But the sheer repetition created an atmosphere of "crisis," and then unnamed sources—including Jared's rivals—started popping off that he must do something to quiet things down.

Kushner might not have been an FBI target but he was a prime target for his White House adversaries, who trashed him anonymously to reporters. Considering that he had clashed with Bannon and Conway, dumped on Spicer, and, earlier, had backed Lewandowski's dismissal, it was payback time through the press.

An extraordinary *New York Times* story by Thrush and Haberman was a grab bag of complaints against Kushner, described as having an "aloof demeanor" and "unfailing self-regard" as he assembled his "vague portfolio" but avoided the "messy" work of government. Trump had started dressing him down in front of other aides, the piece said, especially after the embarrassment of his sister pitching Beijing investors on a New Jersey condo project by dangling the possibility of American visas that could be bought for $500,000. Bannon had been calling him "the air," because he blew in and out of meetings. And the fact that Kushner had thought that Comey's firing would quickly blow over was lost on no one.

The *Washington Post* gave voice to "some White House aides" who "have discreetly discussed among themselves whether Kushner should play a lesser role—or even take a leave" during the uproar. And *Politico* said that within the White House there was "a feeling of resentment among people about Kushner's special status as a family member, and a feeling that it's about time for him to have a turn under the gun."

All this bubbled up into a witches' brew that cast an evil spell on Kushner, without any evidence of wrongdoing on his part. The president had to put out a statement saying that "Jared is doing a great job for the country."

• • •

On May 24, Greg Gianforte, a Republican congressional candidate in Montana, body-slammed *Guardian* reporter Ben Jacobs for barging into a room, sticking a tape recorder in his face, and asking policy questions. The candidate started punching him, shouting "get the hell out," and broke his glasses, according to an eyewitness account by a Fox News correspondent.

The reaction of many commentators to this unprovoked attack was to blame...Donald Trump.

The violence was Trump's fault, they insisted, because of his harsh rhetoric against the so-called dishonest media. So what if Gianforte, who was charged with misdemeanor assault, acted like a thug? Trump must have inspired him!

On CNN, Don Lemon talked over a guest with a contrary opinion, saying "you don't think it's because the guy who's in office now has said very horrible things about reporters and said that reporters are the enemy of the American people?"

On MSNBC, former Bush aide Nicolle Wallace said it was "ridiculous" to deny "a direct line between Donald Trump calling reporters enemies of the state and people beating up a working journalist." Joe Scarborough agreed that Trump's "reckless words have consequences."

And the accusations continued once Gianforte apologized—after he won the election, that is. As a *Washington Post* headline put it: "Reporters Say They Are Being Roughed Up. Observers Point to Trump."

This kind of guilt by association was off the charts. Now anything bad that happened to a journalist was an obvious byproduct of the Trump era.

· · ·

The president had barely tweeted during his foreign trip, but on his first morning back in the White House, confronted with an avalanche of anti-Kushner stories, he let loose: "It is my opinion that many of the leaks coming out of the White House are fabricated lies made up by the #FakeNews media."

Trump also tweeted that it was "very possible that those sources don't exist but are made up by fake news writers. #FakeNews is the enemy!"

Some pundits condemned Trump for that last phrase, saying it was that kind of rhetoric that fostered the climate for attacks on journalists. He had not used the accusatory word "enemy" for three months, so his critics rushed to invoke what happened in Montana.

The press was, in fact, relying too heavily on anonymous sources, who had obvious agendas to push, and Trump was free to call such stories unfair, but it was not true that the sources didn't "exist." Reporters needed to discern which sources were credible, and which were simply trying to undermine the administration or, more commonly, their personal rivals. Kellyanne Conway saw an unmistakable pattern emerging. When Trump asked her whether his foreign trip had been successful, she said, "Yes, that's why the media stopped covering it."

•   •   •

The press loved "White House shakeup" stories, but so far there had been no real shakeup. Sean Spicer was back at his podium after the foreign trip, doing his televised briefings, Steve Bannon was still Trump's chief strategist, and Reince Priebus was still chief of staff, despite *Politico* calling him a "dead man walking" and a cheeky *Drudge Report* headline: "TRUMP READY TO RINCE PRIEBUS?" Kellyanne Conway realized that the first time she was asked about a possible Trump administration shakeup was three days after the inauguration.

For all the leaks and counter-leaks, Conway believed the White House remained a largely collaborative place. The media peddled an image of White House dysfunction, she thought, because it took little effort for reporters to handicap who was in and who was out; and she saw the furor over Kushner and the FBI investigation as classic examples of the media's rush to judgment. The pundits kept screaming about Russia, but after eight months of investigation, in her view, they didn't have much of anything.

Still, Trump was deeply unhappy with how his communications team was handling the press. He wanted a war room to take charge of rapid response. So he summoned Corey Lewandowski to the White House.

As Lewandowski saw it, Trump was working like a dog. When he visited the White House on Memorial Day, the president was in meetings from eight a.m. to eight p.m., this just after his nine-day foreign trip. The reporters were all exhausted, yet Trump kept going. The president was aggravated by the press, and blamed his staff for failing to sell his message.

Lewandowski and his friend Dave Bossie, the former deputy campaign manager and a political streetfighter since the 1990s, had talked to Trump several times about joining the White House staff, and neither wanted to do it. Both were doing well in the private sector, with Bossie having signed on as a Fox News contributor. Both had four kids to support. Both doubted they would have enough influence in a White House infamous for its infighting. Lewandowski was flattered to be considered months after he had been treated so cavalierly, but he didn't want to go inside the building, take all kinds of bullets, and ultimately fail.

Corey's reservations deepened when he spoke separately to Priebus, Bannon, and Kushner. Each asked him whose team he was on.

"I'm not on any team, I'm on his team," he replied.

Ushered into the Oval Office, the president was blunt. "My staff sucks," he said.

Bannon and Priebus had told them that the president wanted Bossie as deputy chief of staff and Lewandowski as a special assistant for political affairs; all they had to do was say yes. But the president had a very different message. "I just don't like that idea," Trump said. Bossie and Lewandowski exchanged puzzled looks.

If things didn't improve soon, Trump said, "I'm going to get rid of everybody, and I don't want you guys to be damaged by that." He said he might make Priebus his ambassador to Greece.

Almost on cue, Priebus walked in. "So this is done, everything is good?" he asked.

Trump said, "If this place isn't working in the next month or so, I'm going to make some changes. And that change is you."

Bannon was disappointed at this turn of events. He told Bossie and Lewandowski: "You two were my ticket out of here."

Lewandowski and Bossie were greatly relieved, and went out for a beer with Kellyanne Conway. Lewandowski got a call from Priebus. He had changed Trump's mind. Both men could start Monday. They politely begged off.

Days later, Trump called Lewandowski again after seeing him on Fox News.

"Look Corey, you're great as long as you're going on TV," he said. "It doesn't matter if you're inside or outside."

• • •

Sean Spicer had a new approach, deflecting questions about Kushner and the FBI. He couldn't comment because the matter was under investigation. That was the emerging strategy: banish such questions from the briefing room and stay focused on the president's agenda.

But there was a moment when Spicer let his frustration show, declaring that the president was fed up with the "perpetuation of false narratives," fueled by "unnamed, unaccountable sources." And he offered a case study: a BBC reporter's tweet—echoed by the *Huffington Post* and retweeted by a new reporter for the *New York Times*—that Trump hadn't been listening to the Italian prime minister at the G7 summit because he wasn't wearing headphones for the translation. Trump was actually using a small earpiece. That, Spicer said, was "fake news," pushed out with "no apology."

Peter Baker, a *New York Times* correspondent respected for his even-handedness, objected: "Sean, none of that was in the newspaper. None of that was on the front page. Your trip was all over the front page. You're making something out of one tweet instead of the vast majority of the coverage."

But "you guys defend your mistakes like that," Spicer said.

"Don't you?" Baker countered.

Spicer was right, though, that such incidents went viral. BBC reporter James Landale's erroneous tweet drew fourteen thousand retweets; his follow-up with the White House denial, forty-two retweets. A *Times* reporter on *Air Force One* told Spicer he was sorry to see the misinformed tweet and was alerting his editors.

Spicer thought this was no minor example. The Italian prime minister had been insulted by the reports. It didn't matter that the story didn't make the paper, for Twitter was now a prime forum for making news. Spicer felt the media were no longer being held accountable for their mistakes.

CHAPTER 19

CLIMATE CHANGE CALAMITY

The media reaction to what President Trump did on climate change was so overheated that there was no pretense of a balanced approach, just a tsunami of criticism.

From the moment that Trump announced on June 1 that he was pulling the country out of the Paris climate accord, the gathering storm reached well beyond the policy or the politics. It was a visceral outcry against the man himself.

There was, of course, plenty to debate about the non-binding agreement, its impact on the economy and America joining only two of the world's 197 countries on the sidelines, and some reporters took that seriously. But the overall tone was captured by Fareed Zakaria, CNN's leading foreign policy voice, who intoned: "This will be the day that the United States resigned as the leader of the free world."

Or perhaps it was the left-wing *Huffington Post*, with its screaming headline "TRUMP TO PLANET: DROP DEAD."

Or maybe it was *Politico Magazine* writer Michael Grunwald, who said Trump was "extending a middle finger to the world" in a slap against "fancy-pants elites and smarty-pants scientists and tree-hugging squishes."

Such dismissiveness permeated much of what was said and written, a journalistic conviction that Trump was uninformed, anti-science, turning his back on the civilized world.

The personal invective was accompanied by alarmist warnings. Mark Preston, editor of CNN's political unit, warned viewers that the seas would keep rising, New York City could be flooded, and the Marshall Islands would completely disappear.

Word of the coming move had dribbled out in advance. Steve Bannon, who press accounts had cast as marginalized, led the charge against the globalist agreement, the epitome of what he was determined to defeat, challenging the more moderate New York wing, whose press-conscious leaders were Jared Kushner and Ivanka Trump. Thus, the *New York Times* quoted "three administration officials with direct knowledge" as saying that Trump was expected to withdraw from the agreement, while "other White House insiders disputed those reports."

But since the president's leanings were clear, the *Times* also ran a "news analysis" that read like an editorial, saying that abandoning the Paris deal "would be a momentous setback" and that the United States "would give up a leadership role when it comes to finding solutions for climate change."

Bannon felt that journalists were shocked and outraged that Trump would do what he said he would do during the campaign. They thought it was just Trump's BS and would never happen. When advocates said the agreement was nonbinding, Bannon told the president that the moment you pull out, you'll see how it wasn't nonbinding at all. He was amused by the press saying he had made a comeback and regained his Svengali role, after having written him off as a hospice patient who would probably expire any minute.

But Bannon hung back toward the end. For three days, he didn't set foot in the Oval Office while Ivanka brought in climate change activists and people like Facebook's Mark Zuckerberg lobbied the president. It was important not to limit his information.

When Trump announced in the Rose Garden that the United States was withdrawing from the Paris climate accord, he also said he would be willing to renegotiate the agreement under terms that would protect American jobs and factories. The press, however, paid little attention to that. And the media barrage that followed was unrelenting.

The *Washington Post* ran such headlines as "Trump's Climate Deal Decision Alarms Leaders Worldwide" and "Trump's Paris Speech Needs a Serious Fact Check." The *New York Times* weighed in with "Trump Hands the Chinese a Gift: The Chance for Global Leadership."

The *Times* op-ed pages ranged from liberal Paul Krugman ("Trump Gratuitously Rejects the Paris Climate Accord") to conservative David Brooks ("Our Disgraceful Exit from the Paris Accord") to environmentalist Bill McKibben ("Trump's Stupid and Reckless Climate Decision").

As long ago as 1987, in my first interview with him, Trump had told me that other countries were taking advantage of America through international agreements. He had made a campaign promise to withdraw from the Paris climate accord, and had long taken a stance in favor of putting American national interests over global agreements. But the media were so worked up that they refused to treat Trump's decision as anything but a national embarrassment.

The outright contempt was crystallized on *Morning Joe*. It was there that Joe Scarborough, who was friendly with the Kushner faction, repeatedly declared that "Steve Bannon is president of the United States. Donald Trump doesn't know anything about policy. Donald Trump doesn't know anything about anything."

Bannon, for his part, thought Scarborough harbored White House ambitions and was insanely jealous of Trump. It was no coincidence that the Republican National Committee, at the White House's request, had just put out a hit piece saying *Morning Joe* had "the worst case of Trump Derangement Syndrome" and had become "three hours of far-left hysteria."

The attacks by Trump-hating celebrities bordered on deranged. Mark Ruffalo, who plays the Hulk, went on a rhetorical rampage, saying the president would "have the death of whole nations on his hands." Actress Alyssa Milano tweeted at Trump, "Oh my God, you really are a monster."

But while many liberals profess there is no higher calling than saving the planet, MSNBC was more interested in damaging Trump. Less than four hours after the president's decision, Chris Matthews led off *Hardball* with the Russia investigation—focusing on Jim Comey's scheduled testimony *a week later*—as did the next three prime-time shows.

A few conservative outlets, like *National Review* and the *Wall Street Journal* editorial page, agreed with Trump that the Paris accord did nothing for the climate but hurt America's economy. Some in the media, however, focused not so much on the details of the accord as on whether Trump was a global warming "denier." On ABC's *Good Morning America*, George Stephanopoulos, the onetime Clinton White House aide, repeatedly asked Kellyanne Conway: "Does the president believe that global warming is a hoax?"

"The president," she replied, "believes in a clean environment, clean air, clean water, he's received awards as a businessman in that regard."

At his White House press briefing, Sean Spicer ducked the question, saying he hadn't talked to Trump about it, but he also thought the question was beside the point. Whether people believed in climate change or not, in his view, the decision was made on economic grounds, which the press refused to consider. A tweet by *Wall Street Journal* reporter Eli Stokols, who during the campaign had called Trump a "mendacious" liar, said it all for Spicer: "Where we're at: Upending the global order and threatening the planet entirely to appease your own base after four months in office."

Threatening the planet?

Spicer called him. "Do you realize that's not reporting?" he asked. Stokols deleted the tweet.

Facing what he considered an increasingly biased and sometimes dishonest press, Spicer answered many questions with a simple "yes," "no," "I don't know." He was pleased with his more disciplined approach.

The briefings were shorter and tighter. And that left many journalists frustrated.

Van Jones, a liberal CNN commentator and former Obama aide, called Spicer "the Incredible Shrinking Man," likened him to a "zombie," and said he "looked like a depressed little kid standing up there."

Spicer found the psychiatric evaluations laughable. Every time he turned around, it seemed, *Politico* was questioning his mental well-being. Who exactly did these reporters talk to? The only person he confided in about his emotional health was his wife, and she wasn't talking to *Politico*.

The pundits tagged Jared Kushner as one of the big losers on the climate decision. A *Politico* reporter later texted an aide: Is Jared considering resigning? I hear it's being talked about.

Kushner actually believed the decision-making process had been terrific. There were many clashing opinions, in his view, but nobody on the inside disagreed that the Paris climate accord was a lousy agreement. The question was whether to bail on the accord entirely or work on its shortcomings. In the end, Kushner felt, Trump had made a gut call that turned out to be right. But Kushner kept such a low profile that no one knew of his quiet agreement with the president.

Besides, the spotlight was on his wife, who had even invited Al Gore to talk to her father about the Paris agreement. The press portrayed her as the voice of sanity—and blamed her for not forcing her dad to bow to the global consensus. Yes, Ivanka believed in climate change; but like her father, she didn't think the Paris accord was well constructed, and actually viewed it as meaningless. What disturbed her was not that her father had withdrawn from the agreement, but that leaks had made it appear that she was trying to puff herself up as a climate change expert, which she made no claims to be. She was not a scientist. She was a millennial who liked nature and believed in environmental policies that protected clean air and water. The media, however, took a harsher view.

"Is Ivanka Trump Getting Tired of Losing?" *BuzzFeed* asked.

Chris Cillizza gave her the "Worst Week in Washington" award.

She also had her defenders, with *Politico* citing "two people familiar with their thinking" as saying that Ivanka and Jared "have taken the defeat in stride" and were playing a "long game."

But the mockery was sometimes malicious. The liberal *New Republic* said that Ivanka's political "brand" was "dead," that she should "stop pretending she ever cared about these issues or acknowledge that she's a massive, world historical failure." And in a particularly elegant phrase, the magazine said her relationship with her father—who was a "moral obscenity"—required her "to piss down our backs and tell us it's raining."

So classy.

• • •

No issue more forcefully brought out Donald Trump's combative side than terrorism. Part of Trump's appeal to voters was that he was willing to take extraordinary steps to protect the country. The press, however, was convinced that he was shattering the norms of diplomacy and blackening America's image.

Reza Aslan was one of those who seethed with hatred for the new president.

During the campaign he had tweeted at Donald Trump Jr., "Like piece of shit father, piece of shit son."

After Trump was in the White House he tweeted: "Oh the joy when this conniving scumbag narcissistic sociopath piece of shit fake president finally gets what's coming to him."

Aslan was not just some bystander; he was a television personality. In fact, he had a show on CNN. And yet he felt free to use the worst sort of gutter language against the president.

After a terrorist attack on London Bridge, in which three knife-wielding men in a van killed seven people and wounded forty-eight, Aslan could not contain himself.

Responding to Trump's tweets, he took to Twitter and wrote: "This piece of shit is a not just an embarrassment to America and a stain on the presidency. He's an embarrassment to humankind."

Aslan's foul-mouthed fury at the president created a problem for CNN, where he hosted a program called *Believer*.

Aslan issued a semi-apology at best, saying he lost his cool and regretted the profanity: "I should have used better language to express my shock and frustration at the president's lack of decorum and sympathy for the people of London." So he had no problem calling Trump an "embarrassment to humankind."

CNN issued the mildest possible statement, saying such discourse was "never appropriate." The network also said that Aslan wasn't an employee. But neither was Kathy Griffin—she appeared once a year—and CNN fired her. A week later, the network quietly canceled Aslan's show.

While Aslan's denunciation was the most extreme, much of the media assailed Trump for his tweeted responses to the London attack. Some of the criticism was legitimate, but it also revealed the continuing culture clash about what constituted appropriate presidential behavior.

First, Trump had turned the attack into a domestic issue: "We need to be smart, vigilant and tough. We need the courts to give us back our rights. We need the Travel Ban as an extra level of safety!"

He criticized London's first Muslim mayor, Sadiq Khan: "At least 7 dead and 48 wounded in terror attack and Mayor of London says there is 'no reason to be alarmed!'" Khan had actually said that the city was increasing its police presence and there was no reason for residents to be alarmed in the coming days.

It was not Trump's finest hour. A *Washington Post* news story accused him of having "reacted impulsively" to the London attack "by stoking panic and fear." *Post* columnist Gene Robinson called the president "out of control" and "dangerously overwhelmed." The *Wall Street Journal* editorial page said the "cycle of Twitter outbursts and pointless personal feuding" could damage his presidency. On Fox, anchor Neil Cavuto scolded Trump: "Mr. President, it's not the fake news media that's your problem, it's you. It's not just your tweeting, it's your scapegoating, it's your refusal to see that sometimes you're the one who's feeding your own beast."

CNN's Chris Cillizza, who admitted he totally misjudged Trump during the campaign, now described him as an "anti-president," one whose attitude "is closer to Jerry Springer than to Gerald Ford. He's more Limbaugh than Lincoln."

Thomas Roberts, an MSNBC news anchor, asked on the air: "Is the president trying to provoke a domestic terror attack with this Twitter rant, because only to prove himself right?" After that comment, which actually suggested that Trump might want to see Americans killed to bolster his political standing, Kellyanne Conway questioned why Roberts still had a job. "People are really losing their minds over this presidency," she said.

Undaunted, Trump returned to Twitter to insist that he won the White House by using social media to circumvent "the Fake News of CNN, NBC, ABC, CBS, washpost or nytimes." It was a megaphone he had no intention of surrendering.

CHAPTER 20

THE MUELLER ESCALATION

Sean Spicer was ticked off from the moment he turned on the *Today* show.

It was June 7, the day before James Comey was to break his silence before a Senate committee. And here was Savannah Guthrie touting "this explosive testimony on Capitol Hill tomorrow." How did she know? And then Chuck Todd told her that "the executive branch is not functioning right now." Really? The entire government?

It had already been a rough week for Spicer. When CBS's Major Garrett asked at a briefing whether Trump had full confidence in Jeff Sessions, the press secretary replied that he hadn't discussed it with the president. The press erupted as if Sessions was about to be booted. But Spicer felt he had to be cautious. It wasn't his job to guess what Trump thought. If he said the president had full confidence in his attorney general and something went wrong, he'd take the hit. His goal was to avoid a replay of that Kellyanne moment, when she gave Mike Flynn a presidential vote of confidence in his final hours at the White House.

The news this morning was that Trump had picked a new FBI director. Trump tweeted the announcement during Spicer's morning staff
meeting. His choice was Christopher Wray.

"Good, we're ready," Spicer said.

Early accounts said that Trump had blindsided his staff, but Spicer
knew in advance and had a packet of information on Wray.

Hours later, Dan Coats, the national intelligence director, testified
in the Senate that he had "never felt pressure to intervene or interfere in
any way" with an ongoing investigation. That statement was at odds
with the lead story on the *Washington Post*'s front page: "Trump Sought
Aid in Pressuring FBI."

The piece, based on unnamed sources, said Trump, in a private
conversation with Coats, "started complaining about the FBI investigation and Comey's handling of it," and that Coats told others that stepping
in would be "inappropriate."

Spicer called a senior *Post* editor. Here was a flat denial by Coats,
he said, demanding that the paper run a correction in the light of his
testimony. The editor stood by the story, saying Coats never said he
wasn't asked to intervene.

Jared Kushner walked into Spicer's office. He grabbed the *Post* story
and started reading from it. Who were the sources for this stuff?

His finger moved down to the next front-page piece, which said "two
senior White House officials" expected that the president might use
Twitter to offer "acerbic commentary" during the Comey hearing. Where
did they get this stuff? No way that was happening, Kushner said.

CNN, meanwhile, reported that Comey's testimony would directly
contradict the president's assertion that Comey had assured him he
wasn't under FBI investigation. Again: Who the hell were the sources?
Was Comey leaking his testimony? Were reporters making it up?

Jared thought the media had gone crazy, and it was driving him nuts.
Major news outlets constantly called his office asking him to confirm or
deny outlandish rumors: Ivanka was becoming UN ambassador. He was
secretly in the Seychelles. She was at a wedding in Italy. Ivanka was
pregnant. Their marriage was in trouble. Ivanka was having an affair

with Justin Trudeau. Every day, it seemed, his office had to knock down stupid gossip.

Kushner tried to walk off with the *Post*, but Spicer snatched it back. His argument with the paper wasn't over. "We're escalating," he told Kushner.

• • •

All the networks—ABC, CBS, NBC, Fox, CNN, MSNBC, and others—went live for what was billed as the biggest Senate hearing since Watergate.

By any reasonable measure, James Comey's testimony was not a good day for Donald Trump. The fired FBI director called the president a liar. He accused Trump of demanding his loyalty, and of saying he hoped that Comey would drop his investigation of Mike Flynn. And Comey, an experienced witness, said he believed he had been fired because he was pursuing the Russia investigation.

But there were major points in the president's favor as well. Comey said he was not accusing the president of obstruction of justice; that was for others to judge. He confirmed that Trump never asked him to halt the Russia probe. And the CNN story that upset Kushner, and a similar report by ABC's Jonathan Karl, turned out to be wrong. Comey said he had in fact told Trump three times that he was not personally under investigation.

Under oath, Comey admitted that he had leaked against the president, giving a Columbia Law School professor a memo, which he wanted him to provide to the *New York Times*. The *Times* had quoted the document in reporting that Trump had asked Comey to "shut down" the Flynn investigation. The mainstream media used this confession to depict Comey as a savvy operative, adept at Washington's dark arts.

For an FBI guy, Comey had left his fingerprints on an array of stories depicting Trump as pressuring him. But if his three hours of testimony were a political mixed bag, the media narrative was not. "Comey Says Trump Lied About Him, FBI," the *Washington Post* blared. The *Politico* verdict: "Comey's Devastating Indictment of Trump." The *Daily News* simply stamped the word "LIAR" over Trump's face.

Sarah Huckabee Sanders had to tell reporters that "I can definitely say the president is not a liar," calling the question "frankly insulting."

The media polarization was unmistakable: The liberals, unable to tie Trump to a Russia conspiracy, focused almost exclusively on his alleged attempt to strong-arm Comey. The conservatives concentrated on the failure to prove the president committed an overtly criminal act, as if that was an acceptable standard.

Kushner had been right: Trump did not tweet all day. But that rare restraint lasted only until early the next morning: "Despite so many false statements and lies, total and complete vindication…and WOW, Comey is a leaker!"

Trump's plan to launch "infrastructure week" was foiled because the media only cared about the scandal. The CNN banner that ran while Trump was giving a speech on infrastructure said, "TRUMP SPEAKS LIVE AFTER CALLING COMEY A LIAR." The MSNBC banner read, "TRUMP TALKS INFRASTRUCTURE AFTER BLASTING COMEY."

Corey Lewandowski suddenly emerged as Trump's leading surrogate. The man was a machine, defending the president and attacking Comey on Fox and MSNBC after the hearing, and the next morning on *Today*, *Good Morning America*, and *Fox & Friends*. He told George Stephanopoulos that Comey represented "the deep state in Washington" and "should be potentially prosecuted" for leaking. NBC's Savannah Guthrie insisted it wasn't "intellectually honest" to cite only the parts of Comey's testimony that helped Trump, but Lewandowski said the bottom line was that the president wasn't under investigation. The *New York Times*, for its part, was calling Comey a "Shakespearean" figure.

With White House officials under orders to avoid substantive comment on the probe, Corey Lewandowski and Dave Bossie were the administration's pit bulls.

The president's comments had bite as well. He held a news conference at which he taunted the media. Before acknowledging Jon Karl, the feisty ABC correspondent, he mused: "Should I take one of the killer networks that treat me so badly as fake news?" And he told Karl: "Remember how nice you used to be before I ran?"

Trump denied that he asked Comey to end the Flynn probe and denied that he asked for his loyalty. Essentially, he accused Comey of perjury. But Karl slipped in a quick follow-up that made headlines everywhere: "Would you be willing to speak under oath to give your version of those events?"

"One hundred percent," Trump said.

. . .

Christopher Ruddy, founder of the conservative website *Newsmax* and a friend of Trump, told PBS's *NewsHour* that he was afraid the president might fire special counsel Robert Mueller. Sean Spicer, worried about possible fallout, called Ruddy and asked him to make it clear that he had not discussed the matter with Trump. Ruddy refused, saying he never implied he had talked with Trump. He declared the press office to be "amateur hour," and accused Spicer of doing "a poor job in defending the president." Spicer was annoyed. He thought he was helping Ruddy and the president, only to find himself castigated.

The Mueller probe was heating up. Newt Gingrich had initially hailed the former FBI chief as a superb choice to lead the investigation. But now Gingrich was ripping him for a severe conflict of interest, because Mueller and Comey were longtime colleagues. Sean Hannity, who constantly attacked the "destroy-Trump media," called on Mueller to resign. Those close to Trump "say he is so volatile," the *New York Times* reported, "they cannot be sure that he will not change his mind" about firing Mueller. The AP reported that according to aides and confidants, the president was "yelling at television sets in the White House" and claiming to be the victim of a conspiracy. This was high-level sabotage by the president's supposed allies.

There was now a definite rhythm to the Mueller scoops, which erupted as evening earthquakes, usually around seven or eight o'clock, in the *Washington Post* or *New York Times*, and the aftershocks would dominate the prime-time programming at MSNBC and CNN. A *Post* or *Times* reporter would join Anderson Cooper on CNN or Rachel Maddow on MSNBC to discuss the story. Both cable networks were eagerly adding reporters from the two papers as paid contributors.

On June 14, the *Washington Post* said that Robert Mueller was now investigating Trump over obstruction of justice allegations. The psychological impact was undeniable, but the details were less dramatic. The paper reported that Mueller intended to interview top intelligence officials about whether Trump had asked them to intervene in Comey's FBI probe. Mueller, of course, would have been guilty of malpractice had he failed to interview these officials about Comey's allegations. In other words, Bob Mueller was simply doing his job.

Early that morning, a heartbreaking story grabbed the nation's attention. A Trump hater named James Hodgkinson had taken a high-powered rifle to a Virginia baseball diamond where Republican lawmakers were practicing and opened fire, nearly killing House GOP Whip Steve Scalise and wounding four other people. It was an attack that stunned the nation, and even as the president and other leaders appealed for unity, much of the media were consumed by a debate over whether harsh left-wing rhetoric had paved the way for the shooting, and whether Trump's own rhetoric had contributed to the toxic climate.

Despite the sense of national grieving, and with Scalise at severe risk of dying, MSNBC remained fixated on the special counsel that night. So what if a congressional leader was almost assassinated? Chris Matthews led off *Hardball* by saying, "Donald Trump and his ties with Moscow remain the big story here, even on a day struck by violence." Maddow did the Russia story about ten minutes into her program, interviewing one of the *Washington Post* reporters.

Kellyanne Conway was deeply affected by the shooting, and it showed. In a segment on *Fox & Friends*, she complained that "as Steve Scalise was fighting for his life and crawling into right field in a trail of blood," some people were trashing Trump. Conway called for "more muted voices," and then she said this: "Look at Twitter. If I were shot and killed tomorrow half of Twitter would explode in applause and excitement." That was a sad glimpse of her emotional state.

But the president was using that very social network to unleash some harsh language of his own. Conway had argued days earlier that the media were paying too much attention to his tweets at the expense of his policies, but these tweets were hard to ignore.

Fed up with the endless Russia investigation, Trump again castigated "Crooked H" for her email scandal, and declared that he was the victim of "the single greatest WITCH HUNT in American political history," which was "led by some very bad and conflicted people!" That was a clear reference to Bob Mueller and his prosecutors, some of whom had donated money to Hillary Clinton's campaign. He rebuked the "Fake News Media" over the "phony collusion" story, and took a strange shot at Rod Rosenstein, the deputy attorney general who had tapped Mueller as special counsel: "I am being investigated for firing the FBI Director by the man who told me to fire the FBI Director! Witch hunt." Every new lightning bolt in this tweetstorm sparked more coverage.

• • •

Another frustration for the president was that his policy agenda was stalled in Congress, depriving the White House of a counter-narrative for the scandal-hungry press.

While issuing executive orders and pruning regulations, Trump had made no progress on tax cuts. Not a single brick had been laid for the border wall. Two versions of the travel ban had been blocked by the courts. And Obamacare repeal was stuck in the Senate. Ivanka Trump made a rare media appearance, promoting a workplace development initiative on *Fox & Friends*. Yet what made news was not the initiative, but her saying that in Washington she encountered "a level of viciousness that I was not expecting."

Some in the press slimed her again, such as *Mediaite* columnist Kylie Cheung, who ripped Ivanka's "unwavering loyalty to a self-admitted sexual serial abuser and crude-mouthed misogynist." Cheung said the president's career was "built on the oppression of just about every woman in this country who doesn't share her privilege."

The *oppression* of just about every non-wealthy woman?

Ivanka's husband was dragged into the hostile media spotlight as well. In the next evening earthquake, the *Washington Post* reported that Mueller was expanding his investigation into Jared Kushner's business dealings. Once again, this was an incremental development treated as huge news. How could Mueller scrutinize Trump aides and their links to Russia without looking at possible transactions by a top official with major real estate holdings? Jared thought the piece was a nothing-burger. But the story ricocheted everywhere.

The same thing happened when Mike Pence hired a lawyer. What top official wouldn't retain counsel when faced with an FBI interview? "Very routine," the vice president told reporters.

But some media outlets treated the move as highly significant. The *Washington Post* questioned whether Pence's approach to his job was one of "serene confidence or willful oblivion" and quoted a senior White House official as saying how important it was that Pence, who "never says no," not be just a "yes man."

· · ·

The battle between Trump and the media was, at bottom, a grand battle over the truth.

To the press, it was a matter of fact that Trump was under investigation, that he had improperly pressured his FBI director, that he had no respect for the independence of law enforcement, that the evidence of a cover-up was strong, that he had a suspiciously soft approach to Russia, that he was acting like a man with much to hide.

To the president, the truth looked very different: that the investigation was a sham, designed by detractors to delegitimize his election, that he had not demanded anything of Comey, that there was nothing wrong with asking aides for loyalty, that illegal leakers were working with the press to undermine him, that he had nothing to do with Russia and therefore had nothing to cover up.

Trump's incessant tweeting, in his eyes, was explicitly meant to combat a negative media narrative over a nonexistent conspiracy. But the press saw it as a self-destructive practice creating self-inflicted wounds.

One truth, however, remained self-evident: the melodramatic coverage of Trump's troubles was blotting out his efforts to change the country.

• • •

What had been fairly obvious to just about everyone in journalism was nonetheless treated as a bombshell.

More than a month after tweeting that Jim Comey had better hope there were no tapes of their conversations, Trump returned to Twitter to admit that, yes, he had no tapes.

It was, of course, a bluff from the start—and a bit of a taunt aimed at Comey. In baseball, you'd call it a brushback pitch. Trump was undoubtedly enjoying all the frenzied media speculation, but clearly underestimated how the echoes of Richard Nixon's downfall would make the story resonate with the press. It was not the wisest decision he'd ever made.

After Trump's admission in late June, NoTapeGate was practically handled as a scandal in itself. On MSNBC, Lawrence O'Donnell said it showed "the president is an utter ignoramus in matters of law and governing." On CNN, Jake Tapper issued a broader criticism: "Was it bluster, witness intimidation, a desire to pressure Comey to be as truthful as possible?" The plan had "backfired," Tapper declared, and was part of a White House effort to spare his staff from having to "go on live TV and defend aberrant behavior on Twitter or explain the false things the president says."

Tapper often thought about the Joe McCarthy era, and the people who stayed silent as the notorious senator smeared innocent people as Communists. He didn't want something similar to be said about him in the Trump era. Tapper fervently believed there weren't two sides when it came to the truth; there was only the truth.

Trump claimed on *Fox & Friends* that his maneuver might have had an impact on Comey's testimony: "When he found out that there may be tapes out there....I think his story may have changed."

"It was a smart way to make sure he stayed honest in those hearings," anchor Ainsley Earhardt replied.

There was no evidence that Comey had changed his account. But the question of Trump's veracity—even though he never actually said he had tapes—became an increasingly prominent media theme. The *New York Times* devoted a full page to a dense list purporting to show nearly every untruth uttered by Trump as president: "Many Americans have become accustomed to President Trump's lies. But as regular as they have become, the country should not allow itself to become numb to them." That was the narrative. (The second example was that Trump said he had been on *Time*'s cover "14 or 15 times," when it was actually eleven.)

A parallel media narrative, powered by self-serving leaks from administration officials, was that Trump's staff was valiantly struggling to save the embattled president from himself.

Politico ran a piece headlined "Trump Gives Priebus Until July 4th To Clean Up White House"—or get the boot. "It's ridiculous, just fake news," the president told him. It's idiots making things up. You're not going anywhere." As the imaginary deadline approached, Trump and Priebus joked that *it must be firing time.*

A *Washington Post* story said White House officials were trying to govern "while also indulging and managing Trump's combative and sometimes self-destructive impulses." These unnamed sources were upset by what they viewed as "the president's fits of rage," and worried about his health as "his mood has been more sour than at any point since they have known him."

The leaks were driving Ivanka crazy. She was from the business world and liked organization and structure, not spending hours each day having to deal with stupid leaked stories. It was one of the reasons that she and her husband wanted Reince Priebus gone, because they held him responsible for either leaking or tolerating other White House leakers, whom Ivanka viewed as building their own brands.

She was especially annoyed by leaks that cast her as an ultra-liberal opponent of her father. The real news, contrary to the media's portrait, was that she wasn't.

• • •

Sean Spicer decided that most press briefings were now going to be off camera—and the media, convinced that they had a right to interrogate the press secretary on camera, threw a fit.

Spicer, undaunted, went further. "There are days I'll decide that the president's voice should be the one that speaks," he said, and on those days he would bar audio recordings.

CNN correspondent Jim Acosta accused the White House of "suppression of information." He told viewers that Spicer was "just kind of useless," so "why are we even having these briefings or these gaggles in the first place?" He compared the press operation to "Pravda." He tried to organize an insurrection, telling the *Huffington Post* that "we should walk out" to stop the "stonewalling."

Spicer found Acosta's protests sad. Sean was, to be sure, trying to dim the harsh spotlight that had enveloped him. But Spicer believed that he and Sarah Huckabee Sanders were providing plenty of information, and by turning off the cameras he intended to discourage showboating reporters who just wanted to generate more YouTube clips for themselves. Some print reporters preferred the more businesslike tone of the off-camera gaggles. Most TV reporters naturally missed their cameras. At one audio-only briefing, CNN subtly protested the camera ban by sending a sketch artist, as news outlets did at courthouse trials. Steve Bannon jokingly texted an *Atlantic* reporter that the real reason the briefings were moved off camera was because "Sean got fatter."

The president was pleased with the pared-back briefings, and Spicer knew that he was playing to an audience of one. He knew as well that Sean Hannity had publicly urged Trump to curtail the briefings. Laura

Ingraham had advised briefing reporters only when the administration had something to push. And Newt Gingrich had suggested that CNN be banned.

Spicer had read stories predicting his ouster practically since the day he arrived. It was though they were saying it would rain, he thought; one day they would be right. But now there was, in fact, an ongoing search for a new press secretary. What journalists didn't know was that Spicer had had a series of conversations with Trump about moving into a senior management role and leaving the press briefings to someone else. That, he figured, could take months, but he was already thinking about making more money on the outside.

Bannon reached out to Laura Ingraham, but she never wanted the job and wasn't going to give up her lucrative media career. David Martosko, U.S. political editor of the *Daily Mail*, announced he had been considered—he was Jared and Ivanka's preference—but had withdrawn his name. "You'll be thrown to the wolves," Bannon had warned him if he took the job.

While the names of his possible replacements kept getting floated in the press, Spicer, with an air of resignation, just kept plugging away.

• • •

If the White House believed the press was firmly in opposition, Glenn Thrush had a way of reinforcing that on Twitter. "FIVE months in: 36% approval, GOP support sags to 71%, no briefings, denialism, ugh policy record, Bannon resurgent," the *Times* reporter wrote.

One reason for the president's unpopularity was the daily media diet of scandalous fare tied to Russia. Kellyanne Conway tried to shift the focus to other issues, but the media wouldn't budge. CNN morning host Alisyn Camerota repeatedly asked Kellyanne what the president was doing about Russian hacking during the election. Conway pushed back hard.

"Alisyn, I know you just like to say the word Russia, Russia to mislead the voters, and I know that CNN is aiding and abetting this nonsense," she said. "You've asked me the same question three times."

"And you're not answering it, Kellyanne."

Conway believed that all this chatter about Russia was irrelevant. They were trying to create jobs, defend the country, support veterans, and help drug addicts—all of which were more important than some unproven Russian conspiracy. And she had a point.

An NBC/*Wall Street Journal* poll found that 50 percent of Americans believed the media coverage of allegations against Trump had been irresponsibly overdramatized. Only 34 percent viewed the coverage as responsible and proper. Such a poll might have prompted some serious self-examination by journalists who again seemed disconnected from much of the country. But most were so consumed with proving that Trump had done something wrong that it did not.

Despite his constant criticism of stories quoting anonymous sources, Trump again seized on one such account in a newspaper he usually disparaged. The *Washington Post* published a lengthy investigation into how Barack Obama sat on intelligence findings for months during the campaign that Vladimir Putin had personally overseen a Russian hacking effort to defeat Hillary Clinton and elect Trump. The paper quoted a former senior Obama administration official as saying, "I feel like we sort of choked."

The president picked up the blind quote in a Twitter barrage about the story: "Why no action? Focus on them, not T!" Trump went so far as to say his predecessor "colluded or obstructed" when it came to Moscow's efforts.

The story said Obama and his aides hesitated because they didn't want to be accused of putting a thumb on the electoral scale and believed Clinton would win anyway. But there was a rich irony in Trump, who had only grudgingly acknowledged the Russians were probably behind the hacking, now embracing that scenario and using the *Washington Post* as his reliable source. Yet the story, which made Obama look weak, somehow didn't get much traction in the rest of the media.

When it came to the Russian scandal, the press was laser-focused on Donald Trump.

CHAPTER 21

INVESTIGATIVE OVERREACH

The media's investigative efforts had grown so intense that even the smallest anti-Trump leads, whose importance was tangential at best, were inflated into full-blown stories.

The *Washington Post*, for example, published a lengthy piece on Jared Kushner's real estate company securing a routine refinancing loan for a property near Times Square. Why was this front-page news?

The $285-million loan, which closed in the final weeks of the campaign, came from Deutsche Bank. That bank was said to be negotiating with New York regulators over allegations "that it aided a possible Russian money-laundering scheme."

There was no suggestion that Kushner had gotten special treatment on the refinancing. There was nothing to indicate that Kushner had even a remote tie to the money-laundering allegations. But, the third paragraph said, the loan "could come under focus" as Robert Mueller reviewed Kushner's business activities. Even that—*could*—was a stretch. Kushner could be criticized for not listing the loan on his financial disclosure form, but he had relied on published guidelines from the Office of Government Ethics.

Jared viewed the story as insane. The *Post* thought it had a big scoop—Kushner bought a building from a Russian guy!—though he emphasized that the purchase had taken place back in 2014.

But for the media, the mere presence of dots, even if they weren't connected, became news if it could be construed as damaging to Trump. Rachel Maddow cited the *Washington Post* piece as she led off her show with the less-than-startling news that Kushner had hired a criminal lawyer.

The *Post* article was a model of good journalism compared to CNN's report, published on the network's website, that Anthony Scaramucci, a close Trump adviser, was under investigation for his supposed ties to a Russian investment fund.

Scaramucci, a wealthy former hedge-fund manager, was feisty, fast-talking, and friends with Trump, making him a fat target. Trump frequently called the Mooch for advice.

The CNN piece, relying on one unnamed source, said Scaramucci had held a secret meeting the previous January with an official from the fund and discussed whether the United States would lift sanctions against Moscow.

But there was no secret meeting. Scaramucci had given a speech on Trump's behalf at Davos, and the Russian had approached him in a restaurant to briefly say hello, with no discussion of sanctions. Scaramucci had never done any business with Russia and had visited the country only once, as a twenty-five-year-old student.

"I was disappointed the story was published," Scaramucci told me. "It was a lie." As the story fell apart, Scaramucci told Jeff Zucker he was ready to go to war, that he was willing to file a major lawsuit. The network quickly deleted the piece, saying it "did not meet CNN's editorial standards," and apologized to Scaramucci. Three journalists who worked on the story, including a Pulitzer Prize winner hired months earlier from the *New York Times*, were allowed to resign.

Trump called Scaramucci after seeing him debunk the story on the air. "You killed them. You're not even in the White House and it's a great comms win for us," he said.

The president asked whether he planned to sue, suggesting he could probably win $15 million. Scaramucci said that would take him off television and he wasn't a fan of lawsuits against journalists.

"I'm not as selfless as you. I would sue the shit out of them," Trump said. But he was impressed by the Mooch's tenacity and quickly claimed vindication on Twitter.

"Wow, CNN had to retract big story on 'Russia,' with 3 employees forced to resign. What about all the other phony stories they do? FAKE NEWS!" he wrote. He retweeted a mock FNN logo (Fake News Network), took a slap at the ratings being way down (which wasn't true), and broadened the indictment: "What about NBC, CBS & ABC? What about the failing @nytimes & @washingtonpost? They are all Fake News!"

Privately, Trump vented that the people at CNN were horrible human beings. He repeated unsubstantiated rumors that Jeff Zucker might resign if AT&T's bid for CNN's parent company Time Warner won federal approval.

Zucker was upset by the botched Scaramucci story and told his troops that they had to "play error-free ball." By publishing such an unsubstantiated piece, CNN handed the president a club to attack the network.

White House spokeswoman Sarah Huckabee Sanders echoed the president's anger after taking a question from a *Breitbart* reporter.

"It's the barrage of fake news directed at the president that has garnered his frustration....If the media can't be trusted to report the news, that's a dangerous place for America," she said.

Brian Karem, editor of Maryland's suburban *Sentinel* papers and a *Playboy* columnist, interrupted her with an angry lecture: "What you just did is inflammatory to people all over the country who look at it and say, 'See, once again, the president is right and everybody else is just fake media.' Everybody in this room is only trying to do their job."

Sanders looked down and hesitated. She was ready to hit back hard, but thought it would be better to use southern charm than come off as an angry mom scolding her kids. Besides, how could she, a thirty-four-year-old woman, be threatening to this fifty-something guy? "If anything has been inflamed," she said evenly, "it's the dishonesty that often takes place by the news media. I think it is outrageous for you to accuse me of inflaming a story when I was simply trying to respond to his question."

Karem became an instant hero, booked on a spate of shows on MSNBC and CNN, and Zucker gave him a contract. He said the White House had "bullied and browbeaten" journalists and, channeling mad-as-hell Howard Beale, declared that "it's disheartening. It's unnerving. I can't take it anymore."

The bullying, the undermining of the First Amendment, as Karem put it, was that the president and his spokesmen criticized the media, sometimes in strong language. But the First Amendment protected their free speech rights as well.

Chuck Todd, looking angry, told viewers that the White House "war on the media" was "nothing less than a war on the truth." By squarely putting his profession on the side of the truth, the NBC anchor suggested that the administration was using lies while journalists played it straight. He did acknowledge that his network and other outlets didn't always get it right but said they took responsibility for their mistakes.

The rush to defend CNN melded into media complaints about the state of White House press briefings. CNN's Jim Acosta heckled Spicer: "Why are the cameras off, Sean?" He essentially accused Sanders of being a minister of propaganda: "Does this feel like America? Where the White House takes Q's from conservatives, then openly trashes the news media in the briefing room."

Actually, political aides in America have every right to push back against media malfeasance. It might have been a stretch for Sanders to turn CNN's debacle into a broadside against the entire press, but the White House had a point that its newsworthy policies—such as making it easier to fire incompetents at the Veterans Administration—got next to no coverage, while each detail of the amorphous Russia probe was endlessly chronicled. And when news outlets got it wrong, they often either downplayed or ignored the error. CNN ignored its retraction on the air, with only fleeting mentions after the White House attack, and

MSNBC ignored it as well; many in the media considered a botched story against Trump to be a non-story.

It had not been a good stretch for CNN. The network had just suffered the humiliation of having reported that Jim Comey would tell the Senate that the president was under investigation, when in fact he testified that he wasn't. Sometimes journalists wished a bit too hard for their Trump stories to be true.

• • •

It was just another day at the office for the *Morning Joe* crew.

Mika Brzezinski seized upon on a less-than-earthshaking *Washington Post* scoop: that clubhouses, at several golf courses owned by Trump, had posted on their walls a mock *Time* magazine cover with a made-up story about *The Apprentice*. "Nothing makes a man feel better than making a fake cover of a magazine about himself, lying every day, and destroying the country," Brzezinski said, adding that Trump's hands looked teensy on the covers.

Minutes later, the president struck back with tweets that would unite virtually the entire media world against him. He had heard (since he insisted he didn't watch) that the MSNBC duo was speaking badly about him.

"Then how come low I.Q. Crazy Mika, along with Psycho Joe, came to Mar-a-Lago 3 nights in a row around New Year's Eve, and insisted on joining me. She was bleeding badly from a face-lift. I said no!"

Blood. Face lift. A woman's looks. It was reminiscent of the blowback he had generated during the campaign when he criticized Megyn Kelly for asking him "ridiculous" debate questions: "You could see there was blood coming out of her eyes, blood coming out of her wherever."

Trump asked Anthony Scaramucci what he thought of the tweets against Mika and Joe: "I know what you're going to say—unpresidential. Then what?"

"I don't think you needed to go there," Scaramucci said.

"Is Korea off the TV?" Trump asked. Yes, the Mooch replied. North Korea's nuclear buildup had been eclipsed.

"Is health care off the TV?" True, the impasse over the Senate bill had faded.

"Sounds good to me," Trump said.

The Mika maelstrom dominated cable news. Even if there was a method to the madness, it was portrayed as madness. Anchors, panelists, guests, including most of those on Fox News, said Trump had gone too far, as did some Republican lawmakers. He was accused of being a misogynist, of being consumed by animosity, of having a personality disorder. Carl Bernstein made this apocalyptic announcement on CNN: "This is the greatest journalistic challenge of the modern era, to report on a malignant presidency."

Some programs replayed the Fox footage of Ivanka saying she had been surprised by the viciousness of Washington, and of Melania calling for an end to cyberbullying.

Brzezinski later insisted that she hadn't had a face lift, that she had told Melania at the Mar-a-Lago meeting brokered by Jared that she'd had skin tightened under her chin and Donald kept asking who her doctor was. He thought the face-lift slap would sting, unconcerned that it might reinforce the media indictment that he liked to denigrate women's looks. Trump always believed in hitting back at his opponents, and he had thrown a hard punch. But as far as the media were concerned, the only face he had bloodied was his own.

Even if Trump was punching down and shouldn't have retaliated against Mika and Joe, they were hardly innocent bystanders. The harsh personal attacks by Scarborough and Brzezinski—calling Trump mentally ill, a liar, a racist, a thug, and a goon—were minimized or ignored in the coverage of Trump's tweets.

Scarborough felt that at times he went too far in ripping Trump, and he regretted it. He knew he wasn't helping his case by sounding angry or emotional on the air. He and Mika had recently discussed whether their rhetoric was getting too strong, but kept it up nonetheless.

One of *Morning Joe*'s sharpest critics was Kellyanne Conway. She thought little of Brzezinski as a journalist and resented being trashed by her in the past. It was Mika she had in mind when she made the on-air crack about face lifts, and was surprised that the plastic surgery story had not come out earlier, since the president had told a group of congressmen about it. Kellyanne believed that Mika and Joe got good press because journalists were the show's target audience, and many wanted to be invited on as guests.

The press was much more sympathetic to Mika than Kellyanne. An associate of conservative activist James O'Keefe had captured on tape CNN's Jimmy Carr, an associate producer on *New Day*, saying that Trump was "fucking crazy" and Kellyanne was an "awful woman" who "looks like she got hit with a shovel." There were no cries of sexism about that.

In her television appearances, Conway condemned the "toxic" attacks on the president by what she called the "jackals and hyenas" in the press. She edged into questionable territory by telling George Stephanopoulos that the harsh coverage of Trump was not "patriotic"— though she meant the harsh personal attacks, not the political criticism.

Sarah Huckabee Sanders had her own resentment toward *Morning Joe*, which had slammed her, and defended her boss: "I think that the president is pushing back against people who attack him day after day after day. Where's the outrage on that?"

The next morning, Joe and Mika responded with what they hoped was a dispassionate approach. Brzezinski said Trump's tweets didn't bother her, but "it does worry me about the country....He appears to have a fragile, impetuous, child-like ego that we've seen over and over again, especially with women."

Scarborough gave the saga a tabloid twist, saying White House aides had warned him that if he wanted to stop an exposé of him and Mika in the *National Enquirer*—owned by close Trump pal David Pecker—he had to call the president and apologize. Some pundits immediately branded this an attempt at blackmail.

The president denied any strong-arming, and said Scarborough had called him, which wasn't true—they hadn't spoken at all. White House sources said Joe had called Jared Kushner, worried about the pending *Enquirer* exposé, and Kushner suggested he take it up with Trump. When

Scarborough said he could not because Trump was mad at him, Jared suggested that maybe he should apologize. That was hardly a quid pro quo.

But that account was just part of the backstory. Scarborough had called a White House official and said he knew what was happening: "I hear Donald is having the *National Enquirer* do a story on us. I want you to know I know: If this story runs, I'm going to know Donald is calling for him to do it."

No, he would never do that, the official said.

"Trust me," said Scarborough. "He would do it, he is doing it, and it's a mistake." And if that happened, Scarborough warned, he would make clear that Trump's fingerprints were all over it.

Two more White House officials got in touch. You need to call Donald and apologize for how tough your coverage has been, they said, and he will kill the story. No way, said Scarborough.

So they started calling Mika. She told them to back off.

Finally, a senior White House official sent Scarborough a last, desperate text: "This is going to be really bad. You really need to give him a call."

Joe and Mika were worried about the story. They both had kids, and they hadn't yet made their romance public. But they were not going to capitulate. (The *Enquirer* piece, which ran weeks later after the previously married hosts announced their engagement, was headlined "'Morning Joe' Sleazy Cheating Scandal.")

Morning Joe became the top cable news morning program for one fleeting day when they responded to Trump's tweets. (Conway thought people tuned in to make their own assessment of Mika's face.) Trump offered an olive branch, tweeting that Joe and Mika weren't "bad people," but that the show was "dominated by their NBC bosses." He couldn't resist adding, however, that Mika was "dumb as a rock."

In the end, Trump gave the cable couple a bonanza of free publicity. The usually supportive Laura Ingraham told him, "No one cares....Stop helping their ratings & jacking up their speaking fees."

Indeed, the lead story that day should have been the Supreme Court's approving parts of Trump's travel ban. Instead, the media focused on Trump's least favorite morning news show.

• • •

Over the July Fourth weekend, Trump posted old footage of him play-tackling his friend Vince McMahon, the WWE boss, at a wrestling match, superimposing the CNN logo over McMahon's head.

It was a crude animation, not particularly funny, and definitely undignified, but more about Trump trying to be entertaining than a serious attack on CNN. The media, however, treated the video as a fundamental threat to journalistic freedom.

In that sense, it was the perfect Rorschach test. Journalists, who always took Trump literally, saw him body-slamming a major news organization; the president and his supporters saw him as having some laughs trolling the media.

CNN didn't see the humor, accusing Trump of juvenile behavior, of encouraging violence against reporters, and scolded him to do his job.

While the video had a farcical look, others feared a more chilling message. Some journalists told me privately that they had been receiving not just obscene vitriol from Trump supporters—often sexually explicit taunts for women—but serious death threats that prompted some to contact local police agencies. Their home addresses had been published. They worried about family members. No public figure can be held responsible for what crazy followers might say or do, but the journalists under online attack were nervous.

On his MSNBC show, Chuck Todd accused the president of dehumanizing journalists and said that if another leader was doing what Trump was doing, the State Department would be saying "that country is inching toward authoritarianism."

CNN commentator Ana Navarro was more succinct: "He is going to get someone killed in the media."

In his *Times* media column, Jim Rutenberg offered a historical lament: Americans could hardly enjoy the Fourth of July "when one of the pillars of our 241-year-old republic—the First Amendment—is under near-daily assault from the highest levels of the government."

The selective bursts of outrage seemed as phony as the WWE itself. The overheated objections were, by an order of magnitude, far more emotional than those that greeted Kathy Griffin's severed Trump head, or Shakespeare in the Park's bloody assassination of Trump as Julius Caesar, both of which suggested murder in a way that a bit of Wrestle-Mania did not.

The famously self-absorbed media cast themselves as brave warriors, guardians of the nation's independence, under siege by a rogue president. Actually, the media were Trump's codependents, addicted to the drama of fighting him at every turn. And Trump's presidency seemed increasingly consumed by an assault on the press that was intended to neutralize criticism of his agenda, but too often overshadowed the agenda itself.

• • •

The speech that Donald Trump delivered in Poland—which combined the sweep of history with a nationalistic call to unite against Islamic terrorism—was described even by many detractors as the best of his presidency.

But there was considerably more media coverage of his attacks on CNN and NBC, eclipsing his major address.

Trump had held a news conference with the Polish president and called on David Martosko of the *Daily Mail*, who asked about CNN's response to the wrestling video, including tracking down its creator on a Reddit message board and warning that the network might expose his identity if he backed off his apology for the stunt and some bigoted postings.

"They have been fake news for a long time. They've been covering me in a very, very dishonest way," Trump said.

And then he pivoted: "NBC is equally as bad, despite the fact that I made them a fortune with *The Apprentice*, but they forgot that"—as if the old show would afford him immunity from critical coverage.

The spectacle of Trump unleashing such criticism on foreign soil sparked a severe reaction. "I'm not sure that the American president should be bashing the American media when he is overseas with a foreign leader who tried to repress the free media in his own country," *Fox News Sunday* anchor Chris Wallace said.

CNN was furious. Jeff Zucker had already declared that Trump was trying to "bully" the network and that he would not be intimidated. Now CNN's Jim Acosta condemned Trump's "fake news conference"—"fake" because Trump dared call on a conservative, not "someone who was going to challenge him on the issues."

Trump had, in fact, also taken a question from NBC's Hallie Jackson, who asked if he would finally accept that Russian hackers interfered with the election. Trump hedged, but scolded the media for reporting that all seventeen U.S. intelligence agencies had blamed Russia for the hacking, when it was only four. "Many of your compatriots had to change their reporting, or they had to apologize or they had to correct," the president said. And he was right—the AP and *New York Times* were among those who had just corrected the frequently repeated but erroneous statistic.

Spicer was often puzzled by how his boss decided who to call on at news conferences. Trump would veto one reporter who had "said some bad stuff" or approve another who had "been really good." But when Spicer noted that *USA Today* correspondent David Jackson had been very fair, Trump told him: "Did you see what *USA Today* said about me yesterday?" Jackson hadn't written the story, but he was made to pay the price.

There was a huge media buildup for the next day's meeting with Vladimir Putin, which was treated like a Cold War summit, with the focus on whether Trump would dare bring up the Russian hacking. As it happened, Trump raised the issue twice during the two-hour meeting. But Trump and Putin's agreement to move on to other issues dismayed anti-Russia hardliners and conservative Trump critics like Steve Hayes, whose *Weekly Standard* piece was titled "Trump Caves to Putin."

Still, Putin had not steamrolled the new president, as some pundits had expected, and somehow that drained the news value from the much-hyped showdown. Since the session, which yielded a partial cease-fire in Syria, appeared to go reasonably well, the press shifted its focus.

The *Washington Post* said that at the G20 meeting, "the growing international isolation of the United States under President Trump was starkly apparent." The *New York Times* said Trump "found the United States isolated on everything from trade to climate change," and that he was a nationalist who "has alienated allies and made the United States seem like its own private island."

But the president was doing precisely what he had promised to do during the campaign on trade, NATO, immigration, and the environment. Whether these were good policies or not, to summarily dismiss them as "isolationist" reflected a media consensus that it was wrong to tamper with the existing world order. A more neutral approach would have been to report that Trump was "challenging" our allies and adversaries rather than turning America into a pariah state.

NBC's Andrea Mitchell called it the worst summit since 1986, charging that Trump was "too chicken" to hold a closing news conference. The *Wall Street Journal*'s Eli Stokols said on MSNBC that Trump's discussion of Russia was "Kremlinesque propaganda."

And then there was Ivanka. She had been edging into a more public role, giving a speech at the State Department to unveil a report on human trafficking, joining a women's roundtable in Saudi Arabia, discussing her job with the *Washington Post*, and writing a *Wall Street Journal* op-ed on family leave.

But then came a fateful moment. When her father asked her to sit in for him at a session in Germany, Ivanka declined. He asked again. No way, Ivanka said; she knew full well the media would lose their minds if she sat in for the president of the United States.

Two minutes after the president left, Treasury Secretary Steve Mnuchin approached her and said her father really wanted her to take the seat. She gave in, and Angela Merkel gave her a fist bump. Ivanka knew what would happen.

There were instantaneous headlines around the globe, such as this one in the *Washington Post*: "Ivanka Trump Takes Her Father's Seat at World Leaders' Table During a G-20 Meeting."

Liberal *New York Times* columnist Charles Blow erupted: "Why the hell is Ivanka Trump sitting in for daddy at G20 meetings? What are her qualifications? Who voted for her?"

Columnist Nick Kristof, also of the *Times*, wrote, "Yes, she's beautiful—but unqualified. When Caligula tried to appoint his horse Consul of Rome, it was a beautiful horse."

A columnist for London's *Independent* harrumphed that "the president runs things like America is just the new family business."

World leaders took the meaningless incident in stride, but Trump had managed to embroil his daughter in yet another media furor.

CHAPTER 22

THE SECRET
RUSSIA MEETING

For nearly a year, the bitter battle between the president and the media turned on his fierce insistence that he had done absolutely nothing to collude with Russia and their unyielding determination to prove that he had.

There had been so many eye-glazing stories about this or that previously private contact between a Trump associate and a Russian official that it had become the background music of his administration, a constant hum that was easy to ignore.

The constant billowing of smoke, with no visible fire, was continuing because the White House had chosen not to release all the information, no matter how damaging, to snuff out the story.

And then, on July 9, came a *New York Times* piece that could not be easily waved away, given the stunning admission that came from Donald Trump Jr. himself. The president's son had taken a first step toward attempted collusion with the Russians, its sting lessened only because the effort apparently went nowhere. He had also pulled Jared

Kushner and Paul Manafort, then the campaign chairman, into the June 2016 session with Russian lawyer Natalia Veselnitskaya.

Don Jr. gave a statement to the *New York Times* that was so incomplete as to be blatantly misleading. Don had wanted to put out more details, but White House officials pushed the idea of what was called a "surgical" statement with minimal information. They drafted it on the plane ride back from the G20 summit, the statement saying that "we primarily discussed a program about the adoption of Russian children."

The next day, the *Times* reporters came back with more information, and the White House told Don Jr. he would have to respond with a fuller statement. He was furious, because that was what he had wanted to do in the first place; now he looked evasive. In the second statement, Don Jr. said that Veselnitskaya indicated she had information on Russians funding the DNC and supporting Hillary Clinton, but she offered only "vague" and "ambiguous" comments. She then turned to her "true agenda"—an effort to change an American sanctions law aimed at Moscow that prompted Putin to end an adoption program—and Don realized "that the claims of potentially helpful information were a pretext for the meeting."

He abruptly ended the sit-down, because his only interest had been whether this Russian had any dirt on Hillary. There was no need for complicated media analysis; these were his own words.

The second *New York Times* story cited "three advisers to the White House briefed on the meeting" between Don and Veselnitskaya "and two others with knowledge of it." These sources were either engaged in damage control or trying to damage the president's son.

Political campaigns, of course, were often on the hunt for "opposition research." Don dismissed the "nonsense meeting," tweeting, "Media & Dems are extremely invested in the Russia story...I understand the desperation!"

On the third day, when the *Times* told Don Jr. that it was about to publish the emails setting up the meeting, he preempted the paper by posting them on Twitter. And they were explicit. A British publicist and former tabloid reporter conveyed an offer from Russia's top prosecutor, through an intermediary, "to provide the Trump campaign with some official documents and information that would incriminate Hillary and her dealings with Russia and would be very useful to your father." And this was part of "its government's support for Mr. Trump." Don Jr.'s response made headlines everywhere: "I love it."

Don made a unilateral decision to sit down with a sympathetic interviewer, Sean Hannity. He defended the meeting as a routine search for opposition research but admitted to Hannity that in retrospect he "probably would have done things a little differently."

Kellyanne Conway was sent off to *Good Morning America*, *New Day*, and *Fox & Friends* to defend the embarrassing disclosures. George Stephanopoulos wanted to know who had misled Conway, since she had previously insisted there were no Russian meetings related to the campaign.

Conway parried by saying the officials involved had amended their disclosure forms, but the best she could offer was that the meeting was a bust: "No information was received that was meaningful or helpful and no action was taken."

Kellyanne wound up in a thirty-five-minute debate with Chris Cuomo on CNN, asking him: "Aren't you the least bit reluctant, if not embarrassed that you now talk about Russia more than you talk about America?"

"No!" Cuomo replied. "Kellyanne, this matters." He tried to score a point for the press, saying viewers "shouldn't believe all of the White House and the surrogates and your alt-right friends that want to destroy the responsible media."

Kellyanne wasn't having it, complaining about "the snarky looks, the furrowed brows, the rolling eyes from so many people on your panels. And you know it. You guys have made a business decision to be anti-Trump."

The press tried to tar Jared Kushner with the latest revelations, even though everyone agreed he had left the meeting within minutes. The pundits started saying without evidence that Kushner could be in legal jeopardy and questioned whether his security clearance should be revoked. The *New York Times* asked whether Kushner had been "forth-coming" in describing the meeting to the president. On MSNBC, Lawrence O'Donnell suggested Jared leaked the story to make Don Jr. look bad. And to make such sabotage sound plausible, he invoked the criminal case in which Kushner's father had entrapped his brother-in-law in a prostitute sting. That was a truly low blow.

Kushner was frustrated that Sean Spicer wasn't defending him and Don Jr. more aggressively. But Steve Bannon wanted all comments on the Russian investigations to come from lawyers or their spokesmen. He didn't want the president's aides sucked back into the Russian morass, as had happened on the plane; otherwise, Spicer and Sanders would have to fight that battle every day.

Kushner's lawyers had discovered the emails setting up the meeting, and Bannon suspected that his team had leaked the story. Bannon thought it mind-boggling that Don Jr. and Jared had taken the meeting. Bannon had spent years on a Navy destroyer, hunting Soviet subs from the South China Sea to the Persian Gulf; he didn't need to be told that the Russians could still be an enemy. Besides, he had all the opposition research he needed from newspaper stories on the Clinton Foundation and the book *Clinton Cash*. When Bannon got to the campaign, it wasn't research they were short of, it was manpower. Trump's skeletal staff, he felt, couldn't even "collude" with the RNC on a ground game.

Bannon realized the Russia probe had become a media soap opera. Before the Don Jr. revelation, the scandal had become so arcane that even anti-Trump journalists were getting tired of it. But now you had these colorful characters: attractive Russian women, an eccentric British publicist, a pop star, quirky billionaires. It had become *The Americans*, the FX drama in which two Soviet agents pose as a married couple to spy on the U.S. government.

Once the special counsel was appointed, Bannon mounted a serious effort to persuade Republicans to shut down the House and Senate investigations as unnecessary. But the lawmakers argued that their inquiries were too far down the road and refused. Bannon felt their egos wouldn't allow them to pass up all that free television exposure.

Bannon's focus was pushing the president's agenda on health care, trade, taxes, and immigration. He didn't want any part of the Russian debacle. He hadn't felt the need to hire a lawyer, and he wanted to keep it that way.

But the press was casting a wide dragnet. Mike Pence's spokesman, for example, made a simple statement of fact—that the vice president was not focused on "stories about the time before he joined the ticket"—which got spun into "Pence Aide Won't Say If Boss Met with Russia," (a *Huffington Post* lead story). Pence, who was offended by the media chatter, had his spokesman clarify that there were no such meetings.

The administration took stinging criticism from both sides of the spectrum. The *Weekly Standard* declared that "the Trump team has lost all credibility on the question of Russia." *National Review* slammed "Don Jr.'s Disgraceful Meeting," saying that after "a journalistic season of hype, innuendo and flat-out error...the *New York Times* finally hit paydirt."

The *New York Times* editorial page accused the president of fostering "a culture of dishonesty." *Time* magazine put Don Jr.'s face on the cover with the headline "RED HANDED." Even the usually supportive *New York Post* declared: "Donald Trump Jr. is an idiot."

Jake Tapper said Don Jr.'s meeting with Veselnitskaya was "staggering" because it was "evidence of willingness to commit collusion," and "can't be dismissed as people out to get Donald J. Trump Jr. or fake news."

Fox News anchor Shepard Smith said that the administration's previous denials of any campaign contacts with the Russians were "mind-boggling": "If there's nothing there, and that's what they tell us...then why all these lies? Why is it lie after lie after lie?" He said the people out there "who believe we're making it up" would one day realize they were not. (The *Washington Post* hailed Shep for a "Cronkite moment," because, well, he went after Trump.)

"The White House has been thrust into chaos," the *Washington Post* announced, with Jared, Ivanka, and Melania pushing for a staff shake-up that would oust Reince Priebus.

The president, however, put the blame on the media, rather than his chief of staff or his son, tweeting that with "highly slanted & even fraudulent reporting, #Fake News is DISTORTING DEMOCRACY in our country." This rang a bit hollow, for it was hardly fraudulent to report information confirmed by his son.

Sean Spicer pushed the White House line with reporters, saying that "there was nothing, as far as we know, that would lead anyone to believe that there was anything except for a discussion about adoption." But that assertion was directly contradicted by the emails to Don Jr., offering Russian dirt on Hillary. What Spicer meant was that even if Don Jr. had been enticed into the meeting by a desire for opposition research, the meeting itself, as it turned out, was a lobbying effort by Natalia Veselnitskaya to encourage the Trump team to support lifting the Magnitsky Act sanctions on Russia in return for an end to Moscow's ban on American adoptions of Russian children. Spicer believed that was the bottom line, and the press was just nitpicking. But CNN's Anderson Cooper called Spicer's answer "flat-out false."

There was no getting around the reality of what Donald Trump Jr. had acknowledged. This wasn't a case of runaway media bias. Had Trump's people disclosed all these Russian contacts months earlier and taken their lumps, they would not have fueled the media narrative of a conspiratorial cover-up.

And the disclosures continued, despite Don Jr.'s insistence to Hannity that he had revealed "everything" about the episode. NBC reported that there was another person in the meeting, a former Soviet military counterintelligence officer named Rinat Akhmetshin, who had been accused in a civil lawsuit of hacking into a company's computer system. Akhmetshin was a naturalized American citizen and now worked as a lobbyist. He gave a strikingly different account of the meeting, saying that Veselnitskaya had actually handed over documents purporting to show improper contributions to the DNC. The picture remained murky.

• • •

On an *Air Force One* flight to Paris for a Bastille Day visit, Trump wandered back to the press cabin and spent ninety minutes chatting with reporters. The session was off the record, so Trump held forth on how he had pressed Putin on Russian hacking but had moved onto other subjects to avoid "a fistfight." He called Don Jr. a "good boy," said "nothing happened" in the meeting and that "honestly, in a world of politics, most people are going to take that meeting."

Trump, as always, actually enjoyed chatting with journalists, assumed he could win them over, and wanted their approval. The president was disappointed that his remarks weren't reported, and asked Sarah Huckabee Sanders to tell the press corps that key parts had been put on the record. Trump even wanted to hold more press conferences, but Steve Bannon talked him out of it, saying the sessions would be dominated by questions about Russia. Trump came round to Bannon's point of view: "I'm beginning to believe more and more what you said. I understand what you meant," he said, about the media being "the opposition party."

• • •

Newt Gingrich was so concerned about the stalled Trump agenda that he decided to send the president a confidential memo.

It was titled "Breaking Out of the Gridlock," and noted that Ronald Reagan had survived the Iran-contra scandal and Bill Clinton had survived the impeachment drive led by the former speaker himself.

The key section was headlined "Communications Strategy in the Middle of Distraction."

"We are being sucked into stupid fights about stupid attacks and being distracted from arousing and organizing the American people on big topics that will change history," Gingrich wrote. He detailed a four-month campaign focused on jobs, higher wages, and economic growth, designed to get around the obstacle that "congressional Republicans can't do anything quickly." This PR campaign, said Newt, would "shrink the media attacks into irrelevancy."

Anthony Scaramucci was equally frustrated, telling Jared Kushner that Trump had the worst White House communications team since the advent of television. Sean Spicer had been put in a nowhere zone, he told Kushner, and should either get his briefings back on TV or be fired.

Trump called Corey Lewandowski, Dave Bossie, and Scaramucci to thank them for defending him. "You're great on the shows," he said. But he was angry that his best spokesmen had to book themselves and weren't being pushed by his own press office. "I've got to fix the comms department," Trump said.

Steve Bannon wanted to create a war room to coordinate legal and political strategy, and tracked down Lanny Davis, the Clinton White House lawyer who handled scandal questions, defended his boss on television, and insulated Clinton's press secretary Mike McCurry from the bad stuff.

Davis gave Bannon a prescient warning: "You've got to remember you need one thing—the discipline to execute the plan." If it were up to Bannon, they would start by abolishing White House press briefings altogether.

· · ·

President Trump's detractors on the left were now in a rage, casting any assessment of him as a character test.

"Is Donald Trump Simply the Worst Human Being We Can Imagine?" *Salon* asked. The answer: "Not only did Trump quickly become the worst president ever, he may just be the most hated person alive."

In a remarkable burst of candor, liberal essayist Thomas Frank admitted in the *Guardian* that "the people of the respectable East Coast press loathe the president with an amazing unanimity." They had "overwhelming contempt for Dumb Donald," and were determined to "outwit the simple-minded billionaire," simply because "so many of them are part of the same class—an exalted and privileged class."

Anti-Trump conservatives, many of them neo-conservatives or Bush loyalists, were part of that class too, members of the political elite, and some declared it their duty to break with the Republican president. Joe Scarborough announced, on Colbert's show, that he was quitting the

GOP, then wrote a *Washington Post* column titled "Trump Is Killing the Republican Party." He ripped party leaders for remaining silent when, in his view, Trump "echoed Stalin and Mao by calling the free press 'the enemy of the people.'"

Michael Gerson, the former Bush White House staffer, titled his *Washington Post* column "An Administration Without a Conscience." The *Wall Street Journal* editorial page scolded that Trump "somehow seems to believe that his outsize personality and social-media following make him larger than the presidency" and that a failure to come clean on the Russia probe meant the Washington establishment would "destroy Mr. Trump, his family and their business reputation."

Fox's Charles Krauthammer said that "it's rather pathetic to hear Trump apologists protesting" that Don Jr.'s meeting with the Russians was "no big deal....Have the Trumpites not been telling us for six months that no collusion ever happened? And now they say: Sure it happened. So what? Everyone does it. What's left of your credibility when you make such a casual about-face?"

A red line had been crossed. The Russian meeting was not just a mistake, an embarrassment, or a breach of faith. It was, in this view, the final proof that Donald Trump and his family could never be trusted.

But whether the media could be trusted, after overdramatizing so many previous incidents, remained an open question.

• • •

The collapse of the health care effort on the night of July 17 was rightly portrayed by the media as a major failure. The president himself had warned Republican lawmakers at a private dinner that they would look like "dopes" and "weak" if they failed to pass a bill. But there was little doubt that the tone of the mainstream media bordered on celebratory.

Had the press been sympathetic to the bill, or sympathetic to Trump's desire for a moderate compromise, there would have been lots of hand-wringing about gridlock choking off progress. Instead, the stories conveyed relief that millions would be able to keep their insurance, melded to a sense of vindication over Trump's failure to master Washington's ways.

The Twitter traffic was revealing. CNBC's John Harwood tweeted that the "demise of GOP health bill is about substance, not Trump's weak standing. No evidence that he's a played a big role, knows or cares what's in it." What's more, he said, Trump's "BS has collided with reality."

Glenn Thrush of the *New York Times* said that "no one's scared of Trump," and he reposted the president's February tweet that he would immediately repeal and replace Obamacare and "nobody can do that like me." He added this schoolyard taunt: "If nobody can do it like you how come you haven't done it already?"

New York Times columnist David Leonhardt, a former Washington bureau chief, wrote that Trump won the presidency "despite a constant stream of falsehoods" and his loss on health care "demonstrated that facts still matter and that truth has some inherent advantages over falsehood."

And Trump critic Rich Lowry said in *National Review* that the debacle was "a lesson in the wages of political bad faith."

The president tried a new fallback position, that Republicans should just repeal Obamacare immediately—as they had voted to do many times when Obama was president—and work out a replacement program later. But everyone knew McConnell could not get enough votes for that approach. Trump told reporters that, if necessary, "we'll just let Obamacare fail," and "I'm not going to own it"—as if the media wouldn't blame him for any disaster in the health insurance market.

If the failure to repeal Obamacare wasn't enough, the press found another reason to attack Trump—Russia, again.

The *Washington Post* reported that Trump had held a second, undisclosed meeting with Putin at the G20 conference in Europe. MSNBC treated this as a nefarious secret rather than routine private diplomacy. There were shouts of "Oh my God!" in Rachel Maddow's office as the news hit. Trump called the story "sick"—Spicer said there had just been small talk—and the encounter seemed less diabolical considering that it took place at a formal dinner in full view of eighteen other world leaders and their spouses.

The press tried switching from Russia to Iran.

The *New York Times* reported that while the president had recertified that Iran was complying with its nuclear agreement, it was "only after hours of arguing with his top national security advisers." Trump had repeatedly vowed during the campaign to tear up Barack Obama's deal. But the clear implication was that the ignorant candidate had been tutored in geopolitical realities by his advisers.

If the press wanted to push an image of Trump as an ill-informed loudmouth, he only added to his woes by proclaiming, "We've signed more bills—and I'm talking about through the legislature—than any president, ever." This led to a front-page *Times* takedown on how he trailed many modern presidents, and that about half his bills were minor and inconsequential. Trump's only caveat was that "I better say 'think'" or the fact-checkers "will give you a Pinocchio."

Lost amid the noise was the administration's latest theme week, touting products "Made in America." The *Washington Post* had already preempted the launch with a lengthy investigative piece on "Ivanka Inc.," saying many of her branded products were made overseas.

For the press, no Trumpian subject was too personal. *Politico* even asked, "Is the President Fit?" But it turned out not to be about his capacity to do the job. Instead, said *Politico,* "No occupant of the Oval Office has evinced less interest in his own health." Virtually nothing about this president, including his diet and exercise habits, was immune from media criticism.

• • •

Trump sat down with Maggie Haberman and two of her *New York Times* colleagues and was about to go off script yet again. With Hope Hicks as his only staffer in the room, he unloaded on Jeff Sessions.

"Jeff Sessions takes the job, gets into the job, recuses himself, which frankly I think is very unfair to the president," he told the reporters.

"How do you take a job and then recuse yourself? If he would have recused himself before the job, I would have said, 'Thanks, Jeff, but I'm not going to take you.'" Trump spoke off the record, but when the interview was over, he agreed, as he often did, that most of it could be published.

Now, there it was, in his own words: he wished he hadn't hired his attorney general. Trump had also said it would be a "violation" for Robert Mueller to look at his personal finances on anything that was unrelated to Russia.

Steve Bannon thought that with that comment, Trump had put a big red flashing light on his business dealings. Why would Trump do that with a *New York Times* group that included Michael Schmidt, an investigative reporter who often got leaks from law-enforcement?

Bannon never underestimated Trump, and thought the move might be intentional. Perhaps Trump was laying the groundwork to fire Mueller if the investigator overstepped his bounds. The media, of course, went ballistic, accusing Trump of not grasping that it was not the attorney general's job to shield him from an investigation. The *Post* alleged that Trump was exploring whether he could pardon his aides, his family members, even himself. Trump lashed out at the "Amazon *Washington Post*"—owned by Jeff Bezos—for "illegal leaks." Trump's top aides faced a dilemma: the only way to keep the president from making headlines with his provocative comments was to keep him off Twitter and away from the media. And that, they realized, was beyond their power.

CHAPTER 23

THE MOOCH'S MOMENT

Sean Spicer had heard the rumors, but it was not until the morning of July 21 that they became a reality.

Trump called Spicer into his office. The president had decided to tap Anthony Scaramucci as communications director, and Spicer would report to Scaramucci. Sean angrily told the president that this was a bad mistake.

Trump asked Spicer to stay on, but he refused. After six months of intense pressure, he had had enough. Trump at least could have consulted him about changing his role, rather than keeping his courtship of the Mooch a secret from him and from Reince Priebus. Working for a businessman with no PR background would be a final humiliation.

Spicer agreed to stay for a transition period before Sarah Huckabee Sanders replaced him at the podium. He felt a palpable sense of relief at the prospect of leaving the building.

Sean Spicer had become a household name. His daily briefings drew high ratings, and late night comedians mocked him, and sometimes the press did as well. As the cable channels went into breaking-news mode over the announcement, the *New York Times* editorial page adopted a juvenile, na-na-na-na-hey-hey-goodbye tone, bidding farewell to "our four-Pinocchio press secretary."

Though Bannon and Priebus had gotten Scaramucci a sinecure at the Export-Import Bank—administration lawyers had earlier blocked a White House job because of his business entanglements—they told Trump it would be a mistake to put him in charge of communications. "He's coming in to support Jared," Bannon told the president. He argued that they needed someone with communications experience. "No, I think he can do it," Trump said.

Bannon also thought Jared and the president were dreaming if they thought Spicer would stay on under these circumstances.

Earlier it had been Trump who had repeatedly resisted hiring Scaramucci. "He was never with me," Trump said, recalling how Scaramucci had criticized him early in the campaign and had supported Scott Walker, and Jeb Bush. "He's a self-promoter."

But Trump changed his mind on Scaramucci after watching him do battle with CNN.

Bannon told Scaramucci: "Dude, this is a pressure cooker. You have no skills." And while shaking his hand after the appointment, Bannon made a prediction: "Mooch, this is going to be a disaster."

The Mooch made his debut in the briefing room, repeatedly proclaiming his love for Trump and praising his "karma." He was naturally effusive in front of the cameras, using humor to deflect Jonathan Karl's question about how he had called Trump a "hack politician" back when he was working for Scott Walker's campaign. "He brings it up every 15 seconds, okay?" Scaramucci cracked. Since his past tweets had praised Hillary Clinton and embraced everything from gun control to gay marriage, the White House put him on a radio show at *Breitbart* to let him rehabilitate himself.

The larger problem was Russia. Bannon himself was staying out of 80 percent of White House meetings to avoid being sucked into that maw. He was bemused by *Politico* writing about "Steve Bannon's Disappearing

Act," saying he was in "self-imposed exile," which Bannon took as a sign that his strategy was working. He didn't understand why Kellyanne Conway was answering Russia questions in TV interviews rather than referring everything to the lawyers.

When Scaramucci told him that the communications team wasn't doing enough to protect Kushner, Steve stiffened. It was not the job of the press shop to defend the president's son-in-law. "If you bring that shit in here, we're enemies," Bannon told him. "You can't be Jared's spokesman." The Russia questions, he felt, could not be allowed to pollute the daily briefing.

Bannon was right to be concerned. Scaramucci told Jake Tapper that an unnamed person had assured him that if the Russians were responsible for the campaign hacking, they were so deceptive that no one would ever find out. The CNN anchor said that was hard to accept from an anonymous source.

Scaramucci admitted that, well, it was Trump, calling him from *Air Force One* to say, "Maybe they did it—maybe they didn't do it." It was a very awkward moment.

• • •

Jared Kushner shed his camera shyness when it mattered most.

Faced with the inevitability of leaks after his closed-door Senate testimony about Russia, Kushner put out his eleven-page testimony before sunrise. By six a.m. the major news outlets were quoting him as saying "I did not collude," a preemptive strike that set the day's media narrative. He provided key details: after being pulled into the Don Jr. meeting with the Russians, he emailed his assistant to call his cell so he'd have an excuse to bail out.

Kushner, knowing he had to feed the media beast, went to the White House driveway after his testimony and read a short version of the statement, which television played in an endless loop.

Kushner felt the press had been killing him for three months, accusing him of treason. His preference had been to avoid the media, and he was stunned when the networks canceled scheduled interviews with his surrogate spokesmen. At last, Ivanka felt, he was excited to be able to tell his side of the story. She knew that her husband never felt the need to defend himself from allegations and anonymous sources, but in politics, sometimes you had no choice.

• • •

It was Jared's father-in-law, however, who dominated the news. The president went on a Twitter rant against his own attorney general—calling Jeff Sessions "beleaguered" and "VERY weak" on Hillary Clinton's "crimes."

Trump confided to friends that he was so angry at Sessions that he couldn't even look at him. Rupert Murdoch, among others, urged Trump to stop the Twitter assault, because he was just hurting himself. Trump said he would tone it down, but he had already created a media spectacle by attacking Sessions and urging a criminal investigation of Hillary. The press speculated that Trump wanted to dump Sessions as a first step toward firing Bob Mueller. Sarah Sanders, who had invited cameras back into all the press briefings, stayed on message and called the Russia probe "a complete hoax."

The conservative media were almost unanimous in supporting Jeff Sessions. *National Review* said Trump's treatment of Sessions was "shameful." Even *Breitbart*, which was usually doggedly pro-Trump, praised Sessions and said the president's approach "only serves to highlight Trump's own hypocrisy." Ross Douthat of the *New York Times* called the anti-Session tweets "an insanely stupid exercise" that showed "this president should not be the president, and the sooner he is not, the better." Peggy Noonan, in the *Wall Street Journal*, likened Trump to Woody Allen, calling him "weak and sniveling…whiny, weepy and self-pitying."

The president's allies were right; he had only undermined himself.

• • •

President Trump was rapidly embracing socially conservative causes. Not only was he taking strong stances on abortion, immigration, and religious freedom, he was moving to fight on other fronts of the culture wars as well.

The administration had conducted a formal policy review on transgender people serving in the military. Reince Priebus called the president at 8:30 in the morning to say that he had prepared a decision memo and explained the four options awaiting the president.

"Great, let's talk about it," Trump said. "I'll be in the Oval Office in about an hour."

Half an hour later, Priebus exclaimed to White House counsel Don McGahn: "Oh my God, he just tweeted this." Trump announced on Twitter that the government "will not accept or allow transgender individuals to serve in any capacity in the U.S. Military"—the third-most severe of the four options. There was no longer a need for the meeting.

The media exploded in thunderous condemnation, interviewing transgender service members and replaying clips of Trump vowing to fight for LGBTQ rights. And some journalists ridiculed the idea of making policy through 140-character tweets.

Ivanka Trump saw that some critics in the press were blaming her for failing to intercede with her father; she had been working on other issues and hadn't even known about the move. Sarah Huckabee Sanders couldn't even say whether currently serving transgender troops would be expelled under Trump's order.

In a single issue of *Politico Magazine,* four of the featured stories were:

"Why Trump's Ban on Transgender Servicepeople is Flatly Unconstitutional"

"13 Trump Scandals You Forgot About"

"To America, It Looks Like Chaos. For Trump, It's Just Tuesday"

"Trump Is a Bad Negotiator"

• • •

Anthony Scaramucci's top priority was to shut down White House leaks—including the man he viewed as the ultimate leaker, Reince

Priebus. He acted like a swashbuckling sheriff, saying in a round of interviews that he would start firing those who were secretly spilling to reporters, even if he had to dismiss the whole communications staff.

When *Politico* reported that Scaramucci still stood to profit from the firm he was selling, SkyBridge Capital, which had paid him $10 million in the previous eighteen months, he had a chief suspect for leaking that information. He tweeted that he would be contacting the FBI "in light of the leak of my financial info which is a felony." And he tagged @Reince45.

Priebus was furious. Scaramucci had just accused him of a criminal act. This was outright defamation. And he'd had nothing to do with it. Reince thought the Mooch's conduct was pure insanity.

After *Politico* said the information came from his newly available financial disclosure form, Scaramucci deleted the tweet. But he didn't regret targeting Priebus.

Scaramucci had been wrong on that story, but he told Trump that mid-level communications staffers had pleaded with him for their jobs, saying they had leaked, but under orders from Priebus and Bannon.

Scaramucci confronted Reince and told him he had "enemies" in the building but offered to serve as the bridge between the factions. Priebus had in fact lost support in the White House—Kellyanne Conway, among others, thought he was too insecure to be chief of staff—but he didn't believe the Mooch for a second.

In an interview with Chris Cuomo on CNN, done at Trump's suggestion, Scaramucci repeated what Conway had told him in confidence on his first day: "There are people inside the administration that think it is their job to save America from this president. That is not their job." She was surprised to hear him go public with it.

Scaramucci knew the establishment wouldn't let him survive, and told Trump it would be a miracle if he lasted a year. But Trump liked his hard-driving style. "You've got some balls on you," the president told him. "You are a tough son of a bitch."

But Scaramucci's downfall was set in motion when he had dinner with the president, Sean Hannity, Kimberly Guilfoyle, and Bill Shine, the former co-president of Fox News. Scaramucci had worked with Shine as a Fox

Business contributor, and wanted him to produce daily television at the White House.

Ryan Lizza, the veteran *New Yorker* reporter and caustic Trump critic, learned of the dinner from a White House official and tweeted about it.

Scaramucci, again convinced that Priebus had leaked the information, called Lizza and asked for his source, which he of course declined to provide.

But Scaramucci made a rookie mistake. He assumed the conversation was off the record without saying so. And when he launched into an expletive-laden tirade, Lizza published it all.

The *New Yorker* piece quoted Scaramucci as saying: "Reince Priebus—if you want to leak something—he'll be asked to resign very shortly....Reince is a fucking paranoid schizophrenic." Priebus, Scaramucci said, was trying to "see if I can cock-block these people the way I cock-blocked Scaramucci for six months." And, he added, "I'm not Steve Bannon, I'm not trying to suck my own cock. I'm not trying to build my own brand off the fucking strength of the president." Bannon was bemused by the anatomical challenge.

As the Mooch saw it, Lizza knew full well that he had intended the comments to be off the record and had broken the bounds of human decency. But he had blundered by trusting him and felt Lizza had gotten him on the letter of the law.

Scaramucci told Trump that the call was mischaracterized; it wasn't an angry rant. On Lizza's tape, the reporter could be heard laughing as the Mooch did his shtick. But he said he'd made a mistake and that he wouldn't be dropping any more F-bombs to journalists. The president lectured him, though not without laughing at times. "You start out as Harvard Anthony, you wound up in the gutter with a crowbar in your hand," Trump said.

• • •

The drive to replace Obamacare had utterly collapsed.

Senate Republicans finally abandoned the effort after one of their own, John McCain—hailed in glowing media accounts as a principled maverick bravely fighting a brain tumor and frequently at odds with Trump—flew back to Washington to cast the deciding vote against the last-ditch bill. He did so delivering a blast against "the bombastic loud-mouths on the radio, television, and the Internet."

Liberal *New York Times* columnist Paul Krugman had denounced McCain as a "world-class hypocrite" for supporting an earlier version of the bill. But now most journalists cast McCain as a hero, and Trump as a humiliated dealmaker.

The new media narrative was that most lawmakers no longer feared the new president, bucking him not only on health care, but giving overwhelming support to a bill, which Trump opposed but signed anyway, imposing tougher sanctions on Moscow.

· · ·

Reince Priebus wanted out. And while reporters assumed he was fighting for his political life, he was calling friends and saying the Scaramucci craziness was giving him the perfect escape route.

Priebus could keep putting up with Mooch madness or he could resign. He was tired of the humiliations he had suffered from the start. He had been prepared to hang on a few more months, but Anthony's antics had created a clear path to the exit.

When Reince told the president he wanted out, Trump tried to dissuade him.

"Let's just play it slow, see what happens," Trump said. "Let's go to Bedminster and talk."

But Priebus said no and suggested a few names as possible replacements.

The next morning, Trump announced on Twitter that John Kelly, the strong-willed retired Marine Corps general who was running Homeland Security, would become chief of staff. Only afterward did Trump thank Priebus for his service. Typically, Trump announced the decision without telling Priebus and without having made a formal offer to Kelly.

The general went radio silent for two hours, calling his family to discuss the matter, but the Twitter preemption had left him little choice.

The press, which never showed Priebus much respect, ran instant eulogies, depicting him as a weak chief of staff whose establishment pedigree had failed to produce a health care victory or tame the Wild West Wing. He played the obedient soldier, telling Wolf Blitzer and Sean Hannity that he wouldn't get into "the mud" by responding to Scaramucci's blasts.

Most journalists were ready to salute Kelly, who had a well-deserved reputation as a leader. "New Chief of Staff Seen as a Beacon of Discipline," the *New York Times* said in writing about a "dysfunctional" White House. "John Kelly Will Bring Plain-Spoken Discipline to an Often Chaotic West Wing," the *Washington Post* agreed, describing a "floundering" administration at its "nadir."

The White House was at war with itself, so Trump brought in a real warrior, a Marine who had commanded troops in Iraq. But many pundits expressed skepticism about whether even a four-star general could rein in this commander-in-chief.

· · ·

Things suddenly took a nastier turn for Scaramucci. The *New York Post*'s Page Six reported that his wife had filed for divorce when she was eight months' pregnant, supposedly complaining about his "naked political ambition," and noted he hadn't been there for the birth of their son. The Mooch suspected, without evidence, that Priebus, the day after he was ousted, had leaked that story through intermediaries, since the filing had been public for weeks.

Scaramucci had predicted he wouldn't survive a year. He lasted eleven days.

He never saw it coming. Although Scaramucci had bragged, as a slap at Priebus, about dealing directly with the president, he sent John Kelly a message that he would happily report to him.

But the president's view had changed. As much as he enjoyed the Mooch's brash style, he hated the media fallout. "Please stop talking," Ivanka told Scaramucci. "You're not the press secretary."

At eight a.m. on Monday, Scaramucci knew he was toast when his White House phone stopped working. Kelly was sworn in, and then asked for his resignation at 9:30. The president tweeted that morning that there was "no WH chaos!" Reporters, however, gave Scaramucci's dismissal saturation coverage. Liberal media outlets were overjoyed. "TRUMP SCREWS THE MOOCH," the *Huffington Post* banner blared.

The man who had vowed to fire all the leakers was now the target of nasty White House leaks. The *Washington Post* reported that Kelly told associates he had found Scaramucci's phone call to Lizza "abhorrent and embarrassing for the president." *Politico* quoted an unnamed White House official as saying Scaramucci's "antics over the past week were crazy by any standard."

In a bizarre way, once Scaramucci had completed his suicide mission against Priebus, his usefulness came to an end. It was now John Kelly's mission to stop the leaks and bring order to the White House.

• • •

A growing number of journalists were calling Donald Trump a liar—not just commentators but anchors and beat reporters. It was repeated like a mantra, as an established fact.

It began with an evening earthquake from the *Washington Post,* which reported that the president himself had "dictated" Don Jr.'s first minimal, and misleading, statement about his meeting with Natalia Veselnitskaya. The president's lawyer, Jay Sekulow, had denied that Trump was involved, but Kellyanne Conway conceded the point with a pro-family twist, saying "the president weighed in because fathers do that."

Around the same time, Trump said he had received positive calls from Mexico's president and the head of the Boy Scouts, though both denied making the calls.

"So he lied?" ABC reporter Cecilia Vega asked at a briefing. Sarah Huckabee Sanders called that a "bold accusation," saying the president was referring to personal conversations, not phone calls.

On CNN, anchor John King said, "Is basic truth-telling too much to ask?...I'm waiting for my children to tell me, 'It's okay that I fib, Daddy, the president does it all the time.'"

"There is evidence," said CNN's Anderson Cooper, "that Donald Trump likes to make things up."

The *New York Times* offered the thirty-thousand-foot view: "Many Politicians Lie. But Trump Has Elevated the Art of Fabrication." While acknowledging the history of presidential prevarications, the piece said the scope of Trump's falsehoods raised questions about whether "the consequences for politicians' being caught saying things that just are not true have diminished over time"—much to the paper's frustration.

NBC's Chuck Todd offered a stinging indictment: "Why is it so difficult for this administration to tell the truth the first time?"

Todd often wrestled with whether he was going too far, whether they would be as tough on any president who behaved this way or were treating Trump differently. He felt they had to be careful not to play into the president's hands. Todd worried that Steve Bannon had put them in a box by dubbing the media the opposition party, that any criticism would make them sound like political partisans.

The paradox was that Chuck Todd had never had more access to a president. He could get Trump on the phone and was invited to off-the-record chats in the Oval Office. The sessions always began the same way, with Trump yelling at him over some NBC story or something he'd said, and Todd often shouting back. But after the first twenty minutes, they would settle down to a cordial conversation. It would begin with a tirade and end with a charm offensive.

During one visit, Trump complained about journalists using fake sources.

"You know we don't make things up," Todd told him. "Mr. President, you know we couldn't report this story without people talking to us."

Hope Hicks quickly chimed in: "I keep telling him the call is coming from inside the building."

Todd thought Trump's view of journalism had been distorted because, as a businessman, he had dealt with New York's gossip columnists, and Washington journalists wouldn't play ball the same way. Chuck had a running joke with Hope about his tempestuous relationship with the president: "We can't quit each other."

. . .

For many in the media, Donald Trump was risking nuclear war.

The North Korean regime was conducting advanced nuclear missile tests and making increasingly provocative threats against its neighbors and the United States. On August 8, the president told reporters on camera that further threats "will be met with fire and fury like the world has never seen."

The mainstream media, which greatly preferred quiet diplomacy, immediately depicted Trump as bringing the country to the brink of a nuclear confrontation with Kim Jong Un. He repeated the harsh words at the second of two impromptu news conferences at his New Jersey resort, and later said that the military was "locked and loaded" if North Korea acted unwisely. There were breaking-news banners with each tough comment, such as that Kim "will regret it fast" if he kept up the threats.

While Trump's language might have been calculated to make Kim back down, it was obviously unsettling. CNN went on a war footing, reporting from a bunker in Hawaii after Kim said the islands were in range of his nuclear missiles and experts calculated the missiles could hit within twenty minutes of launch. On MSNBC, Brian Williams said his job was "actually to scare people to death on this subject."

The crisis "has been exaggerated and mishandled by the Trump administration to a degree that is deeply worrying and dangerous," Fareed Zakaria announced.

Other outlets questioned Trump's sanity in ways large and small. A *Huffington Post* banner called him "M.A.D. MAN," playing on the acronym for mutually assured destruction. *Politico* ran a piece titled "The Madman and the Bomb," harkening back to Nixon and the question of an unstable president controlling the nuclear codes.

Trump-hating celebrities launched their own missiles. Chelsea Handler appeared to call for a coup against the president, tweeting: "To all the generals surrounding our idiot-in-chief...the longer U wait to remove him, the longer UR name will appear negatively in history." So much for elections.

CHAPTER 24

CHARLOTTESVILLE CATASTROPHE

The television crews were on high alert in Charlottesville, Virginia, for a Saturday morning protest by white supremacists and neo-Nazis. When it was over, one woman had been killed, three dozen people wounded, and Donald Trump's presidency stained.

That was the overwhelming media consensus, across the political spectrum, after the president chose to denounce the violent outbreak, which included one man ramming his car into a crowd, in generic language. "We condemn in the strongest possible terms this egregious display of hatred, bigotry and violence on many sides, on many sides," Trump said. But as the press was relentless in pointing out, only one side had killed anyone.

From the right, *National Review* ran an editorial titled "Condemn the White Supremacists, Mr. President." From the left, a *New York Times* editorial said: "Let's discard the fiction that President Trump wasn't placating white supremacists by responding so weakly."

Trump's critics were ablaze with anger. "What a pathetic statement," Joe Scarborough said. "We have a president who is scared of calling out racism and terrorism. Disgraceful and disgusting." CNN's Chris Cillizza said that "it's hard to overstate how unpresidential it is to not condemn white supremacy and paint Charlottesville as a 'both sides do it' issue." *Times* columnist Paul Krugman flat-out declared that "the current president of the United States isn't a real American."

CNBC's John Harwood began a piece by saying Trump's father had been arrested at a Klan rally ninety years ago—a disputed fact based on an ambiguous 1927 *New York Times* story, and denied by Trump—and ended by raising the possibility "that Trump's presidency itself will be cut short."

Even Jimmy Fallon, the only late-night host not regularly skewering Trump, called the remarks "shameful."

The president was again defying political convention and then refusing to back down. By declining to name the fringe groups, Trump allowed his detractors to charge that these were his people, that he was determined not to alienate his base. Many journalists noted that he was quicker to blast Mitch McConnell or Mika Brzezinski than people marching with swastika flags. And it was the mirror image of Trump's criticism of Barack Obama for not naming radical Islamic terrorists, a cause the media had never embraced.

It was true that the press was far more consumed by Trump's reticent language than by the violence in Virginia. All sense of proportion had been lost. But Ivanka Trump tweeted that there was "no place in society for racism, white supremacy and neo-Nazis"—and privately urged her dad to step up his criticism. Mike Pence and many other Republicans condemned the groups as well. And that allowed journalists to bring up Trump's apparent hesitancy during the campaign to criticize David Duke, who was at the rally.

Steve Bannon had been having his regular Saturday coffee meeting with Robert Costa when the *Washington Post* reporter glanced up at the office television and said, "Man, this Charlottesville thing." Bannon, who grew up in Virginia, didn't know what he was talking about. He quickly called the editor of *Breitbart* and told him to dispatch a team there.

On Monday morning, as the staff debated whether the president needed to say more, Bannon argued against it. Trump, he told Kelly, was close to having another racially charged uproar like the campaign blow-ups over his calling Judge Gonzalo Curiel biased over his Mexican heritage and his harsh criticism of Gold Star father Khizr Khan.

While other aides pushed for a more explicit denunciation of the hate groups at the University of Virginia, Bannon warned that things would spin out of control. Trump would read the scripted words without enthusiasm and the press would dismiss whatever he said as too late and not enough.

He did not prevail. That afternoon, the president finally said that "racism is evil" and included "the KKK, neo-Nazis, white supremacists and other hate groups." The media reaction was pretty much as Bannon had predicted. Trump was "LATE ON HATE," the *Huffington Post* scoffed. MSNBC complained that he hadn't used the word "terrorism." NBC's Katy Tur said Trump hadn't spoken "from the heart." CNN's Jim Acosta shouted a question about why he hadn't named the groups earlier. "You know," said Trump, "I like real news, not fake news. You're fake news."

The next day, the White House was planning a Trump Tower event on pruning regulations for infrastructure projects. Bannon, again, argued against it. The announcement was a nothing-burger, he said, and Trump would inevitably take some questions. CNN would bait him and there would be a meltdown.

Bannon recalled a prescient warning from Corey Lewandowski: You can't just let Trump be Trump, but at the same time you can't control him too tightly without having a pressure valve, or else he would erupt.

As if on cue, the president, who was not scheduled to take questions, went rogue. In another act of defiance disorder, he stunned his advisers—John Kelly was looking down, grim-faced—by staging an impromptu news conference and appearing to equate the white supremacists in Charlottesville with the counter-protestors. "You had a group on one side that was bad, and you had a group on the other side that was also very violent, and nobody wants to say that, but I'll say it right now," Trump told the press. Some of the marchers were "very fine people," and "if you were honest reporters, and in many cases you're not," the stories would say that they "were there to protest the taking down of the statue of Robert E. Lee."

That, of course, prompted the networks to show footage of torch-bearing marchers shouting anti-Semitic slogans, with no sighting of "nice" folks among them. And while some of the left-wing "Antifa" counter-protestors had hit the marchers with clubs, the press hardly viewed them as equivalent to the raging band of neo-Nazis.

What followed in the media was the fiercest and most sustained eruption of moral outrage since Trump took office. The mask dropped and journalists who had long insinuated or suggested that Trump was a racist came out and called him just that. "Mr. Trump Gives Comfort to Racists," said a *Washington Post* editorial. Jake Tapper called the comments "unpatriotic" and "un-American." The even-tempered Willie Geist said on MSNBC that Trump's message "was extraordinary and it was despicable." And Jim Acosta said on CNN, "he has united the country against the views that he espoused today, which were right there on the edge of white nationalism."

Mika Brzezinski went the furthest, saying Trump had "created a permissive climate for violence" and "the blood and carnage will be on his hands." That was the most audacious of charges, one that had some-times been hurled at Obama after violence committed by blacks against police officers.

But the condemnation was almost as loud on the right. "A moral disgrace," Fox's Charles Krauthammer said. Fox News host Kat Timpf said, "I have too much eye makeup on to start crying right now. It's disgusting." Former Bush aide Nicolle Wallace said on MSNBC that the president had "so disgraced not just the Republican Party, but the country."

Some no doubt were expressing deep feelings. I was also disap-pointed that Trump had made the divisive remarks. But many of the denunciations were marked by an exasperated, we-tried-to-warn-you tone.

So many corporate executives bailed on Trump's advisory councils that the president had to abolish them, winning the business titans instant media praise. CEOs were "testing their moral voice," the *New York Times* said, and Trump was "inspiring C-suite moral courage," in the *Washington Post*'s words. As the likes of Marco Rubio and Ted Cruz and Presidents George W. and George H. W. Bush issued tough statements, it was easier for the press to portray Trump as isolated.

Trump had made at least some reasonable comments. In a series of tweets, he wrote, "Sad to see the history and culture of our great country being ripped apart with the removal of our beautiful statues and monuments. You can't change history, but you can learn from it. Robert E Lee, Stonewall Jackson—who's next, Washington, Jefferson? So foolish!"

But to the media, he was on the wrong side of a cultural civil war.

And, once again, his own administration was at war with itself, with some aides using leaks as a vote of no confidence in the president. The *New York Times* had this killer paragraph: "The president's top advisers described themselves as stunned, despondent and numb. Several said they were unable to see how Mr. Trump's presidency would recover, and others expressed doubts about his capacity to do the job." And General Kelly, initially hailed for his military discipline, was said to be "frustrated." The *Washington Post* reported that chief economic adviser Gary Cohn, who had been standing near Trump at his impromptu news conference, was "disgusted" and "frantically unhappy."

Bannon was livid too—but for other reasons. He told colleagues that Cohn and his compatriots were wrong to leak against Trump. The leakers were pouring gasoline on the fire, giving cover to Republican lawmakers to talk about censuring the president, and that, Bannon felt, could be a preamble to impeachment.

Trump called "shame" on the media for distorting his position, but as with a number of other controversies, his wounds were largely self-inflicted, and legions of pundits raced to pour salt in those wounds.

It was another turning point. The media had declared him a domestic policy failure when the health care bill collapsed. The media had declared him an ethical failure when the Russia investigation enveloped his inner circle. The media had declared him a foreign policy failure when he threatened to annihilate North Korea. Now the media were declaring him a moral failure as he spread the blame beyond the white supremacists to the Antifa counter-protesters for the violence at Charlottesville. And his first summer in office wasn't even over.

• • •

Steve Bannon knew that part of the media backlash was aimed at him, since he had been counseling the president throughout the weekend and was viewed as the alt-right guy in the White House. Despite the hailstorm of negative coverage, Bannon thought Trump was providing a strong example of cultural leadership.

He had no use for these extremist creeps with their Nazi slogans, but he believed that Trump was outsmarting the Democrats, who seemed to be obsessed with making everything about race. Bannon believed that bringing back manufacturing jobs would do more to help the black, white, and Hispanic working class, than any number of speeches about racism. But palace intrigue, Bannon knew, was much more alluring for the press than substantive issues. Charlottesville was a proxy war, and he was target.

Pundits and pols called for him to be fired. Rupert Murdoch, who spoke to Trump about every ten days, had been urging him for months to dump Steve Bannon, viewing him as a leaker and a dark influence on Trump. Bannon had his own resentments, recalling that Murdoch had initially opposed Trump while *Breitbart* had been firmly behind him. It was true that Trump was not Murdoch's first choice, but he preferred him over Ted Cruz and there was no way he would have backed Hillary Clinton.

Breitbart opined that no one, including Steve Bannon, was bigger than Trump, but that "getting rid of Bannon would be the strongest signal to his voters that Trump has sold them out."

What no one knew was that two weeks earlier, Bannon had met with John Kelly and offered his resignation. It was clear that Kelly wanted him out. The strategist knew that his usefulness was about to expire, that the Marine general Kelly would rein in the old Navy officer Bannon. And he believed that you could only fight so many battles without bleeding out.

Had Priebus remained, Bannon felt, he probably would have stayed on, if only to support Reince after they had forged a pragmatic alliance. But Kelly was running a tight ship for everyone; even Ivanka, Bannon would say, couldn't run to daddy and cry. Bannon had been right on target when he told friends that he would probably last eight months.

He realized he had made too many enemies inside the mansion, from Jared and Ivanka, who had wanted him out for months, to Gary Cohn and H. R. McMaster, who he was fighting virtually every day. And Bannon was losing more battles, from his push to raise taxes on the rich to dropping the militaristic approach toward North Korea.

Bannon knew he still had clout with the president, but felt it waning. In the end he was just another *schmendrick* in a meeting, arguing against what he called "the apparatus." In the White House he had influence, but if he returned to *Breitbart*—if he once again ran his own media operation—he would have power. *Breitbart* was a machine. He could seize an issue and put it on the national radar without the shackles of an administration bureaucracy.

Bannon went back to Kelly and said he definitely wanted to leave. But, he said, "You can't tell the boss."

He knew that Trump would chat about it with everyone and the news would quickly leak. But Bannon also confided in one of the president's lawyers, John Dowd, and the next day Trump found out. The president called him and said he wanted to think about it. Bannon figured Trump wanted to make sure that he wouldn't go buck wild on Jared and Ivanka after leaving the premises.

Bannon tried to justify his disruptive style. "I am going after the guys who are stopping your program, because you are dead in the water," he told Trump. He also warned the president that he was not feared or respected on Capitol Hill.

The press was starting to play up Trump's feud with Mitch McConnell, and things were worse than the headlines suggested. Trump told Bannon that he wanted McConnell out as majority leader.

Bannon and Trump eventually agreed to announce his departure on Monday, August 14. But that weekend, Charlottesville erupted.

He and Trump agreed to delay the announcement. Bannon did not want to be painted as a white nativist leaving in the middle of a racially charged mess. Bannon told Maggie Haberman off the record that he was on his way out. He might have detested the press, but at the moment he felt he needed the *New York Times*. She wrote that Bannon was in "a kind of internal exile."

Trump told reporters that he liked Bannon as a friend and that "he is not a racist, I can tell you that. He actually gets a very unfair press in that regard." What Trump conspicuously would not say was that his friend would stay in the job.

Bannon had a five-hour dinner on Long Island with billionaire financier Robert Mercer, who bankrolled *Breitbart*, and was assured that his old job as executive chairman of the website was waiting for him. They had met three times over the summer, and Mercer had urged Bannon to stay in the White House. But the next night, after dining with Trump, Mercer called Bannon. "I want you out of there right away," he said.

In a bizarre twist, Bannon made an out-of-the-blue call to Robert Kuttner, the liberal co-editor of the *American Prospect* (whose first issue after the election was "Resisting Trump"). He knew that Kuttner was a hawk on trade with China and wanted to put that issue in play. He ripped Gary Cohn and said some administration officials he had targeted were "wetting themselves." He also called the white supremacist movement "a collection of clowns" and argued that "the media plays it up too much."

But Bannon's real strategy was in undercutting the president on North Korea, saying, "There's no military solution here, they got us." He knew that would cause people's heads to explode.

Despite the media chatter that Bannon might have pulled a Mooch—and thought he was off the record—he knew exactly what he was doing, drawing fire away from the president. He gave quotes to the *New York Times* and *Washington Post* as well.

Kelly was outraged by the comments to Kuttner. On August 18, after word dribbled out to *Drudge*, the White House confirmed that Steve Bannon was out.

Most of the press misconstrued Bannon's influence by viewing him as a malevolent force. He didn't push Trump anywhere that the president didn't want to go. But he was a disruptive figure precisely because he believed that was the only way to force change on an entrenched establishment.

The press practically cheered Bannon's ouster. With few exceptions "the Bannon presidency was a colossal failure," the *Wall Street Journal* editorial page said. MSNBC's Nicolle Wallace said his legacy could not be separated "from racism and from Charlottesville."

Reporters on Twitter insisted that the real problem was his former boss. "Ultimately you don't need a Bannon when you are a Bannon," Glenn Thrush wrote. And CNBC's John Harwood said: "Bannon's departure can't resolve core problems of Trump WH: his selfishness, impulsiveness, inattention, ignorance."

With Spicer, Priebus, Scaramucci, Bannon, and Bannon ally and national security aide Sebastian Gorka gone within weeks; Jared distracted with the Russia probe; and outside advisers no longer allowed to stroll into the Oval Office; the atmosphere in the White House changed. Kellyanne Conway was now a stabilizing force; Hope Hicks was elevated to communications director, and there was no drama churning around her.

Conway thought the media were being grossly unfair by using Trump's language as an opportunity to impugn his character. It would have been better if he had ripped the protesting neo-Nazis and then talked about bad people generally, but that was not the way he spoke. And what if the president *had* gone too far with his Charlottesville remarks—how did that affect the average voter?

The biggest problem, Kellyanne thought, was that nobody had the guts to stand up to those who falsely accused Trump of being a racist.

· · ·

Bannon, meanwhile, had shrewdly stage-managed his relaunch. Five hours after leaving the White House, he walked back into the *Breitbart* townhouse on Capitol Hill and chaired the evening editorial meeting. And he started making news.

"The Trump presidency that we fought for, and won, is over," Bannon told the *Weekly Standard*. This stirred up some uninformed media speculation that he would exact revenge by attacking Trump. His real plan was to keep whacking his White House antagonists and others who opposed his populist agenda, and to harness his notoriety to make *Breitbart* a dominant force in conservative media.

He was now Bannon the Barbarian, unchained from the White House, and more excited than he'd been in months. He concluded that the press had normalized him in just twenty-four hours as they pivoted to saying he wasn't all that important.

He knew that he wasn't the media's ultimate target. That, of course, was Donald Trump.

CHAPTER 25

TACKLING THE SPORTS WORLD

By the media's conventional yardstick, Donald Trump was in deep trouble. His approval ratings were mired in the mid-30s. Republican lawmakers were openly criticizing him. His congressional agenda was stalled. Corporate executives he had counted on for cooperation were running for the exits. Charities canceled events at Mar-a-Lago. Entertainers shunned him, prompting him to pull out of the Kennedy Center Honors. Rabbis canceled a Jewish New Year conference call. A Democratic state senator in Missouri even hoped on Facebook that Trump would be assassinated, with little uproar. The president blamed much of this on the media. Most elected Republicans stuck by him, as did an overwhelming majority of Republican voters, despite calamities that would sink an ordinary politician.

Trump represented one side of a cultural civil war, with the press clearly on the other, which is why the president's supporters loved his attacks on a media establishment that viewed them with such condescension. It was a view summed up in the headline, "Dear Trump Voters:

You're a Bunch of Idiots," which ran over a column by conservative Trump critic Matt Lewis in the *Daily Beast*. The more that Trump was under media assault, the more his base rallied around him.

True, *Breitbart* was quick to accuse Trump of a "flip-flop" when, in his first major speech since Bannon's departure, the president yielded to the advice of his generals and announced that he was reinforcing American troops in Afghanistan rather than withdrawing them. Trump said his instinct to pull out American troops had to change because the vantage point is different "when you're sitting behind the desk in the Oval Office." Rather than accuse him of flip-flopping, the *Washington Post,* like much of the rest of the mainstream media that approved of his decision, said it "marks a new willingness to take greater ownership of a protracted conflict that he had long dismissed as a waste of time and resources."

Yet twenty-four hours later, Trump wiped away the Afghanistan story with a long and stinging indictment of the media that exceeded even his own history of high-decibel attacks. Senior officials had begged him not to hold a rally in Phoenix, Arizona, because they knew he would use the occasion to defend his response to the Charlottesville violence. But he went anyway, and once there Trump denounced journalists as "sick people" who "don't like our country," insinuating that they were unpatriotic. Since they had painted him as polarizing, he told the cheering crowd: "If you want to discover the source of the division in our country, look no further than the fake news and the crooked media." They were the ones, he said, "giving a platform to these hate groups." It was a form of media Jiu-Jitsu, flipping the blame to those who accused him of encouraging racism.

In his half-hour rant, Trump engaged in some hyperbole and exaggeration. "I said, racism is evil. Do they report that I said that racism is evil?" Actually, yes. News outlets reported it again and again because it was part of his scripted statement naming neo-Nazis and the KKK. And Trump's recital of what he had said left out the most controversial passages, such as that there was violence "on many sides." Trump just couldn't let it go.

Some anchors and commentators took the bait Trump offered them and revealed the depth of their hostility. Don Lemon declared that Trump "is unhinged, it's embarrassing and I don't mean for us, the media, because he went after us, but for the country." Lawrence O'Donnell literally interrupted the president's speech to say that "uh, this is the president lying about the media."

Even former anchors felt compelled to join the fray. Tom Brokaw charged the president with a "cheap shot," saying he'd never met a journalist who didn't love America. Katie Couric announced that "I am truly afraid for our country."

And the amateur psychiatrists went, well, insane. One CNN commentator, Maria Cardona, said Trump might be "psychologically demented." Another, Ana Navarro, said the president might be suffering from "early-onset dementia," and if he wasn't, "then he is just such an incredible, self-centered, narcissistic, unfit jerk." *New York Times* columnist Charles Blow, called him a "cretin" and said, "I honestly hate this man, and I do mean HATE!"

In the eyes of his supporters, such journalists validated Trump's argument that they were the recklessly divisive ones.

• • •

The mainstream media viewed Hurricane Harvey as a major political test for Trump—and assumed that, as a government novice, he couldn't possibly be up to the challenge.

Even when he quickly visited the flood-ravaged areas of Texas and huddled with local officials, and federal emergency services ran smoothly, he never got credit for passing the test—and he drew media flak for insufficient empathy. That word, "empathy," was heard over and over, with the likes of Lawrence O'Donnell saying that "President Trump visited Texas but he forgot to bring any empathy with him, but he did bring a hat, a hat that is for sale." The *Washington Post* said that "yet again, Trump managed to turn attention on himself" rather than "on the millions of Texans whose lives have been dramatically altered by the floodwaters."

The media ideal of a compassionate president was Bill Clinton, biting his lip and feeling the victims' pain, or Barack Obama, hugging everyone in sight and delivering an eloquent speech. Trump had a CEO's approach, checking up on his managers, setting priorities, making sure the operation was functioning properly. So even though FEMA was performing well, the press shifted the goalposts and made feelings, not results, the mandatory standard in hurricane relief. And for good measure, the pundits ridiculed Melania because she boarded *Marine One* in six-inch stilettos (before later switching to sneakers). Not until Trump met victims and handed out lunches in a second visit four days later did the media allow that he was fulfilling the role they had prescribed.

The monster storm stirred the political waters as well—with help from the president, who used the occasion, when he knew TV ratings would be skyrocketing, to announce his controversial pardon of former Arizona sheriff Joe Arpaio. The conservative *Washington Examiner* broke ranks with Trump on the pardon, since Arpaio had defied a court order against stopping and questioning Latinos, saying the self-described "law and order" president was really about "busting heads."

Even as rescuers were struggling to reach residents trapped on rooftops, MSNBC devoted much of its prime time to Russia, consumed by stories breaking in the *Washington Post* and *New York Times*. They disclosed that Trump's personal lawyer, Michael Cohen, had written to Vladimir Putin's spokesman during the campaign to try to revive a stalled proposal to build a Trump Tower in Moscow. And the *Times* obtained a bragging email from a Russian-American businessman and Trump associate named Felix Sater, telling Cohen: "Our boy can become president of the USA and we can engineer it. I will get all of Putins [sic] team to buy in on this."

While it hardly looked good for Trump's company to be pursuing a Russia deal while the candidate was speaking positively about Putin, the stories actually underscored the lack of collusion with Russia. Cohen didn't know who to contact, so he e-mailed the general address for Putin's press office. He got no response and the proposal died—hardly evidence of the candidate being well wired with the Kremlin.

By then, news outlets had settled on a new narrative, portraying Trump as increasingly isolated and unable to control his own top deputies. When Gary Cohn, after Charlottesville, said the administration "must do better in consistently and unequivocally condemning" hate groups, the *Washington Post* reported that Trump was "furious." After Secretary of State Rex Tillerson said on *Fox News Sunday* that "the president speaks for himself" on American values, *Axios* reported that Trump was "fed up" with Tillerson. Steve Bannon, who remained in touch with Trump—and attacked his former rivals in a *60 Minutes* interview—thought Tillerson should have been instantly fired for insubordination.

· · ·

According to leaked reports in the press, President Trump was chafing at General Kelly's restrictions. He missed having his friends saunter into the Oval Office, and he was binge-watching Fox News. He was also reported to have made his displeasure known to his new chief of staff. The *New York Times* said Kelly had told colleagues that no one had ever dressed him down the way Trump had, and that "he would not abide such treatment" again.

Reince Priebus was bemused by the flood of stories about Kelly's strict "process." Priebus had the same procedures, the same rules to restrict access to the Oval Office, but Trump did whatever he wanted. "If you were still in the White House the last three months," Bannon told him, "the press would be saying you're the worst chief of staff ever."

Another former staffer, Corey Lewandowski, had formed a new advocacy firm. He had quit his previous company after unauthorized appeals were sent out that used his name to seemingly offer overseas clients access to Trump. The *New York Times Magazine* slapped Corey on its cover, accusing him of becoming a hypocritical Washington swamp creature. But Lewandowski, a surrogate for a pro-Trump PAC, did less than legions of Beltway lobbyists. He insisted he had never asked Trump for anything. "People want to see me fail," he said.

• • •

For all their periods of hostility, the media were never more passionately united against Trump than over his decision to end the Dreamers program for the children of illegal immigrants—even with a six-month delay to give Congress time to authorize the program in the face of court challenges. One news outlet after another stoked public sympathy by playing up the plight of individual Dreamers, especially those in their twenties or thirties with stellar jobs and others who aided in the Houston flood rescues. Journalists were tapping into broad public support for the nearly eight hundred thousand people brought to America illegally before they were eighteen.

White House leakers painted the president, who had let Jeff Sessions make the announcement, as looking for "a way out," as one unnamed official told the *New York Times*. He was determined to enforce American immigration law, but did not want to seem callous or cruel.

What was missed or minimized by much of the media was that Barack Obama, during the 2012 campaign, unilaterally shielded the Dreamers from deportation through an executive order, which he always said was a temporary measure. Trump wanted Congress to come up with an actual law, since Congress had never passed the DREAM Act and Obama's policy of "Deferred Action for Childhood Arrivals" had long been derided by Republicans as an abuse of executive power.

Nevertheless, Trump was denounced as cold and uncaring across the media and entertainment landscape. Facebook founder Mark Zuckerberg called the move "particularly cruel." "You are garbage," said Sarah Silverman. And Rob Reiner opined that "Donald J. Trump is a heartless prick."

The president responded to the harsh reaction by softening his tone. He told reporters he had "a love for these people" and that "hopefully" Congress will help them. Rupert Murdoch, who was friendly with Jared and Ivanka—both of whom wanted to preserve the program—suggested that Trump tweet something sympathetic about the Dreamers. The president reassured them on Twitter that "you have nothing to worry about."

A day later, the Beltway press was stunned when Trump cut a budget deal with the Democrats, siding with Chuck Schumer and Nancy Pelosi over Mitch McConnell and Paul Ryan. The agreement—tying a three-month extension of the debt ceiling to immediate hurricane aid—was mainly tactical. But Trump, keeping an eye on TV, raved about the "incredible" coverage of the compromise, telling Schumer that Fox News was praising the senator and the other cable networks were praising *him*. For the president, the details were less important than the pundits finally giving him a win.

Rather than crediting the president with a moment of bipartisanship—and the media usually worship bipartisanship—many news outlets reveled in the way Trump blindsided Republican congressional leaders. "Trump's Deal Is a Nightmare Come True for the GOP," a *New York Times* headline said. The *Washington Post* said the president had "burned" his ostensible allies, that "some" would call the move "untrustworthy," and that "he is ultimately loyal to no one but himself."

Fox's coverage was generally positive. "Isn't it refreshing to see them work together?" Ainsley Earhardt said on *Fox & Friends*. But others on the right were appalled.

"Trump tosses Republicans and conservatives under the bus," said Bill Kristol, who had openly denounced Trump during the campaign and had briefly tried to run a third-party candidate against him.

Bannon's *Breitbart* dissed the Democratic deal with a "Meet the Swamp" headline, saying it "Jacks Up Debt, Punts Agenda, Snubs GOP."

That was merely a dress rehearsal for Trump's next move, which was striking a tentative deal with "Chuck and Nancy" to legalize the Dreamers program in exchange for tougher border control, though funding for a border wall was notably absent. *Breitbart* went ballistic. "AMNESTY DON," blared a red-letter headline.

Some of Trump's strongest media supporters on the right felt betrayed. Laura Ingraham mocked his campaign chant: "'BUILD THE WALL! BUILD THE WALL!'…or…maybe…not really."

"At this point," Ann Coulter tweeted, "who DOESN'T want Trump impeached?"

Radio titan Rush Limbaugh expressed shock: "Is he this tone deaf? Is he this ignorant? Does he not know what got him elected?"

The mainstream media loved the compromise—there was barely a mention that Trump had reversed a campaign promise—because it boosted the Democrats and could potentially save the Dreamers. The media also touted it as evidence that Trump was a lousy negotiator, forced to cave to the Democrats because of his strained relations with his top leaders, Ryan and McConnell.

What the media could have said was that Trump, who never campaigned as an orthodox Republican, was leveraging both parties to make some progress after the GOP had failed to deliver much of anything. But many pundits were too busy relishing the spectacle of him antagonizing his own party.

• • •

Politics in the Trump age had become a blood sport. And perhaps it was inevitable that even sports commentators felt the need to attack the president.

Jemele Hill, the co-host of ESPN's *SportsCenter*, unleashed a Twitter rant against Trump, calling him a "white supremacist," a "bigot," "unfit," and "the most ignorant, offensive president of my lifetime." The network, which had protested his candidacy by canceling a celebrity tournament at Trump's California golf club, punted with a wimpy statement that her actions were merely "inappropriate." And the African American analyst refused to apologize, saying only that she regretted casting ESPN in an unfair light.

Despite the racially incendiary nature of the attacks, the *New York Times* and *Washington Post* initially ignored the story, as did CNN and

MSNBC and much of the media. It was not until a *Post* reporter raised it at a White House briefing, and Sarah Huckabee Sanders said the "outrageous" comments were a "fireable offense," that the press jumped on Hill's attack—and to her defense.

The *Huffington Post* practically endorsed the slander: "WHITE HOUSE GOES AFTER ESPN HOST!" after she "GOT REAL ABOUT TRUMP."

As the controversy mushroomed, Trump tweeted that ESPN, with its political bent and bad programming, should "apologize for untruth!" Yet many journalists managed to put the onus on the White House.

"Does that mean that he's willing to apologize" for his "birtherism claims?" one reporter asked Sanders.

Another asked: "Did it give you any pause to make those comments about a private company from the podium here at the White House?" Sanders said she was talking about an individual, and about ESPN's hypocrisy in firing or suspending conservatives for controversial comments.

It had come to this: a major sports anchor had called Trump a white supremacist, her network refused to throw a penalty flag, and reporters reserved their ire for the Trump team.

But the president wasn't done with the sports world. Hours after John McCain announced he would vote against a revised health care bill that would turn Obamacare over to the states, Trump gave the National Football League a swift kick in the pants.

At an Alabama rally on Friday, September 22, he rebuked football players who refused to stand for the national anthem. The most prominent had been Colin Kaepernick, an out-of-work quarterback who said he was protesting racial injustice.

Trump told the cheering crowd: "Wouldn't you love to see one of these NFL owners, when somebody disrespects our flag, to say, 'Get that son of a bitch off the field right now. He is fired. Fired!'" He ratcheted up the attack in a series of tweets, suggesting that fans boycott teams that refused to punish the protestors.

As he ignited one media firestorm over the NFL, Trump tried to slam-dunk the NBA champion Golden State Warriors as well. When superstar Stephen Curry expressed doubts about his team's ritual appearance at the White House, Trump abruptly disinvited him—and the Warriors voted to scrap the visit.

Trump had thrown himself into a new culture war featuring politics, patriotism, sports, and race. Much of the press felt he was dismissing the right to call attention to injustice and police brutality. The *Huffington Post* went all in: "Trump's Racial Crusade Against the Black Athlete." CNN's Chris Cillizza said he was "playing with racial animus." Trump insisted to reporters that it "had nothing to do with race."

But the president was picking on players with their own massive media platforms. LeBron James, Curry's NBA rival, actually called Trump "u bum" in a tweet that drew more than a million likes—and posted an accompanying video.

There was pushback from anti-Trump conservatives too, and mockery in late night comedy. *National Review* called Trump's assault "unseemly"; Seth Meyers announced that "our president is an asshole." NFL Commissioner Roger Goodell made headlines for scolding Trump. Even the president's pal Tom Brady, the New England Patriots quarterback, called his remarks "just divisive." On Sunday dozens of players, in solidarity, refused to stand for the anthem, with three teams staying in the locker room. Stevie Wonder and other celebrities made a similar gesture. "Taking a knee" became instant shorthand for protesting Trump.

Cable news, with its bipolar model, savored the great debate: whose side are you on, the patriots or the protestors? It was the lead story on show after show, day after day. On *Anderson Cooper 360°*, the host began with "a very full program tonight, including new reporting from Puerto Rico where the human need is so great in scope and so urgent.... We begin, though, tonight 'Keeping Them Honest,' with the president's latest take on the wave of protests sweeping the NFL." He soon aired a prime-time special on the football flap.

When a Reuters reporter asked Trump whether he was "preoccupied" with the NFL at the expense of Puerto Rico, the president said he wasn't, he was just "ashamed" of the league. The media accused Trump of being fixated on the issue, but they were the ones who couldn't let it go; it was too perfectly formulated for their theme that Trump had divided America—even over football.

A *New York Times* news analysis said Trump had abandoned any attempt at unity, instead turning himself into "America's apostle of anger, its deacon of divisiveness." But the president had picked the fight he wanted, one that wrapped him in the flag and energized his supporters on the right. Trump may have had trouble scoring points with his legislative agenda, but he had won the season's biggest sports showdown.

CHAPTER 26

THE FIGHT OVER "FAKE NEWS"

When Sean Spicer made a surprise appearance at the Emmys, wheeling out the podium and joking with Stephen Colbert about the record-breaking size of the crowd, a *Huffington Post* banner screamed "GET. LOST." *Slate* called the appearance a "Sickening, Cynical Laugh Grab." CNN's Chris Cillizza said it was "a validation that purposely misleading on the taxpayer's dime is a-OK." Rob Reiner said that since Trump was a "sick liar, if we reward Sean Spicer for enabling his sickness, we are saying we accept a mentally ill POTUS."

Spicer was stunned. He had insisted that any skit he appeared in not be mean, and had thought the bit was a cute moment that poked fun at himself. He was not on some rehabilitation tour. The pundits were wrong, he thought, in claiming the brief bit had some deeper, esoteric meaning. The haters, he concluded, were always going to hate.

Spicer's detractors were so deeply afflicted by Trump Trauma that they lost any semblance of a sense of humor. They wanted Spicer to wear a scarlet letter forever and never show his face in public.

But even friends thought it was too soon for Spicer to be joking about what was widely deemed a lie. Reince Priebus called his old protégé, saying: "What were you thinking?"

Sean spoke briefly to Glenn Thrush, who reported in the *New York Times* that the ex-spokesman regretted his decision to criticize "accurate news reports" about the size of Trump's inaugural crowd. "Of course I do, absolutely," Spicer was quoted as saying, though Spicer later said that he had unfairly truncated the quote. He'd said he could have done a better job and been more prepared, not that he regretted what he had done. The reporter brushed aside that criticism, but he did make an unexpected move.

Thrush had previously drawn flak for his harsh tweets about Trump. He had been cautioned by his editors about his snarkiness and had even deleted a couple of postings. Now he finally decided to pull the plug on his Twitter account. The *Times* executive editor, Dean Baquet, soon tightened the paper's social media policy with Trump very much in mind, saying it might appear "we're trying to take him out... if I have 100 people working for the *New York Times* sending inappropriate tweets."

Still, it appeared that the press would not forgive anyone who had worked for Trump. *Politico*'s media man Jack Shafer decreed Spicer a "pariah."

"Sean Spicer doesn't have to lie anymore," Anderson Cooper announced. "Now he just seems to be doing it recreationally." An NBC story said all the networks were passing on hiring him. A *Good Morning America* interview turned into an inquisition, with reporter Paula Faris asking: "Have you ever lied to the American people?" "Did the president ever ask you to lie or manipulate the truth?" "Do you think you have a credibility issue?"

Spicer had seen his job as expressing Trump's opinions. Journalists, he felt, wanted him to call balls and strikes, and call out his own boss. No press secretary would ever do that.

Even now the press hounded him. When veteran reporter Mike Allen of *Axios* texted him about a story that Robert Mueller might be interested in notebooks he had compiled while in the White House, Spicer wrote back: "Do not email or text me again. Should you do again I will report to the appropriate authorities."

The truth was, he hadn't even bothered to read the text. Spicer had helped Allen over the years, but he was tired of Mike peppering him with negative questions and stories, some of which were sent to his wife, Rebecca. Still, Spicer had lost his cool, and he apologized for his outburst. He canceled several television interviews and decided to lay low.

• • •

No one noticed at first, but Donald Trump was feeling a bit more generous toward the press.

Hope Hicks had encouraged him to spend more time talking to reporters, and he did just that, regularly stopping for questions during his public appearances, especially when he was about to board *Marine One* and had to raise his voice over the engines.

Trump enjoyed mixing it up with journalists, and lately had felt he was getting better coverage, receiving grudgingly high marks for his handling of two hurricanes, for making deals with Democrats, and for his meetings with leaders at the United Nations. Even if the press didn't like his tax-cut plan, Hicks thought, most of the headlines were about substantive policy.

There were, as always, bumps in the road. The *Washington Post* disclosed that Jared, Ivanka, and other officials were occasionally using private email for official business. Kushner was bemused by the charges of hypocrisy—there was no classified material involved, as there had been in Hillary Clinton's celebrated email scandal, and he had forwarded the notes to his White House account—but it was an embarrassment nevertheless. And the press suddenly seemed fixated on how Jared's public role, at least, seemed greatly reduced. When the *Times* reported that John Kelly had not only slashed his portfolio but wanted him and Ivanka out of the White House, the general had to provide an on-the-record denial of any such thoughts—while Kushner countered to the *Washington Post* that he was now trying to dig deeper on just a few issues.

The press declared a major Trump setback when his candidate, Senator Luther Strange lost Alabama's Republican Senate primary and Steve Bannon's man, Roy Moore, won, with Bannon and *Breitbart* touting Moore's victory as the harbinger of their effort to derail the GOP establishment. A *Washington Post* review of two books questioning Trump's mental health featured a disturbing sketch of the president in a straitjacket. That was soon surpassed by *Newsweek* comparing Trump to murderous cult leader Charles Manson.

And Trump was enraged at his secretary of Health and Human Services, Tom Price, when *Politico* disclosed that Price had blown more than $400,000 on private jet travel to the Aspen Ideas Festival and other less-than-urgent destinations. The dead-on reporting prompted the president to fire him.

But then came Puerto Rico, which had been hit by another monster hurricane. Trump was spending a long weekend at his Bedminster, New Jersey, golf club, seemingly more focused on kneeling football players.

As the magnitude of the devastation became clear, news outlets asked why Trump hadn't been quicker to mobilize the military to help in relief efforts. Initially, the media had shared the president's fixation on the NFL over Puerto Rico, but now that the story was about Trump and not just the lack of food and electricity, it was suddenly fodder for cable news arguments.

When the liberal mayor of San Juan, Carmen Yulín Cruz, ripped the administration's response on CNN, saying that "people are dying," the media were filled with Katrina comparisons. And when Trump slammed the mayor on Twitter for "nasty" comments and "poor leadership," the pundits chided him for picking on her during a crisis. On *Meet the Press*, African American host Joy Reid said Trump "has a particular reflex to attack women, to attack women of color." Most of the media nodded in agreement. A CNN banner blared, "Trump Attacks San Juan Mayor as She Begs for Help." He was counterpunching against a harsh critic, but that didn't matter.

Rachel Maddow, whose anti-Trump program had briefly surged to number one in cable news, told Jimmy Fallon: "Three and a half million

Americans in Puerto Rico, and the president was really preoccupied with trying to make a racial issue out of the NFL while he wasn't doing anything about that." It was untrue that Trump "wasn't doing anything"— in fact, Puerto Rico's governor praised Trump for his handling of the relief efforts—but the football controversy, which the media had fervently embraced, now made a useful weapon against him.

Trump went after "the Fake News Networks" for depressing morale in Puerto Rico, singling out CNN and NBC—"Shame!—over their negative coverage. The truce with the media, such as it was, was over.

• • •

Puerto Rico was a natural disaster, but on the night of October 1, a disaster of human depravity erupted, as a man armed with automatic weapons committed the worst mass shooting in American history, leaving fifty-nine people dead and more than five hundred wounded.

The president delivered a somber, even eloquent speech. He declared the Las Vegas massacre "an act of pure evil," called for unity and prayers, quoted the Bible, and said, "though we feel such great anger at the senseless murder of our fellow citizens, it is our love that defines us today— and always will, forever."

But much of the media refused to give him credit for matching the moment, believing, along with Hillary Clinton and other Democrats, that anything short of an immediate demand for greater gun control was an abomination. *Politico* allowed that Trump's response "didn't make a tragic situation worse," but lamented that his words "were in line with what any National Rifle Association-backed president would do." When CNN's John King called Trump's speech "pitch-perfect," he drew flak from lefty pundits. While common-sense gun restrictions had broad public support, the press was clearly holding Trump to an ideological standard. And the late-night hosts—Colbert, Kimmel, Meyers, and others—denounced the president's party for not embracing stricter gun control.

Trump did have some stumbles the next day on his visit to Puerto Rico. He lauded the federal effort, and said the island should be "very proud" because its official death toll of sixteen was way below that of Katrina. He added that "you've thrown our budget a little out of whack" but that was fine. An awkwardly arranged photo op of him helping to distribute relief supplies—with Trump throwing rolls of paper towels into a crowd—went viral.

The media went into hypercritical mode. Joe Scarborough said Trump was showing "a basic lack of humanity." David Gregory said on CNN that it was "callous and absurd" to compare the death toll to Katrina and "trying to stir up hatred for the media." A *Salon* headline called Trump's Puerto Rican response "monstrous," and said that any journalist who disagreed with that assessment was "naive, dishonest," or "willfully delusional." The president was trying to lift spirits on the crippled island, and once again, the media verdict was that he couldn't do anything right.

· · ·

Much of the mainstream media believed that Trump was dangerously uninformed on foreign policy and that his generals and advisers were keeping him on a tight leash.

NBC reported that Secretary of State Rex Tillerson had considered resigning and had privately called the president a "moron." Tillerson called a televised news conference to deny the story, but rather than dispute the moron comment, he said it was too petty to discuss. (His spokeswoman later denied it on his behalf.)

Trump was furious at NBC, and branded the report bogus, even as the *New York Times* also quoted "associates" of Tillerson as describing "his deep frustration with the president and talk of resignation."

Trump seemed to give the stories of a rift between the two men some confirmation when he tweeted that Tillerson was "wasting his time trying to negotiate" a diplomatic back channel with North Korea, or, as Trump put it "with Little Rocket Man. Save your energy, Rex, we'll do what has to be done!"

Trump also took this shot: "Why Isn't the Senate Intel Committee looking into the Fake News Networks in OUR country to see why so much of our news is just made up—FAKE!" He was clearly venting, but the mere suggestion that the government should investigate the press showed how low things had sunk.

That was just the beginning. NBC reported that the moron comment followed a meeting in which the president stunned his national security team by asking for a tenfold increase in the nuclear arsenal, supposedly unaware of decades of arms-control treaties. Trump insisted the unnamed sources behind this report were made up. Anchor Lester Holt said they included three people in the room. Trump then ratcheted things up.

"With all of the Fake News coming out of NBC and the Networks," he tweeted, "at what point is it appropriate to challenge their Licenses? Bad for country!"

What Trump missed is that the FCC doesn't license national networks, only local stations. But the notion of using government muscle to pull the plug on offending media companies was a step too far, a slap at the First Amendment.

"It's frankly disgusting the way the press is able to write whatever they want to write, and people should look into it," Trump told reporters.

"You might want to look into it too, Mr. President," Jake Tapper said on CNN, brandishing a copy of the Constitution.

When Trump tweeted insults against retiring Republican Senator Bob Corker—who accused him of moving the country closer to "World War III"—the *Washington Post* said an angry Trump was "lashing out, rupturing alliances," and had "torched bridges all around him." Next the paper reported that Trump was "livid" and "threw a fit" when his team pressed him to accept Barack Obama's nuclear disarmament deal with Iran. H. R. McMaster helped craft a compromise where Trump could denounce the deal—and refuse to "certify" it—while leaving the agreement intact unless Congress intervened.

This could have been reported as boosting pressure on the Iranian regime without unraveling an international pact. But the media were wedded to the idea of the generals restraining Trump.

When the president unilaterally halted billions in Obamacare subsidies, the AP—in a straight-news story—described his approach to governing as "wreaking havoc." Chris Matthews said Trump was reversing Obama's legacy out of "spite." Don Lemon questioned whether he had "an Obama obsession." The notion that Trump believed in changing these policies was rejected in favor of the notion that he was motivated solely by personal animosity.

There were so many stories along the lines that Trump is impossible, and restrained only by his staff, who were always on the verge of quitting, that John Kelly felt compelled to appear in the briefing room to announce he was "not quitting," and calmly suggest that reporters "develop some better sources." It was, Trump's new chief of staff declared, "astounding to me how much is misreported."

CHAPTER 27

THE ERA OF HARASSMENT

With one poorly framed answer in the Rose Garden on October 16, President Trump unleashed a war about war, which consumed an entire week of his presidency, and underscored how he was treated far differently than his predecessors.

During a Rose Garden news conference called to demonstrate that Trump and Mitch McConnell were "closer than ever before," a reporter asked why the president hadn't addressed the deaths of four American soldiers in Niger twelve days earlier. Trump chose to respond by pointing the finger at others.

He said that "if you look at President Obama and other presidents, most of them didn't make calls, a lot of them didn't make calls" to the families of soldiers who were killed. "I like to call when it's appropriate." When pressed again, he retreated to "that's what I was told."

Trump was wrong; Obama visited with some families as well as calling and writing them. On CNN, which no longer seemed to care about cursing if Trump was the target, Ryan Lizza said the president just "makes shit up." Former Obama counselor Dan Pfeiffer called him a "deeply disturbed ignoramus" and "pathological liar," while Obama's former deputy chief of staff Alyssa Mastromonaco said he was "a deranged animal."

Such over-the-top attacks fueled the media denunciations, but that was just the beginning. The next day Trump called the widow of one of the men ambushed in Niger, Sergeant La David Johnson, launching a cycle of charges and countercharges that overshadowed the deaths of four American heroes. And the mainstream media, which had provided scant coverage of the deaths in Niger, were obsessed with the political sniping. Just as with the hurricane in Puerto Rico, a tragedy wasn't big news until it became a Trump story.

Frederica Wilson, a Democratic congresswoman who heard the call, launched a television blitz to attack Trump for insensitivity, saying the president told Johnson's widow that her husband "must have known what he was signing up for." The soldier's mother told the *Washington Post* the president had disrespected her son, and his widow, Myeshia Johnson, told *Good Morning America* that his tone had made her cry.

Trump, in turn, denounced the "wacky" congresswoman for having "totally fabricated" the account (though it turned out he had uttered those words). And Sarah Huckabee Sanders told reporters it was "a disgrace of the media" to try to distort "an act of kindness."

Journalists were all too willing to believe that Trump, even if there were awkward moments, was incapable of handling a condolence call. They started asking other Gold Star families about Trump—CNN aired a tear-filled interview with two parents who said the president hadn't called them—imposing a standard to which no previous president was subjected.

There was a powerful moment when John Kelly, who had always been reluctant to talk about losing a son in Afghanistan, delivered an emotional defense of the president's condolence call. But Kelly's emotional appearance was marred by a misstep. He drew fierce media criticism after inaccurately describing a speech the African American lawmaker had once given—including from Congresswoman Wilson, who charged that "the White House itself is full of white supremacists."

The media view of Kelly quickly shifted. For all the talk about him "as a moderating force," the *New York Times* said, he had turned out to mirror Trump's "hard-line views" on "patriotism, national security and immigration."

The press also turned with a vengeance on Sarah Sanders for a rare misfire. When a reporter pressed her on General Kelly having misstated some facts about Wilson, Sanders replied, "If you want to get into a debate with a four-star Marine general, I think that that's something highly inappropriate."

Wolf Blitzer said Sanders should apologize for claiming that generals were above criticism. Jake Tapper called her remarks "one of the most shocking things I've ever heard from that podium." Another CNN anchor, Erin Burnett, went so far as to say "a military dictatorship—that appears to be what the United States is."

What Sanders was trying to say was that Kelly had an impregnable moral standing when it came to fallen soldiers, not that journalists should never question military brass. But the toxic relationship between Trump and the press had turned even condolences for a soldier's ultimate sacrifice into political sniping.

· · ·

Steve Bannon was suddenly riding a wave of positive press.

And the man who openly disdained the "opposition party" knew why. He was the same curmudgeon, but now he was trying to destroy something the media wanted destroyed: the Republican establishment. The press was promoting him because he was trying to blow up Mitch McConnell. He had been transformed from creep to crusader. By recruiting insurgent candidates to challenge wavering GOP lawmakers, Bannon hoped to create a Trump-centric populist party, which many pundits thought would clear a Democratic path to victory.

The president called to congratulate Bannon after a fiery appearance on Fox, but he was growing a bit worried about him. Trump asked Sean Hannity, Rand Paul, and others the same question: "Is Steve still with me? He is, isn't he?"

Bannon believed he was, but he had given Trump fair warning. On the day he left the White House, he told the president: "I'm going after Mitch McConnell." Bannon was explicit, saying the goal was "to bring him down. You can't go after him halfway."

Trump said that was fine, that Bannon should go ahead.

But now Bannon was denouncing the majority leader and some of his allies when Trump needed their votes to pass tax reform.

After Bannon criticized Luther Strange, the appointed Republican senator in Alabama, Trump told him that Strange was his "friend."

"You don't have any friends," Bannon shot back, not unless they went to the microphones to take on his critics like Senator Bob Corker.

Corker had pounded the president on the morning shows, saying Trump was "debasing our country," and Arizona Senator Jeff Flake joined him in announcing his retirement, saying he could not remain silent in the face of Trump's "reckless, outrageous and undignified behavior" that was "dangerous to our democracy." The media reveled in the narrative that leading Republicans were questioning Trump's character, which justified their own dark portrait without them having to make the case.

"Should you be more civil as the leader of this country?" a reporter asked Trump.

"Well," the president replied, "I think the press makes me more uncivil than I am."

Even as the press hailed Flake as a man of conscience, *Breitbart* confirmed that Bannon felt he had gotten another "scalp" in his effort to oust establishment Republicans. The party seemed to be consumed by civil war. A lead story in the *Washington Post* was headlined: "Republicans Target Bannon."

While Bannon had the luxury of being a populist purist, Trump had to practice Beltway politics. Bannon was agitated when Trump caved to Chuck Schumer and Nancy Pelosi on short-term funding for the border wall, and agreed to delay the ending of the Dreamers program. He felt Jared and Ivanka had gotten to him on protecting the Dreamers.

He loved Trump but often found him too much of a pragmatist. When Bannon's candidate, former judge Roy Moore, beat Trump's man, Luther Strange, in an Alabama primary, Steve realized that the populist conservative movement was not a cult of personality focused on Trump, it was about policy. Trump, he felt, had to deliver. The president's supporters wanted results before the 2018 elections. And the immigration issue was at the core of Trump's political appeal.

"Don't think you're getting away without building a wall," Bannon told Trump. "You said it too many times at too many rallies. Nancy Pelosi will get the House. They're going to swear themselves in and fucking impeach you."

• • •

Sarah Huckabee Sanders often questioned the credibility of the *Washington Post*. But when the *Post* delivered an evening earthquake that Sanders liked, she enthusiastically tweeted a link to the story.

The paper confirmed that Hillary Clinton's campaign and the DNC helped fund the research that led to the salacious and unsubstantiated dossier on Donald Trump that had been published by *BuzzFeed* and that was a key element in the Democrats' Russian "collusion" case against Trump.

A lawyer for the Clinton camp and the Democratic National Committee had hired opposition research firm Fusion GPS, which in turn hired a former British spy to gather Russian dirt on Trump. While it was not clear that Hillary and her top aides knew about the dossier, the story said, the Democratic payments were an embarrassment that linked the party to the radioactive dossier. The president told reporters near *Marine One* that this was a "disgrace," that "it's very sad what they've done with this fake dossier."

One allegation in the dossier suffered a blow when word leaked to NBC about House testimony by Trump's longtime security director Keith Schiller. He said that during their 2013 trip to Moscow for Trump's Miss

Universe pageant, a stranger with a foreign accent had offered to send five women to Trump's room, but Schiller had immediately dismissed the idea and considered it a joke. As the *Washington Post* piece got widespread coverage, Trump had finally caught a break. Thanks to the mainstream media, the Russian collusion plot line had just been turned on its head, with the Democrats shown to be colluding with a sleazy attempt to link Trump to misconduct in Russia.

But that fleeting story was blown off the radar by another leak, this one disclosed by CNN. Anderson Cooper's show reported that Robert Mueller had delivered his first indictment, but one rather crucial detail was missing: who was the mystery target? That didn't stop CNN, and MSNBC, from devoting endless hours of speculative analysis to this "landmark development."

Throughout the weekend it was a metaphor for the media's pursuit of the probe: *One of Trump's people must have been involved in something terrible with Russia—but we're not quite sure who it is.*

Early Monday morning, Trump aides got news alerts on their phones: Paul Manafort had been indicted. Bob Mueller had hit the president's former campaign chairman with twelve counts of conspiracy to launder money, tax evasion, lying, and illegal lobbying—all over a decade-long period ending in 2015, before he had any involvement with the Trump campaign. His business associate, former campaign aide Rick Gates, had been charged as well, and both men pleaded not guilty.

While the press had to concede that the charges had nothing to do with Russian collusion, pundits and reporters said the special counsel could be trying to flip Manafort against Trump—which assumed Manafort had incriminating evidence to offer.

"Why was Paul Manafort involved in this campaign," Jeff Toobin asked on CNN, when he was "doing Vladimir Putin's bidding in Ukraine."

The opposing spin was framed by @RealDonaldTrump himself: "Sorry, but this is years ago, before Paul Manafort was part of the Trump campaign. But why aren't Crooked Hillary & the Dems the focus?????" And, he said, "the Fake News is working overtime."

Commentators sympathetic to the president brushed off the charges, questioned Mueller's credibility or, as in a number of Fox segments, changed the subject to Hillary Clinton's past controversies. Sean Hannity, who had regained the top spot in cable news, called the indictments "the best evidence yet that the Russiagate witch hunt has come up pretty empty."

One complicating factor was the unsealing of a guilty plea by an obscure figure named George Papadopoulos, described by the press as a Trump campaign adviser. He admitted lying to the FBI about his contacts with people linked to Russian officials in floating a possible meeting between Trump and Putin. One such contact told Papadopoulos that the Russians had "dirt" on Hillary, including "thousands of emails," but despite the initial encouragement of a campaign supervisor, he never met with the Russians involved.

"How is it not collusion," Jim Acosta demanded at the White House press briefing, when Papadopoulos was in touch with people "promising dirt on Hillary Clinton and a series of events that closely mirrors what occurred with the president's own son?"

Sarah Sanders minimized the importance of Papadopoulos, as Sean Spicer once did when he was asked about Manafort.

"This individual," Sanders told the CNN reporter, "was a member of a volunteer council that met one time over the course of a year."

Corey Lewandowski was grilled on the *Today* show, repeatedly calling Papadopoulos a "low-level volunteer" and saying that as a constantly swamped campaign manager he didn't recall any emails or conversations with him about potential contacts with Russia. "I have nothing to hide," he said.

On one of the most challenging days of his presidency, the White House proved to be as leaky as ever. Trump spent the morning in the residence stewing over the television coverage, refusing to come to the Oval Office until almost noon. He was "playing fuming media critic," unnamed officials and friends told the *Washington Post*, watching his flat screen with "rising irritation" that turned to visible "anger."

The president was so annoyed by the story that he called Maggie Haberman at the *Times* to say that "I'm actually not angry at anybody," and besides, "I'm not under investigation."

Steve Bannon urged Trump to disregard his lawyers' advice and take a far more aggressive stance against Bob Mueller.

"You're not going to be able to fire Mueller," Bannon warned. "They'll impeach you. They'll have tons of Republican votes." But, he added, "you have to contest his budget. You have to contest his mandate."

"You know me, I can be aggressive," Trump said. He explained that he just wanted to play things out and get his "letter."

Bannon thought it was a fantasy that the special counsel would wrap things up quickly and cough up a letter saying Trump wasn't under investigation. He believed the president didn't fully grasp the magnitude of the challenge.

"This must be the new Trump," Bannon scoffed. "I don't remember you being passive on these things."

Trump said there was no problem because he didn't know any Russians.

Bannon said Mueller had twenty all-star assassins and they had to come up with a scalp.

Trump said they didn't have any evidence of collusion.

Bannon said that witnesses trying to save their skin would make stuff up.

Now that he was no longer in the West Wing, Bannon felt, all he could do was sound the alarm.

The Mueller investigation had a long way to go. But as Paul Manafort posted bail, the media were split into all-too-familiar warring camps, one side defending the president regardless of inconvenient facts, the other trashing him despite a pair of indictments that literally failed to mention his campaign. The truth was once again elusive.

• • •

On the morning of November 1, after an Uzbek supporter of ISIS used a truck to kill eight people on a Manhattan bike path, Trump echoed a commentator on *Fox & Friends* by appearing to blame the attack on "a Chuck Schumer beauty." The media were apoplectic over this partisan tweet right after the tragedy, because Trump was referring to the alleged killer's admission to America under a 1990 "diversity visa" program—Schumer was one of many bipartisan sponsors—signed into law by George H. W. Bush.

Journalists were within their rights to accuse Trump of politicizing a tragedy, but there was a double standard at work. Trump "now has the world record for injecting politics into the aftermath of a terror attack," said CNN's Jim Acosta, who had chided Trump for not talking about gun control right after the Las Vegas massacre. That, in the media's view, wasn't injecting politics, while assailing lax immigration policy most certainly was. And front-page stories accused the president of jeopardizing the prosecution by saying the attacker should get the death penalty.

Next Trump repeatedly insisted that the Justice Department should be investigating Hillary Clinton and the Democrats over such controversies as a possible link between donations to the Clinton Foundation and Obama administration approval of a Russian agency's purchase of American uranium assets—even as the president admitted "the saddest thing" was his frustration that he couldn't just order Jeff Sessions to do so. Instead he told reporters that "a lot of people are disappointed in the Justice Department, including me," and tweeted that "everybody is asking" why the DOJ "isn't looking into all of the dishonesty going on with Crooked Hillary."

Trump may have merely been venting, but since he was urging agencies that worked for him to investigate his former opponent, the media revolted against what they saw as an abuse of power. On CNN, Jake Tapper decried "President Trump's shocking statements on the rule of law in the United States of America." MSNBC host Ari Melber said that orchestrating prosecutions of political enemies "is what authoritarian regimes do."

The president was again playing to his strongest supporters, some of whom had chanted "lock her up" during the campaign. But the renewed attacks on Hillary allowed the press to depict Trump as fostering a banana republic atmosphere.

• • •

On the first anniversary of Trump's election, the media seized an opportunity to declare him a political failure. When Republicans lost gubernatorial races in New Jersey and especially in Virginia—where former Republican Party chairman Ed Gillespie had distanced himself from the president—much of the coverage had an enthusiastic tone.

"Democratic Wins Are Stinging Rebuke of Trump One Year after His Election," a *Washington Post* headline declared. The *New York Times* called it "the first forceful rebuke of President Trump."

There was no question, based on exit polls, that Trump was a factor in the Virginia contest as energized Democrats turned out to cast a protest vote. But many pundits were quick to extrapolate that because Republicans had lost in a state carried by Clinton and Obama, their hold on the House, where many red-state seats were in play, was threatened in 2018. That, of course, depended on the state of the Trump presidency twelve months down the road, whether he could pass tax reform after the Senate joined the House in handing him a long-sought victory with a sweeping bill approved in a two a.m. party-line vote.

Still, the mainstream media finally had their preferred narrative, that one year after the election that had shocked them, Donald Trump was a flop, just as they had been insisting, and the voters were finally catching on.

If the media's measurement was legislative victories and poll standing, Trump had largely fallen short. But the press failed to grasp that many voters gave Trump credit for a record-breaking stock market, for slashing regulations, and for a cultural crusade on issues ranging from illegal immigration to football protests. Journalists were far more consumed with the Mueller probe, especially when Mike Flynn pleaded guilty to lying to the FBI about his contacts with the Russian ambassador, triggering waves of media speculation about whether he could implicate his former boss. The chasm that had blinded most journalists to Trump's appeal during the long campaign had grown even wider.

The president's attacks on the media were delivered with such clockwork precision that they became, in a sense, less newsworthy even as they intensified. He suggested awarding a "fake news trophy" to the network that was "the most dishonest, corrupt and/or distorted in its political coverage of your favorite President (me)." After his Asia trip, he complained that "CNN International is still a major source of (Fake) news, and they represent our Nation to the WORLD very poorly"—prompting pushback because its foreign correspondents operated in hostile areas and giving an opening to Jake Tapper. Trump, he declared, acutally "hates that which is honest and precise." CNN decided to express its disgust by boycotting the White House Christmas party for the press on December 1—a snub that seemed to parallel Trump having thumbed his nose at the White House Correspondents' Dinner. Even social occasions were now verboten.

• • •

When the *New York Times* and the *New Yorker* disclosed graphic allegations of sexual assault and harassment against movie mogul Harvey Weinstein, the story seemed far removed from the Trump presidency. But that didn't last long.

As the press dug up more accusations of sexual misconduct against actors, producers, entertainers, and journalists—from Kevin Spacey and Louis C. K. and Charlie Rose to Glenn Thrush, who was suspended by the *New York Times* over allegations of harassment—there was a cultural explosion that, for once, had nothing to do with the White House. When the president told reporters that he had known Weinstein for a long time and was "not at all surprised" by the allegations, a CNN correspondent followed up by asking how Weinstein's behavior differed from Trump's raunchy comments on the *Access Hollywood* tape.

"That's locker room," the president replied. The media hadn't waited long to make the connection. The *Washington Post* interviewed some of the dozen women who had accused Trump during the campaign of unwanted touching or kissing—allegations the candidate had dismissed as "pure fiction"—and quoted one of them as saying that "my pain is every day." The headline: "After Weinstein's Fall, Trump Accusers Wonder: Why Not Him?"

A *Chicago Tribune* columnist questioned whether "the election of Donald Trump" had in part "led to this avalanche of sexual harassment and sexual assault allegations against powerful men." For some in the media, the president was somehow responsible for abusive behavior toward women, from Hollywood to Silicon Valley to the nation's newsrooms.

On November 9, the *Washington Post* quoted a woman named Leigh Corfman as saying that Roy Moore, the Senate candidate from Alabama, had befriended and sexually molested her when she was fourteen. Moore vehemently denied the allegations, which were alleged to have occurred nearly four decades earlier, when he was a thirty-two-year-old prosecutor, and said he was the victim of "liberal media lapdogs." Another woman, Beverly Young Nelson, said at a televised news conference that Moore had sexually accosted her in a car when she was sixteen. Seven more female accusers spoke to reporters.

As Mitch McConnell and other leading Republicans urged the nominee to withdraw, Trump felt compelled to address the controversy.

Sarah Huckabee Sanders said in a statement, "The president believes that we cannot allow a mere allegation—in this case, one from many years ago—to destroy a person's life. However, the president also believes that if these allegations are true, Judge Moore will do the right thing and step aside." She read the remarks to reporters on an *Air Force One* flight in Vietnam, and it made far more news than Trump's visit over the previous week to Japan, South Korea, and China. The president had been disciplined and restrained on the Asia trip, and that had yielded only modest coverage.

Trump spoke to reporters on the next flight, to Hanoi, and stirred controversy by saying that he had asked again about Russian hacking of the election during an informal conversation with Vladimir Putin: "Every time he sees me he says I didn't do that and I really believe that when he tells me that, he means it."

Many commentators argued that Trump had embarrassed the country by expressing his belief in Putin's denials. The White House disputed that interpretation and the president had to clean it up, saying all he meant was that Putin believed it, while Trump himself believed the American intelligence agency findings on the hacking—and adding a blast at the "haters and fools" who opposed a better relationship with Russia. (The story got more complicated when the *Atlantic* reported that Donald Trump Jr. had secretly communicated with WikiLeaks during the campaign, complying with its request to have his father tweet a link to the shadowy group's posting of Clinton campaign chairman John Podesta's hacked emails.)

During the same in-flight gaggle, a reporter asked Trump whether the Republican Party should ditch Roy Moore as its candidate. Ivanka would annoy her father by saying there was "a special place in hell" for people like Moore "who prey on children."

Trump said he had been too busy on the trip to follow the details of the story back home. But, he added, "even when I'm in Washington and New York, I do not watch much television. I know they like to say, people that don't know me, they like to say I watch television. People with fake sources—you know, fake reporters, fake sources. But I don't get to watch much television, primarily because of documents. I'm reading documents a lot."

It was a fleeting snapshot of his presidency. The media again tried to put Trump on the defensive over what most journalists considered his strangely cordial relationship with Putin at a time when a special counsel remained in hot pursuit of any improper collusion with Russia. The media were also trying to draw him into a tawdry sex scandal involving a candidate he had tried to defeat in a Senate primary, with some resurrecting the harassment allegations that had flared up at the end of Trump's own campaign. And Donald Trump had hit back with a shot at "fake reporters."

But while Trump kept ignoring reporters' questions about Moore, he displayed no such restraint when Al Franken, the Democratic senator and onetime *Saturday Night Live* star, had to apologize for sexual harassment. A Los Angeles radio host said he had aggressively tongue-kissed her a decade earlier during a USO show rehearsal, and a photo showed him groping her breasts while she slept on a plane; three more accusers soon emerged.

"The Al Frankenstein picture is really bad, speaks a thousand words," the president tweeted, and "to think that just last week he was lecturing anyone who would listen about sexual harassment and respect for women."

That served as an engraved invitation to the press to accuse the president of selective morality, and to again invoke the women who had accused him of sexual harassment a year earlier. The *New York Times* ran a front-page headline, "Sneering without Shame." CNN news anchor Kate Bolduan said "this has officially become a the-president-doesn't-get-to-do-this moment. He doesn't get to question Al Franken and stay silent on Roy Moore and no one should allow it"—though it wasn't clear how the press was supposed to stop it.

Steve Bannon, a major force behind Moore's campaign, ducked messages from top Trump officials and made a point of not calling the president, so no one could say he was pressuring the White House. But he applied considerable pressure by sending the aides polling data showing that Moore would win, and urging Sean Hannity to tone things down after the Fox host gave Moore twenty-four hours to knock down the allegations. Bannon's unmistakable message to Trump: You can again find yourself on the losing side in Alabama, or you can tilt in his direction and take credit when Moore wins.

Trump soon shifted his stance. First he sent out Kellyanne Conway, who had earlier said "there is no Senate seat worth more than a child," to tell *Fox & Friends* that Moore's Democratic opponent Doug Jones was a liberal who would oppose tax reform, and that "we want the votes in the Senate to get this tax bill through." That set the stage; when a reporter asked the president whether "Roy Moore, a child molester," was "better than a Democrat," Trump replied: "Look, he denies it…He totally denies it. He says it didn't happen."

Those comments triggered a wave of media disgust. MSNBC prime-time host Chris Hayes began his program by saying "today the president of the United States effectively endorsed an accused child molester for U.S. Senate. I'm just going to repeat that to let it sink in." And CNN news anchor John Berman brought the indictment full circle by saying that Trump "apparently doesn't believe the eighth accusation of sexual misconduct against Roy Moore, nor does he believe the thirteen women who have come forward to tell their own stories of being sexually harassed by Donald Trump."

Once again, a story about questionable conduct by others ultimately became a story about Donald Trump, because Trump had opened the door and journalists were determined to pull their favorite target into the muddy realm of controversy.

The president couldn't resist piling on moments after NBC abruptly fired *Today* anchor Matt Lauer for serious sexual misconduct. He went on a tweetstorm that reflected his deep animus toward his former network, calling for NBC executives, including MSNBC President Phil Griffin, to be fired for fake news. He made a vague insinuation about NBC News Chairman Andrew Lack, saying "Check out Andy Lack's past!" And he seized on an old, discredited conspiracy theory in asking whether the network would "terminate low ratings Joe Scarborough based on the 'unsolved mystery' that took place in Florida years ago? Investigate!" Scarborough, who had been talking that morning about Trump's embrace of conspiracy theories, was stunned that he would bring up discredited gossip about an intern in his Florida congressional office who was found to have died of natural causes in 2001.

The Twitter barrage came just as news organizations were flatly depicting the president as detached from reality, based on the boomerang from his own experience with sexual harassment allegations. The top newspapers reported that Trump was privately telling people he wasn't sure that was his voice on the *Access Hollywood* video, that the tape might be bogus or doctored—despite the fact that he had apologized for the remarks and NBC had confirmed its authenticity.

The *Washington Post* said, "Trump simply rejects facts—and his own past admissions—as he spins a new narrative." The *New York Times*, saying Trump was again questioning Barack Obama's birth certificate, called it "part of his lifelong habit of attempting to create and sell his own version of reality," and quoted "advisers"—unnamed as usual—as saying "he continues to privately harbor a handful of conspiracy theories that have no grounding in fact."

They were now blatantly calling each other liars, with the pretense of politeness often giving way to outright disdain. And the constant combat was no longer a surprise. The president and the press were each clinging to their own version of the truth.

AFTERWORD

The media siege against Donald Trump, whether justified or not, has become so embedded in our psyche that sometimes it takes a detached observer—in this case a ninety-three-year-old Democrat—to bring a moment of clarity.

No less a figure than Jimmy Carter, who endured more than his share of bad press, told columnist Maureen Dowd that "the media have been harder on Trump than any other president" he had seen and "feel free to claim that Trump is mentally deranged."

I've been pretty tough on my profession in this book, and I know that will bring a ton of personal criticism my way. Fair enough. But I believe I'm standing up for the fundamental values of journalism, which have gotten sadly twisted in the Trump era.

Some journalists have done important work in chronicling the misstatements and excesses of this president, and strive to be fair. I covered half a dozen administrations before Donald Trump took office, have done plenty of investigative reporting, and know that prying loose information that government officials would prefer to keep secret is an arduous and often thankless task.

I am, in short, not a media-basher.

But too many journalists and media executives, dwelling in a bubble of like-minded opinion, became convinced that they had a solemn duty to oppose Trump. The normal rules of balance and attempted objectivity were suspended, dismissed as a relic of a calmer time. And they justified the new approach by telling themselves and the world that they had a duty to push back—perhaps even push out—a president they viewed as unqualified, intemperate, and insistent on pursuing harmful policies. They also took on the mission of proving that the president obstructed justice and possibly colluded with Russia, with limited results as 2017 drew to a close.

There is simply no factual dispute that the coverage of Donald Trump has been overwhelmingly negative in tone, tenor, and volume. Some of these stories have been legitimate, some generated by Trump himself, but many others are tendentious, or biased, or minor developments magnified out of all proportion. And on the commentary side, many conservatives as well as liberals remain downright hostile in their criticism of Trump.

To be sure, Trump has at times made mistakes, stretched or obscured the truth, and gone too far in attacking journalists and painting them as enemies of the country.

And while the media still play a vital role in separating fact from fiction, the president's criticisms—and their own blinders and blunders— have cast that role in doubt.

The media have become more tribal, their outlets often serving as a badge of personal identity. Conservatives and liberals, Trump fans and Trump bashers, have split into ideological camps, unwilling to tolerate the slightest deviation from their side, wedded to their version of the truth.

A common refrain among Trump's antagonists in the press is that they must resist normalizing his presidency. But in the process, they have abnormalized journalism.

Perhaps the gravest offense is the disdain and derision, if not outright revulsion, that seep into so many reports and segments about the president—especially in the entertainment culture that, by osmosis, spills into the media culture as well.

Just to be clear: I'm making this case not because I resent journalism, but because I love journalism and believe it has lost its way, choosing sides in a politically charged struggle, practically earning the label of opposition party against an unlikely leader. Too many journalists have subjected him to trial by Twitter, overreacted to his personal invective, and lost sight of what truly matters in people's lives.

Donald Trump will not be president forever, but the media's reputation, badly scarred during these polarizing years, might never recover.

ACKNOWLEDGMENTS

My thanks to Rafe Sagalyn, my longtime friend and literary agent, without whom this book literally would not have been possible, given the resistance in the publishing business to an unvarnished look at the battles between President Trump and the media. I'm grateful to Harry Crocker and his team at Regnery for instantly grasping the potential of this book and skillfully bringing it to market. My colleagues at Fox News have supported my media criticism and my independence, even on the most sensitive subjects, and many are valued friends. The rest of you who have put up with me know who you are.

INDEX